LEADERSHIP
AND
ORGANIZATIONS

LEADERSHIP
AND
ORGANIZATIONS

ALAN BRYMAN

Lecturer, Department of Social Sciences
Loughborough University of Technology

ROUTLEDGE & KEGAN PAUL
London, Boston and Henley

First published in 1986
by Routledge & Kegan Paul plc

14 Leicester Square, London WC2H 7PH, England

9 Park Street, Boston, Mass. 02108, USA and

Broadway House, Newtown Road,
Henley on Thames, Oxon RG9 1EN, England

Set in Sabon 10/11pt.
by Columns of Reading
and printed in Great Britain by
St Edmundsbury Press, Bury St Edmunds, Suffolk

Library of Congress Cataloging in Publication Data
Bryman, Alan.
Leadership and organizations.
Bibliography: p.
Includes index.
1. Leadership.   2. Organization.   3. Executive
ability.   I. Title.
HD57.7.B79   1986   658.4'092   85–19342

British Library CIP data also available

ISBN 0-7102-0324-1
0-7102-0800-6(p)

For Sue and Sarah

CONTENTS

PREFACE

On Tuesday, 13 March 1984, the then Chancellor of the Exchequer, Nigel Lawson, conducted his first budget and received wide acclaim for the presentation of his speech as well as its content. A few days later, a commentator in the *Financial Times* remarked upon speculation that Mr Lawson was in the running for the Tory succession as a consequence of his performance: 'That seems to me to be absurd. He is not without ambition, but he is not a leader.' (*Financial Times*, 17 March 1984, p. 30.) He is not a leader. It is so easy to see this comment as unremarkable and move on to another item in the paper. But if the phenomenon of leadership, its nature and its forms, is something which attracts us, such a comment is of interest. In everyday life, the words 'leader' and 'leadership' recur with surprising frequency, yet not always with the same content and meaning. Take a remark such as 'I don't like his style of leadership at all'. Is it denoting the same kinds of attributes as those to which Mr Lawson's commentator was alluding? Possibly not, for the comment upon Mr Lawson seems to refer to him as a person, whereas the other remark seems to refer to what someone does. Suppose that, instead of talking about the Tory succession, the reference was to the Tory *leadership*. Here again we are confronted with another meaning of the idea of a leader, that is, as a lofty position within a hierarchy.

Defining what leadership is or comprises, it should be apparent (if it was not already), is a complex and elusive problem. Within the study of organizational behaviour, the examination of leadership has been a prominent issue, and it is this aspect of the study of leadership which is the focus of the book. The *leitmotif* of this field of research is the quest for the effective leader, although as we shall see there has been a slight drift away from this over-riding emphasis in recent times. The succeeding pages will dwell upon the various theories, approaches and findings relevant to the study of leadership in organizations, the vast bulk of which work has been preoccupied with the issue of leader effectiveness. As such, the book will only deal with a portion of the general study of leadership. The study of leadership in general is well served by Bass's (1981) compendious handbook, which contains slightly under 200 pages of references! As a result, the author will deal either very briefly or not at all with some topics or issues relating to leadership. Indeed, even within the sub-field of leadership in organizations, the aim is to be selective. An attempt has been made to emphasize the main, and in my view most interesting, approaches and ideas, as well as the main and most interesting findings relating to the selected approaches and ideas. The aim has been to be discursive rather than encyclopaedic, to equip the reader with a facility for talking about leadership such that he or she is sensitive to the complexity of the phenomenon rather than what amounts to a complete but superficial annotated bibliography. Ultimately, then, some controversial choices have been made. Further, this is not a handbook for learning how to become a leader. Indeed, many of the implicit themes of the book will point to the difficulty of developing such programmes.

In addressing the various controversies surrounding the leadership research to be examined here, it has been decided not to side-step the methodological issues involved. Leadership research reflects the whole gamut of methodological approaches in the social sciences, though some are more prominent than others. However, the various research designs and methods have posed interpretive problems for leadership researchers, albeit ones which are common to students of organizational behaviour in general. Very often debates about methodology are as critical to an understanding of research on leadership in organizations as the theoretical and interpretive discussions which abound in this area of study.

This is a textbook in respect of the literature on leadership in organizations. As such, it is oriented to two main groups: students of management who, as part of their course, invariably need to examine theory and research relating to organizational behaviour and the management of human resources; and students of what is variously called social psychology of organizations, industrial psychology, or organizational psychology. In each case, students often find a single chapter on leadership in their respective textbooks; but very often the need to cover a wide range of topics prevents the authors of the more general texts from examining a wide range of issues in connection with the study of leadership. Too often, the single chapter in a textbook glosses over the complexity of the issues. This book seeks to provide a more discursive and more wide-ranging discussion than such very general treatments can usually present. It is hoped that the book will also be of interest and use to students of the sociology of organizations and industry.

It has been very difficult to rid this book entirely of 'sexism'. Some sentences end up looking incredibly tortuous when an attempt is made to moderate sexist language. Wherever feasible, I have sought to combat the problem of sexism.

Finally, I wish to acknowledge some debts. Michael Bresnen and Michael Billig helped me a great deal to curb some eccentric language and to sharpen many ideas; to David Stonestreet of Routledge & Kegan Paul for his help and encouragement; to Peter Lawrence for helping me to get this book under way; to the various authors and publishers who have allowed me to reproduce their work; and to Gwen Moon and Marjorie Salsbury for unstinting devotion to deciphering my handwriting. None of these people, however, can be held in any way responsible for any deficiencies contained within these covers. I have often noted that the acknowledgments authors present of the contribution of their spouses and children are tinged with guilt. I now know why. My gratitude for the immense sacrifices that my wife and daughter have had to make can only be recorded; to express it would require another volume.

Alan Bryman
Loughborough
19 March 1985

1

THE IDEA OF LEADERSHIP AND THE METHODOLOGY OF LEADERSHIP RESEARCH

It is tempting to reject the usual starting point for discussions of leadership – namely with its definition – if only because it tends to be a daunting induction for the uninitiated. Writers typically point (quite properly) to the wide range of pertinent definitions (e.g. Gibb, 1969; Stogdill, 1974; Yukl, 1981) and proceed to examine a sample of them. The basic problem is that not only is there a range of definitions, but there is also no consensually agreed one. The absence of a common definition of leadership means that the initial treatment of the topic can very easily become bogged down in a definitional quagmire, providing the reader with an unattractive introduction to a promising area. It is a promising area because in everyday life people seem to believe that leadership matters, that it is important to the realization of a desirable state of affairs. This is what people mean when they bemoan the absence of 'good' or 'strong' leadership or when industrialists seek to recruit to their firm people with the 'right' leadership qualities.

However, this book examines the literature relating to the study of leadership in organizations (firms, schools, the military, etc.) and is not concerned with the totality of leadership research *per se*. Within this domain of study, there is a tendency for there to be a fair degree of concordance among writers. Consider the following definitions:

Leadership may be considered as the process (act) of influencing the activities of an organized group in its efforts toward goal setting and goal achievement. (Stogdill, 1950, p. 3)

leadership is a process of influence between a leader and those who are followers. (Hollander, 1978, p.1)

Leadership . . . is the behaviour of an individual when he is directing the activities of a group toward a shared goal. (Hemphill and Coons, 1957, p. 7)

The statement, 'a leader tries to influence other people in a given

1

direction' is relatively simple, but it seems to capture the essence of what we mean by leadership . . . (Korman, 1971, p. 115)

'Leadership' is defined as the process of influencing the activities of an organized group toward goal achievement. (Rauch and Behling, 1984, p. 46)

The common elements in these definitions imply that leadership involves a social influence process in which a person steers members of the group towards a goal. Many of the studies which will be examined in this book seem to employ this conception as a working definition of leadership. The emphasis on 'the group' is a common one in leadership theory and research, which conjures the image of a leader with a small coterie of followers. In this connection, many researchers have examined the activities of supervisors or managers in industry and the implications of their behaviour for the sentiments and performance of the subordinates for whom they are responsible. This level of analysis creates a relatively small-scale emphasis in leadership research, for the organization comes to be seen as comprising a plethora of groups and attendant leaders. The organization as a whole, or as an entity *sui generis*, recedes from view in this context. Another aspect of the working definition is that the leader/non-leader distinction is a clear-cut one which is taken to be indicative of role differentiation within the group. This role differentiation may occur in a number of ways, but two chief notions tend to prevail in the literature. Much of the early research on leadership was concerned with the 'emergent' leader, that is the person who becomes a leader in leaderless contexts. Many studies exist which sought to create the conditions for emergent leadership in psychology laboratories, wherein unstructured groups worked on tasks assigned by the experimenter, and the characteristics which distinguished emergent leaders from followers were then assessed. In addition, there have been studies of emergent leadership in natural settings, such as Whyte's (1943) pioneering study of an American street corner gang. In this *prima facie* leaderless context, the process of emergent leadership and its subsequent retention were directly observed. Thus, one form of leadership which has been examined is that which emerges from situations in which there is no formal leadership. The second way in which the leader/non-leader distinction is likely to occur is in the context of formally designated roles. People are appointed to positions in which the exercise of leadership is a prime requirement and it is this context with which the bulk of research into leadership in formal organizations is concerned. As Stogdill and Shartle put it:

It is assumed that it is proper and feasible to make a study of leadership in places where leadership would appear to exist and that if a person occupies a leadership position he is a fit subject for study. (Stogdill and Shartle, 1948, p. 287)

In this conception, the leader is a person who is formally designated as such. The formal organization throws up a range of such positions for whom 'goal oriented group activities' (Stogdill and Shartle, 1948, p. 287) are an important responsibility. Researchers concerned with leadership in organizations have tended to adopt this strategy, particularly when examining the behaviour of leaders. As a result, as the succeeding chapters will reveal, there tends to be relatively little discussion of informal leadership in organizations, i.e. leadership processes which occur outside the formal blueprints of organizations. The neglect of informal leadership by most investigators can be attributed, not only to a research strategy which focuses on leadership positions, but also to a pervasive preoccupation with leadership effectiveness. Researchers have been particularly concerned with the factors (personal or behavioural) which distinguish the effective from the ineffective leader, 'effectiveness' being construed in a variety of ways but generally taken to involve indications of group productivity, subordinate satisfaction and involvement, and the like. Such research has typically been guided by a belief that it would be possible to refine the selection or training of leaders, if it were known which factors contribute to leadership effectiveness. Because informal leadership is relatively idiosyncratic and not always directed to official organizational goals (Blau, 1956), its relevance for the study of leadership effectiveness was not obvious.

Leadership and influence

The working definition of leadership which, it has been suggested, has provided a general orientation for leadership researchers concerned with organizations, is not without its problems. Quite aside from the fact that the definition includes notions like 'group' and 'goal' which are not as uncontentious as they first appear, it is difficult to distinguish it from other forms of social influence. In particular, it is difficult to distinguish leadership from kindred concepts like power and authority, not least because people in leadership positions typically exert (or have the capacity to exert) power and authority over their immediate subordinates. Indeed, in some approaches to the study of leadership, a deliberate attempt is made to fuse it with the concepts like power (e.g. French and Snyder, 1959; Janda, 1960). The problem of distinguishing leadership from other influence processes has been addressed by Kochan, Schmidt, and De Cotiis (1975) who follow Gibb's (1969, p. 270) assertion that leadership involves 'influencing the actions of others in a shared approach to common or compatible goals'. Similarly, Etzioni (1965) has sought to distinguish leadership from power by suggesting that the former is an influence process which changes the preferences of those being influenced. In terms of such views, leadership is not simply a matter of effecting changes in other people's behaviour, but more to do with enhancing their voluntary compliance. This notion relates to the leader's ability to motivate, an ingredient which is often taken as the *sine qua non* of leadership. While Etzioni's definition subsumes this conception very readily, many of the definitions which were quoted earlier do not obviously absorb it. This suggests that the working definition which underpins much of the research to be explicated may be at variance with the popular conception of leadership as involving the motivation of others.

This notion is reinforced by a classic study of the work activities of managers by Mintzberg (1973) in which ten managerial roles were delineated as a result of his observations. One of these roles is described as the 'leader role', the key purpose of which

> is to effect an integration between individual needs and organizational goals. The manager must concentrate his efforts so as to bring subordinate and organizational needs into a common accord in order to promote efficient operations. (Mintzberg, 1973, p. 62)[1]

The problem with assessing the manager's leader role is that it infiltrates a great many of his activities which renders leadership a difficult area to study *per se*. When we seek to distinguish leadership from other influence activities, we are effectively attempting to distinguish it from the mere incumbency of a position or status in a formal organizational structure ('headship' as it is often called) to which power and authority accrue. When people talk about the 'leadership of the Conservative Party' they are invariably making a reference to positions of authority within the party; if they say that the Conservative Party lacks leadership, they are unlikely to be referring to the absence of persons in formal authority positions, but to a deficiency in the capacity of Party leaders to motivate and guide backbenchers and, possibly, supporters. It would seem important to maintain a distinction between the leader who is in a leadership position and who has power and authority vested in his or her office, and leadership as an influence process which is more than the exercise of power and authority as Etzioni, for example, suggests. However, as the reader will come to recognize, a great deal of leadership research rides roughshod over these distinctions. Studies abound on the subject of the behaviour of leaders in which the strategy involves discerning the activities of people in positions of leadership, with little reference to how these activities might be indicative of leadership *per se* as distinct from the exercise of power and authority.

The organizational context

Of course, issues associated with power are very relevant to what leaders do, since the power at their disposal affects what they can do. For example, an important component of leadership behaviour, according to some writers (see Chapter 4), is the use by designated leaders of rewards or penalties, for as Mintzberg, observes: 'Each time a manager encourages or criticizes a subordinate he is acting in his capacity as *leader*' (Mintzberg, 1973, p. 61). But the leader's opportunity to encourage or criticize may be affected by how much power he has and organizational policies in connection with the assessment of subordinates. Nor is the power structure the only constraint on how leaders can behave, for organizations frequently encumber the occupants of offices with rules, job definitions, and a catalogue of procedures which restrict and restrain them (Weber, 1947). Further, research shows that the behaviour of designated leaders is substantially affected by the expectations held of them by their own bosses, subordinates, and peers (e.g. Pfeffer and Salancik, 1975). The climate of an organization may constrain the leader's range of options too.

It was in the light of these issues that Katz and Kahn offered the following useful definition of leadership:

> we consider the essence of organizational leadership to be the influential increment over and above mechanical compliance with the routine directives of the organization. (Katz and Kahn, 1978, p. 528)

This definition directs the researcher to an examination of leadership processes which are over and above conformity to organizational routine and prescription. However, leadership research is disappointing in this respect too, for it often fails to distinguish the routine compliance component of what designated leaders do, from the influential increment ingredient.

Management and leadership

Much of the early research on leadership was concerned with the investigation of the personal traits of leaders (see Chapter 2). The inability of investigators to discern unambiguous traits which permitted discrimination between leaders and non-leaders, or between good and bad leaders, ushered in a lengthy period from the later 1940s onwards in which the behaviour of leaders was the prime focus (see Chapter 3). The main emphasis of the programmes of research during this period was the type or types of leader behaviour associated with group or organizational effectiveness. The most prominent research strategy of this period was that exemplified by Stogdill and Shartle's (1948) proposal, quoted earlier in this chapter, which orientates the investigator to people in *prima facie* positions of leadership. Stogdill and Shartle were themselves prominent figures in the development of the strategy in that they participated in giving birth to the Ohio State Leadership Studies, one of the best-known and most influential programmes (see Chapter 3). Unfortunately, the strategy made it extremely difficult to distinguish between leadership and management. It involved treating managers or supervisors in industry and elsewhere as though they were leaders with little questioning of how one might discriminate between management and leadership. Indeed, there is even a sense in which the authors took the view that this distinction does not matter: 'The question of whether *leaders* or *executives* are being studied appears to be a problem at the verbal level only' (Stogdill and Shartle, 1948, p. 287).

During the period in which leadership behaviour has been a major focus of investigation it has been very difficult for an outside observer to ascertain whether it is leadership or management that the innumerable studies of 'leader behavior' have been examining. Terms like 'leadership style', 'supervisory style', and 'managerial style' tend to be used interchangeably, and seem to all intents and purposes to be addressing the same phenomena. The failure to distinguish between leadership and 'headship' (see the preceding section) and leadership and management in the majority of investigations has prompted the following apt comment:

> Despite these distinctions, leadership research continues to be dominated by studies which in fact deal only with a restricted range of *managerial* behaviours. This may well be a reflection of the difficulties involved in pursuing definitions which do not tie leaders to particular role titles, such as supervisor. (Hosking and Morley, 1982, p. 10)

In recent years, a number of authors have sought to forge a distinction between leadership and management. Zaleznik (1977) draws a distinction between managers and leaders. The former are reactive organization men concerned with routine and short-term projects, whereas

> Leaders adopt a personal and active attitude toward goals. The influence a leader exerts in altering moods, evoking images and expectations, and in establishing specific desires and objectives determines the direction a business takes. The net result of this influence is to change the way people think about what is desirable, possible and necessary. (Zaleznik, 1977, p. 71)

According to this view, leadership entails the creation of a vision about a desired future state which seeks to enmesh all members of an organization in its net. This view is consonant with the view that leadership is distinguishable from the exercise of authority and routine compliance with organizational protocol, by virtue of being an influence process which seeks to secure voluntary compliance to agreed goals and which transcends a slavish acquiescence to routine. A congruent view to that of Zaleznik has been expressed by Bennis who suggests:

> The leader must be a social architect who studies and shapes what is called 'the culture of work' – those intangibles that are so hard to discern but so terribly important in governing the way people act, the values and norms that are subtly transmitted to individuals and groups and that tend to create binding and bonding. (Bennis, 1976, p. 15)

Managing, by contrast, tends to involve a preoccupation with the here-and-now of goal attainment. Not only do these definitions enable one to distinguish leadership from management, they also dovetail well with the interest in the values and culture of organizations (Bryman, 1984b) which has developed in recent years. Further reference to this issue will be made in Chapter 7.

It should be apparent by this juncture that there is evidence that it is difficult to distinguish leadership from kindred notions of headship, the exercise of power and authority, and management. Moreover, while various writers have attempted to forge distinctions, they have often not been embodied in empirical research, so that the working definition presented above has had a wide currency. In order to discuss the research literature relating to the study of leadership in organizations it is necessary to suspend any attachment to the more refined definitions, and to deal with the relevant literature as it is conventionally recognized. This expedient is necessary because such a large proportion of the literature, as conventionally defined, fails to take the distinctions that have been addressed on board. Instead, they have tended to be underpinned by the loose working definition of leadership. Stogdill (1974) may be correct in his view that there are as many definitions of leadership as there are writers on the subject. However, in the more specific domain of the study of leadership in organizations, the focus on leader-influencing-group-towards-goals has been a core notion for researchers, especially those concerned with the elucidation of leader behaviour. Indeed, one of the main reasons why a decision was made not to present the reader with a catalogue of definitions, and an extended discussion of them, was precisely that it would be of limited use in coming to terms with the research discussed in the later chapters. However, the problems raised by the failure to make fine distinctions between, say, leadership and management, and the implications thereof, will be addressed *en passant*.

Leadership and exchange

The tendency thus far, following the prevalent orientation among researchers, is to refer to leadership as an activity which involves the leader doing something to others, usually subordinates. However, there is a strong case for suggesting that leadership may be a two-way influence process. The work of Hollander is most clearly associated with this idea which he tends to refer to as a 'transactional approach'. In order to be allowed to continue in a position of leadership, the leader must be responsive to the needs of his followers (Hollander and Julian, 1969). In his observation study of a street corner gang, Whyte made the following observation which sheds light on the transactional nature of leadership:

> The man with a low status may violate his obligations without much change in his position . . . On the other hand, the leader is depended upon by all the members to meet his personal obligations. He cannot fail to do so without causing confusion and endangering his position. (Whyte, 1943, p. 257)

Similarly, a study of emergent leaders at Antarctic scientific stations (Nelson, 1964) found that the most liked leaders were those who were motivated to be efficient group members. It is important to bear in mind, then, that leadership is not a one-way influence process and that the leader must be responsive to the group for his position to be viewed as legitimate.

Hollander has recognized that the suggestion that the leader must conform to the wishes of the group and not transgress its norms implies that he can never be innovative in that he is trapped by his need to maintain his position. In order to deal with this conundrum, Hollander proposes an 'idiosyncrasy credit' model. According to this idea, in their early contacts with a group, leaders or prospective leaders gain 'credits' by virtue of the competence they display in connection with the group's primary task, and also their conformity to the group's norms (see, e.g., Hollander, 1978, pp. 40-3). Once a fund of credits has been accumulated the leader is in a position to be innovative and can depart from normal group practice to a certain degree. Indeed, there is a sense in which the leader will be seen as deficient if he does not move in an innovative direction. Hollander (1978, p. 42) cites research which indicates that the leader must not allow himself to fail to meet his role obligations; for example, he must not act in his own self-interest and must be seen as fair.

While Hollander's ideas seem to have been formulated largely in the context of emergent leadership, they are of relevance in the formal organizational context too because they suggest that leaders need to be responsive to their subordinates' needs and wishes. Further, it may provide a framework for the highly neglected issue of informal leadership in organizations, particularly the conditions for its emergence and maintenance. However, the idea of leadership as a social exchange has not had a major impact upon researchers who have tended to focus on what leaders do *to* subordinates. An exception to this generalization is the Vertical Dyad Linkage Model (e.g. Danserau, Graen and Haga, 1975) which will be discussed in later chapters. The main thrust of the model is to suggest that the vertical dyads between a leader and each group member become structured at a certain stage, such that there develops an 'in-group' of subordinates close to the leader and an 'out-group' of those who are more distant. Members of the in-group are much more likely to be able to influence the leader than their peers in the out-group. Interestingly, a phenomenon missing from most of these models is any account of leadership in a lateral context. Most of the ideas which have been encountered thus far, as well as the ones to come, perceive leadership in vertical terms, albeit occasionally as a two-way process. Yet it is not in the least difficult to visualize the possibility in a formal organization that leadership relationships may occur among putative equals. To a large extent, this observation harks back to the suggestion that informal leadership is often neglected by researchers. This disregard for leadership in a lateral context in organizations is surprising in the light of the interest among organization theorists in power differentials among sub-units of apparently equal power (e.g. Hickson *et al.*, 1971).

The purpose of the discussion until now has been to introduce the reader to a number of definitional and conceptual issues which abound in this area of study. A foretaste has also been provided of some of the problems and difficulties which pertain to much of the work to be described. Three practical problems with which the working definition does not really cope were mentioned; namely, the difficulty that is encountered in distinguishing leadership in an organizational context from the exercise of power and authority, from conformity with organizational protocol, and from management and managerial activities. While writers were mentioned who have sought to address these points, it was observed that much leadership research rides roughshod over them. However, there are methodological issues to face as well and the rest of this chapter will be devoted to a discussion of some of them, particularly those which pertain to the design of research on leadership in organizations.

Some methodological issues in leadership research

The study of leadership in organizations shares many of the same methodological problems which beset researchers in the social sciences as a whole. It is intended in this section to provide a brief overview of some of these issues. There is a possibility that a concern for methodological issues at this juncture of a textbook may appear perverse. However, it is necessary to make a number of points relating to methodological concerns throughout this book, so that an early familiarity with them is of considerable use to the reader.

It is intended to focus in particular upon methodological issues which pertain to the study of leader *behaviour*. The point has already been made in passing that the early interest in the personal traits of leaders (Chapter 2) gave way from the late 1940s to an emphasis on what leaders do, a focus which is evident in the research covered in Chapters 3 to 5. In view of the prominence of this approach, the methodological issues will be addressed primarily in relation to it.

A particular dimension of leader behaviour that is frequently addressed by researchers is that which is often called 'participative leadership' – the extent to which a leader provides his subordinates with latitude and involves them in decision-making. It is often assumed that participative leaders have happier, more productive subordinates because people prefer to have control over events and are more likely to feel involved in a group enterprise when this occurs. The attention accorded this aspect of leader behaviour will be particularly evident from some of the research covered in Chapters 4 and 5. But how do we go about confirming the veracity of the contention that participative leadership is superior? There are two broad approaches which tend to be used by researchers – the 'cross-sectional' (or 'correlational') design and the 'experimental' design. The predominant emphasis in both contexts has been to conceive of participative leadership as an independent variable which enhances various 'outcomes' like the productivity or job satisfaction of subordinates which are taken to be dependent variables, as Figure 1.1. implies.

Figure 1.1   *The study of leader behaviour*

The cross-sectional approach

This means of examining the contentions implicit in Figure 1.1. is so called because measures of the independent and dependent variables are obtained more or less simultaneously, thereby providing a static cross-section of events. It is often called 'correlational' because it seeks to correlate the two types of variable, although more recent studies are more sophisticated than this statement implies. In order to obtain a measure of participative leadership, researchers have used questionnaires to elicit the degree of participativeness exhibited by leaders, whether as viewed by designated leaders themselves or from the perspective of their subordinates. The latter has tended to be the more favoured approach, in large part because of the possibility that leaders' own reports of their behaviour may be tainted by a tendency towards 'socially desirable' answers.[2] Examples drawn from questionnaires used in such research will be found in later chapters. Thus, one very prominent way of examining the effects of leader behaviour is that evident in Figure 1.2, which will be called Design 1.

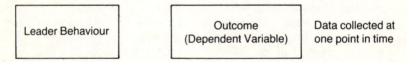

Figure 1.2   *The cross-sectional approach (Design 1)*

This approach is plagued with a number of problems. First, it may be that the correlation between the two variables is being caused by the mutual association of each variable with a third variable. Second, when subordinates are the source of descriptions of both leader behaviour and an outcome variable (e.g. job satisfaction), there may be a problem of response bias, such that contented subordinates tend to view their superiors as participative and to report higher levels of job satisfaction. Third, there is the problem of 'reverse causality'. Since Design 1 involves the correlation of two variables, which determines which cannot be ascertained with any certainty. It could be that if a sizeable correlation is found between a group productivity and participative leadership the latter may not be the cause of the former, but that leaders tend to behave more participatively when faced with productive subordinates and less participatively when they are poor performers. The cross-sectional approach can be adapted to deal with this problem by collecting data at two or more points in time, i.e. a longitudinal design. This design (Design 1A) is outlined in Figure 1.3.

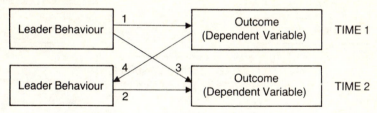

Figure 1.3 *The longitudinal approach (Design 1A)*

Design 1A, which has been employed on remarkably few occasions, is basically two cross-sections in which data on the same respondents are collected on at least two different occasions. It enables the researcher to examine the cross-sectional impact of leader behaviour on a particular outcome on two different occasions (arrows 1 and 2); the impact of leader behaviour over time (its 'lagged' effect as indicated by arrow 3); and the contention that leaders respond behaviourally to properties of their subordinates (like their performance or levels of satisfaction as indicated by arrow 4). Design 1A is not without its problems in that the decision concerning how much time ought to elapse between the two data collection waves is somewhat arbitrary, and there is the possibility that the results obtained are at least in part a product of the choice made.

Design 1 is often adapted to take into account the possibility that the effectiveness of, say, participative leadership is partly affected by the context or situation which pertains. It may be that a researcher examines the degree of participative leadership exhibited by the designated leaders in a number of firms and the productivity of their subordinates, but finds the correlation to be small. Further investigation might reveal (holding the problem of reverse causality in abeyance) that among those subordinates working on simple, routine jobs there is a very low correlation between the two variables. The amount of participative leadership has little effect on their productivity. However, when more complex work is involved, participative leadership can have a more pronounced effect and so enhance productivity. In this context, the correlation between participative leadership and productivity might be quite high. Such a finding would indicate that the correlation between leader behaviour and outcome is 'situationally contingent', that is, it depends on the circumstances which obtain. The research examined in Chapter 5 has the contingent nature of the effects of leader behaviour as its chief focus. The research associated with approaches examined in that chapter seeks to discern those variables (such as the complexity of a task in the hypothetical example above) which 'moderate' or 'mediate' the effects of particular types of leader behaviour. This general orientation to leadership research instils an 'it all depends' tone into leadership research, and can be expressed diagrammatically as in Figure 1.4. It can be examined in the context of a Design 1 or 1A approach, though the former is much more prevalent.

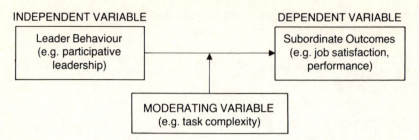

Figure 1.4   *The contingency approach*

The experimental approach

Studies using a cross-sectional design tend to be carried out in relation to samples of designated leaders and their subordinates in real-life contexts such as industry, the military, commerce, or educational establishments. Researchers employing experimental designs can and do conduct their investigations in the laboratory or in natural environments. One could examine the effectiveness of participative leadership in either of these contexts. Each carries with it its own problems. In the laboratory situation, the researcher has much more direct control over the conduct of the experiment and as a result tends to be in a much stronger position to impute a cause-and-effect relationship (or its absence). In Campbell's (1957) terms, the 'internal validity'[3] of such a study tends to be strong. By contrast, because of the artificiality of the laboratory and the pervasive tendency among social scientists using experimental designs to use students as subjects, its external validity (i.e. generalizability) tends to be weaker. In the more natural environment of the field experiment, the researcher tends to have less control over events so that internal validity is often weak, but the fact that field experiments are located in real-life environments provides a more pronounced aura of generalizability and relevance. The latter is important, for the study of leadership in organizations has often been carried out with a view to providing findings which could improve leadership effectiveness. Research conducted in the same environment as that to which it is supposed to be applied is likely to seem more convincing than that carried out in laboratories on university students, so that there is a fairly strong practical appeal attached to investigations carried out in natural environments.

The possible effects of participative leadership on group productivity can be treated as our hypothetical problem once again. In order for a piece of research to be genuinely experimental, there must be at least one control group which acts as a point of comparison so that confounding factors can be eliminated. A study could be envisaged in which just one group was examined as follows: the initial level of group productivity was ascertained, the amount of participativeness exhibited by the leader might then be enhanced, and the group's productivity then re-assessed after the passage of some weeks or months. The problem with this design is that even if group productivity did increase, one could not be sure that it was the enhanced participative leadership alone which caused it (Campbell, 1957). Consequently, a control group is required in which there is no enhanced participative leadership, but which has all the same conditions as the experimental group. Two kinds of basic design can be envisaged (see Figures 1.5a and 1.5b).

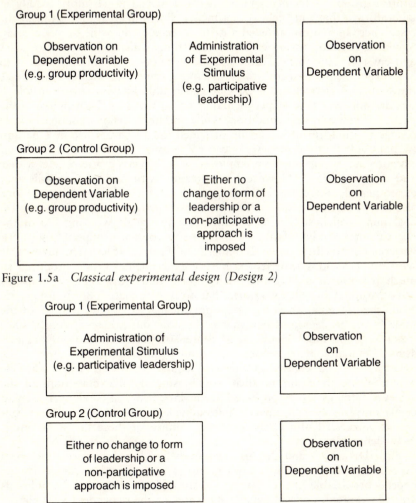

Group 1 (Experimental Group)

| Observation on Dependent Variable (e.g. group productivity) | Administration of Experimental Stimulus (e.g. participative leadership) | Observation on Dependent Variable |

Group 2 (Control Group)

| Observation on Dependent Variable (e.g. group productivity) | Either no change to form of leadership or a non-participative approach is imposed | Observation on Dependent Variable |

Figure 1.5a   *Classical experimental design (Design 2)*

Group 1 (Experimental Group)

| Administration of Experimental Stimulus (e.g. participative leadership) | Observation on Dependent Variable |

Group 2 (Control Group)

| Either no change to form of leadership or a non-participative approach is imposed | Observation on Dependent Variable |

Figure 1.5b   *Post-test only control group design (Design 2A)*

In both instances, there are at least two groups, one of which receives the experimental stimulus (participative leadership) while the other does not. This latter group, the control group, is likely to receive an alternative form of leadership, which is often that which pre-dates the start of the experiment. Control groups in natural settings are often comparison groups which retain the form of leadership to which they are accustomed. It is essential that the two groups are equivalent in two senses. First, the nature of the personnel should be equivalent in respect of such factors as job experience, ability, and the like. Second, the tasks and environments of the groups should be as near to identical as possible. The first requirement is best achieved by random assignment[4] of people to experimental and control groups, a facility which can be achieved much more readily in laboratories than in field experiments since in real-life settings the researcher is often not allowed a *carte blanche* to do as he or she pleases. Similarly, it is not always easy to establish equivalence in respect of tasks and environments in field experiments. A response to this problem is to have experimental and control groups in the same organization to enhance the similarity of circumstances. One can readily imagine a firm in which one division acts as an experimental group in that it is the recipient of the participative leadership condition; while another division experiences little change to the form of leadership provided (or a non-participative pattern is imposed) and provides a control group. Indeed, this kind of experimental set-up has been employed in some classic studies (e.g. Morse and Reimer, 1956). However, a difficulty with this approach is that experimental and control groups may have mutual knowledge of one another. A stark instance of this problem is provided by a study in a US coal mine which sought to enhance the quality of working life of the experimental group relative to that of the control groups whose work patterns remained the same (Blumberg and Pringle, 1983). The favourable working conditions experienced by the experimental group produced so much resentment among the other miners that work and relationships were disrupted and the experiment had to be terminated. But if groups are established in separate firms, or geographically separated divisions of the same firm, the degree of equivalence is more difficult to establish, since wider organizational factors (e.g. degree of bureaucratization, organizational climate) may render the groups non-equivalent. Insofar as experimental and control groups lack equivalence there will always be doubts about the fruits of such studies, since rival explanations of the achieved findings can be proffered. In the laboratory, it is relatively easy to create purposively two separate but equivalent leadership conditions, but as was suggested above, the external validity of these investigations is more debatable.

Both Designs 2 and 2A are intensively used in laboratory and field experiments. In the former, both groups are measured in respect of the dependent variable at the start of the study; the experimental conditions are then created; and subsequent measures of the dependent variable are taken. Design 2A is identical except that there is no pre-testing of experimental and control groups. The absence of pre-testing means that it is not feasible to devise a complete picture of the degree of change that the experimental stimulus effects in respect of the dependent variable.[5] A contingency framework of the kind outlined in Figure 1.4 can readily be incorporated into either design. If one wishes to examine the possibility that task complexity moderates the effects of participative leadership, groups experiencing high and low levels in respect of this variable under conditions of both participative and non-participative leadership would need to be created. A basic design would include four groups: participative leadership under conditions of either high or low task complexity; non-participative leadership under conditions of either high or low task complexity. It might be anticipated, once again, that the researcher's ability to introduce these more sophisticated designs will be more readily realized in the laboratory than in the field.

The chief advantage of experimental over cross-sectional designs is the greater facility with which the former can impute causality and a time order to variables. However, field experiments frequently have to depart from strict canons of experimentation (Cummings, Molloy and Glen, 1977), some of the reasons for which have been briefly reviewed here. Consequently, cross-sectional designs, which are often relatively quick to administer, have had a very considerable following among many leadership researchers in spite of the dubious nature of the causal relationships they engender. It should also be noted that the experimental approach shares with its cross-sectional counterpart a tendency to focus on designated leaders and subordinates, with an accompanying disinclination to ask fundamental questions about the nature of leadership as against what designated leaders do as incumbents of positions to which managerial responsibilities and the exercise of authority adhere.

In this discussion it has been necessary to deal briefly with the issues relating to the use of cross-sectional and experimental designs. To deal with them in greater depth would change this text into a treatise on research methodology. The designs explicated are those which have been used intensively by researchers seeking to distinguish effective from ineffective leader behaviour patterns. However, it is not an exhaustive list in that there is a group of research techniques which have been used in the context of seeking to describe the nature of managerial work and which are often perceived to have relevance for the study of leadership in organizations (Yukl, 1981, ch. 5). Firstly, there is *observation* in which managers are observed more or less unceasingly over a period of time. This technique may involve either 'structured' observation, whereby data are collected and recorded in the context of predetermined behavioural categories, or 'unstructured' observation, in which data are recorded in a less formal way on the basis of what appears interesting to the researcher. Secondly, there is the *diary* method which is often used in tandem with observation. This technique involves the recording by the manager himself of more or less everything that he does, usually in terms of predetermined categories. On the basis of data derived from observation and diaries researchers have been able to ascertain how much time is spent in meetings, on the telephone, at the desk, in formal and informal meetings, with subordinates or with superiors, etc. (see, e.g., Stewart, 1967; Mintzberg, 1973; Cohen and March, 1974; Lawrence, 1984). Other techniques have been used in the context of research into managers, but they have been in large part fairly marginal to this area of study.[6]

The problem with these techniques is that it is not always clear what they have to do with leadership. Mintzberg's (1973) work has already been cited as being of interest by virtue of attempting to disentangle the leadership element of managerial work. But even this investigation is of limited use in that it does not tell us whether some organizational positions involve the exercise of the leader role more than others or whether some individuals exercise it more than others irrespective of their position. The question of whether variations in the extent to which the leader role is exercised has implications for the manager's performance or that of his subordinates is side-stepped. It is manifestly the case that studies of managerial work are relevant to the study of leadership (cf. Stewart, 1982), but how and in what ways they are relevant cannot be determined until leadership and management are no longer seen as synonymous by researchers.

Overview

The purpose of this chapter has been to introduce the idea of leadership and some of the methods used for studying it. The fuzziness of the concept has not been ignored and the tendency for it to overlap with kindred ideas, such as management and the exercise of authority, has been noted and not dodged. However, the observation has also been made that it is necessary to hold many of the terminological difficulties in abeyance and the remainder of the book will focus on what, in the author's view, is generally taken to be the study of leadership in organizations. In Chapter 2, the tradition of examining leadership in terms of the traits of leaders will be addressed. In Chapters 3 and 4, the literature on leader behaviour, which emerged as disillusionment with the prominence given to traits grew, is examined. The idea that the situation in which leaders find themselves is an important determinant of the effects of particular styles of leadership provides the focus for Chapter 5. Chapter 6 tries to relate the study of leadership in organizations to ideas and developments in organization theory. Finally, Chapter 7 seeks to examine some more recent approaches.

There can be little doubt that the study of leadership in organizations is a field in flux. There is deep dissatisfaction with its fruits as the following often quoted statement suggests:

> Of all the confounding areas in social psychology, leadership theory undoubtedly contends for top nomination. And, ironically, probably more has been written and less is known about leadership than about any other topic in the behavioural sciences. (Bennis, 1959, pp. 259-60)

Little has changed since Bennis made this statement and many writers working within and outside the field of leadership have commented since then upon the inconclusiveness that pervades much of the literature. To some extent, the problem may derive from leadership researchers claiming too much for their speciality. For example: 'The successful organization has one major attribute that sets it apart from unsuccessful organizations: dynamic and effective leadership' (Hersey and Blanchard, 1977, p. 83). An assertion such as this seems vastly to overstate the potential influence of leadership to organizational effectiveness, particularly when one bears in mind the many other factors which are likely to impinge on it.

In this book, an attempt will be made to reflect the uncertainty with which the field is suffused. However, wherever feasible, the contributions of particular approaches will be dealt with so that readers will not be overwhelmed by a morass of equivocality. In recent years, the response to the disillusionment with much leadership research has been the proliferation of new perspectives, approaches, and paradigms. This trend is exemplified by the International Leadership Symposia series, whose most recent volumes in particular (Hunt, Sekaran and Schriesheim, 1982; Hunt, Hosking, Schriesheim and Stewart, 1984) contain many papers advocating new approaches. Thus the 1984 Symposium is described as 'the embodiment of the editors' philosophy of "Let a thousand flowers bloom", which we think is clearly called for in the current transitional period of leadership research' (Hunt *et al.*, 1984, p. 2). As might be anticipated, new approaches have also appeared outside of the pages of these volumes. These developments pose a problem to the textbook writer since it is neither feasible nor desirable to include all of them, if only because quite a large proportion are likely to have only a limited impact upon leadership research in the future. In the light of the author's view that only relatively major developments ought to be covered in a textbook and of the fact that he has limited powers of foresight, an attempt will be made to concentrate upon those approaches which are of particular interest to the study of leadership in organizations and which show signs of developing into research traditions.

The formalities are now over.

2
TRAITS AND ABILITIES

No amount of learning will make a man a leader unless
he has the natural qualities of one. (General Archibald Wavell,
The Times, 17 February 1941)

General Wavell seems to have subscribed to the view that leaders are born
not made. The idea that there are natural leaders is deeply ingrained in
many people's thinking. It is easy to see why many people responsible for
recruitment subscribe to this view, for if it were possible to specify the
factors which go to make up the natural leader, then the acquisition of
good leadership in organizations and elsewhere would be a matter of
screening people. Such an approach was consistent with the emergence of
psychological techniques in the 1930s and 1940s, the period during which
this approach to the study of leadership was in evidence.

However, as occasionally happens in the social sciences, decades of
research which addressed the question of whether there are natural leaders
failed to provide conclusive evidence that general qualities or abilities
could be discerned. In the 1940s, three reviews of the literature on
leadership 'traits' came to this conclusion. The reviews were conducted by
Bird (1940), Jenkins (1947), and Stogdill (1948), the last of which was the
most influential. Stogdill carried out a subsequent review of the literature
up to 1970 which was published along with his 1948 article in his
Handbook of Leadership (1974). Both of these reviews, along with yet a
further update were published in Bass's (1981) revised and expanded
edition of the *Handbook*, published after Stogdill's death in 1978. These
three 'editions' of the review of research on leadership traits, along with
other useful assessments such as Gibb's (1947; 1969) and Mann's (1959),
provide a comprehensive account of this approach to the study of
leadership, upon which the author will borrow heavily. All references to
Stogdill's (1948, 1974) work will be cited in terms of Bass (1981).

Research on leadership traits

The bulk of research on leadership traits has sought to establish the
personal features of leaders which distinguish them from non-leaders or
followers. It might be argued that such a question is of only limited use in

18

the context of the study of leadership in organizations where one would hope to identify the characteristics of effective, as against less effective, leaders. This latter issue had been addressed in a relatively small number of studies at the time of Stogdill's (1948) review. Unfortunately, reviews of the literature on leadership traits often fail to distinguish the two issues in their assessments (e.g. Bass, 1981, p. 75). It could be argued that effective leaders exhibit the identified traits in greater quantity (in terms of both number of traits and the quantity of each) than do non-leaders. Such a correspondence would need to be demonstrated rather than assumed, but is nonetheless implicit in a good deal of the literature.

What kinds of 'trait' have researchers tended to examine? There are three broad types of trait which the literature has addressed. Firstly, there are *physical* factors such as height, weight, physique, appearance and age. Secondly, researchers have examined *ability* characteristics such as intelligence, fluency of speech, scholarship, and knowledge. Thirdly, a wide range of *personality* features have been examined. These have included conservatism, introversion-extroversion, dominance, personal adjustment, self-confidence, interpersonal sensitivity, and emotional control.

Early reviews

A great many of these traits had been examined by Stogdill in 1948 and the implications of his assessment were broadly pessimistic. While he was able to point to a variety of leadership traits, i.e. variables which distinguished leaders from non-leaders, Stogdill also asserted: 'The qualities, characteristics and skills required in a leader are determined to a large extent by the demands of the situation in which he is to function as a leader' (Bass, 1981, p. 65). In other words, the situations or contexts in which leaders find themselves are key determinants of whether particular traits are appropriate. Similarly, Gibb (1947, p. 270) concluded that:

> the particular set of social circumstances existing at the moment
> determines which attributes of personality will confer leadership status
> and consequently determines which members of a group will assume the
> leadership role, and which qualities . . . function to maintain the
> individual in that role.

If the situation is so important then the quest for universal leadership traits would seem fruitless. A research programme under the direction of L.F. Carter, which was more or less contemporaneous with the publication of these views, seemed to provide support for the conclusions which were emerging from these literature reviews. Using experimental studies of school boys in three different work task conditions, Carter and Nixon (1949) found that leaders who were effective in one condition were not necessarily as effective in another, although the boys who emerged as leaders for clerical tasks tended to do so for intellectual tasks too, but not for mechanical tasks.

Later reviews

Stogdill's 1948 review is often cited as a major cause, albeit in conjunction with those of Bird, Gibb and Jenkins, of a disillusionment with research into leadership traits. Even Stogdill (Bass, 1981, p. 73) recognized in 1974 that they 'sounded the seeming deathknell of a purely traits approach to the study of leadership'. Indeed, these reviews are often cited as causes of a loss of interest in such research. It is certainly true that they were a contributory factor to a surge of interest in leadership styles and behaviour, discussed in later chapters, but they certainly did not kill off trait research. Stogdill's review of the 1949-70 literature was able to uncover 163 studies, hardly evidence of a moribund field. In particular, research into the traits of effective managers seems to have thrived during this period. Of particular interest is that on the basis of his second review, Stogdill (Bass, 1981, p. 73) asserted that his own and others' earlier reviews had over-emphasized the situational element and under-emphasized the universal traits which leaders seem to exhibit. This assertion was consistent with a review by Mann (1959) of personality factors alone and their relationship with leadership. Mann's review indicated that leaders tend to be more intelligent, extrovert, dominant, masculine, and interpersonally sensitive than non-leaders. They also tend to be better adjusted and less authoritarian. However, Mann found contradictory evidence in respect of all of these variables, as well as a very large number of findings which did not attain acceptable levels of statistical significance. However, the general tenor of this review was much more positive about the potential of personality variables to discriminate between leaders and others. Similarly, in contrast to the 1948 review, Stogdill's (Bass, 1981, p. 81) second survey resulted in a somewhat less tentative conclusion:

> The leader is characterized by a strong drive for responsibility and task completion, vigour and persistence in pursuit of goals, venturesomeness and originality in problem solving, drive to exercise initiative in social situations, self-confidence and sense of personal identity, willingness to accept consequences of decision and action, readiness to absorb interpersonal stress, willingness to tolerate frustration and delay, ability to influence other persons' behaviour, and capacity to structure social interaction systems to the purpose at hand.

Stogdill retained his views about the importance of the situation in the study of leadership traits, but sought to attach greater significance to traits as such than in his earlier work. It is worth pointing out that in his later survey, Stogdill chose to pay little attention to studies which did not confirm the importance of a particular trait because of the probability that disconfirming evidence is less likely to appear in print, since drawing conclusions from an unknown universe of evidence would be hazardous. This applies equally to confirming evidence, but due to the disinclination of researchers to publish negative findings, and often research journals editors' disinclination to publish them, the problem of drawing conclusions from studies which do not confirm the importance of a particular trait is particularly hazardous. The problem with his chosen strategy is that the reader is not given a strong feel for the possible *un*importance of a certain trait.

Table 2.1 summarizes some of the relationships and is based on Stogdill's own summary (Bass, 1981, Table 5.1). It excludes traits which, in the 1948 survey, seemed to exhibit a lot of disconfirmation, relative to the degree of confirmation, and those which have received little treatment. An asterisk means that there is broad confirmation of the importance of a trait in the 1948 or 1970 reviews.

Table 2.1 *Personal traits associated with leadership*

	1948	1970
Physical Characteristics		
Activity, energy	*	*
Appearance, grooming	*	*
Social Background		
Education	*	*
Social status	*	*
Mobility	*	*
Intelligence and Ability		
Intelligence	*	*
Judgment, decisiveness	*	*
Knowledge	*	*
Fluency of speech	*	*
Personality		
Adaptability	*	
Adjustment, normality		*
Aggressiveness, assertiveness		*
Alertness	*	*
Ascendance, dominance	*	*
Emotional balance, control	*	*
Independence, non-conformity		*
Objectivity, tough-mindedness		*
Originality, creativity	*	*
Personal integrity, ethical conduct	*	*
Resourcefulness		*
Self-confidence	*	*
Strength of conviction	*	*
Tolerance of stress		*
Task-Related Characteristics		
Achievement drive, desire to excel	*	*
Drive for responsibility	*	*
Enterprise, initiative		*
Persistence against obstacles	*	
Responsible in pursuit of objectives	*	*
Task orientation	*	*

	1948	1970
Social Characteristics		
Ability to enlist cooperation	*	*
Administrative ability		*
Cooperativeness	*	*
Popularity, prestige	*	
Sociability, interpersonal skills	*	*
Social participation	*	*
Tact, diplomacy	*	*

This table is based on Bass (1981, pp. 375-6). An asterisk indicates significant support for a trait in Stogdill's 1948 and 1970 reviews.

Many of the traits listed under 'Task Related' and 'Social' characteristics are ones which are often subsumed under 'Personality' by many writers. It is worth noting that, as Yukl (1981) has observed, the 1970 collection includes a larger number of studies in which technical and administrative skills figure strongly. It is questionable whether these attributes are 'traits' in the usual sense of the term, in that they border on many of the phenomena investigated by researchers concerned with leadership styles and behaviour, for example, a leader's task orientation. Further, it is difficult not to be overwhelmed by both the comprehensiveness and complexity of the list. Given that a great deal of research into leadership traits was motivated by a desire to promote instruments for screening leaders, it is not easy to see how one would choose from this bewildering (and growing) array. Of course, many are situation-specific, as Stogdill and others have long recognized, but in view of the fact that the relative importance of many situational contexts in relation to leadership traits is still not fully appreciated, this is not a great comfort. Nor are the additive and interactive effects of various combinations of traits fully documented.

General reflections

There can be little doubt that the mixed results which emerged from much trait research led to a disenchantment with the approach among leadership researchers in general and was, as has already been suggested, a factor in the surge of interest in leadership styles from the late 1940s onwards. This shift has occurred, and in large part has been maintained, in spite of the fact that many of the findings which have emerged from the study of leadership style have been just as mixed and also found to be context specific (see Chapter 5).

One other possible reason for the disillusionment with much leader trait research has to do with the nature of the methodology employed. A great deal of the research was based on discerning who became leaders in leaderless contexts,[1] which were often created in psychologists' laboratories or alternatively observed in school classrooms and other natural environments of limited generalizability. The differences, in trait terms, between these emergent leaders, whether formally acknowledged as such by the group or not, and their followers were then examined. This kind of procedure was employed by Cattell and Stice (1954) who found that, for example, leaders elected voluntarily by experimental groups engaged in a variety of tasks (e.g. construction, committee decisions, tug-of-war) had greater character integration, were less anxious, and exhibited a greater will to control than followers. In Nelson's (1964) study of men in Antarctic scientific stations, group leaders were discerned on the basis of nominations by supervisors, based on responses to questions to the effect that a particular man displayed a 'marked ability to lead his fellows' and 'always follows, never leads'. These nominated leaders were found to be more self-confident, alert, and aggressive than followers. Peer nominations of leadership are probably more frequently found in the literature than are superiors' nominations, though numerous examples of assessments of emergent leadership by observers also exist.

The difficulty with the focus on emergent leadership, quite apart from the inconsistent or statistically insignificant findings, is that its relevance for 'real-life' situations was not always clear. Can we assume that a personality type that emerges as a leader in a leaderless tug-of-war will also be an effective captain of industry? While some of the early leadership style research, like the work of Bales (e.g. Bales and Slater, 1955), reflected an interest in emergent leadership in leaderless contexts, albeit with a greater emphasis on what leaders *did*, most research was on 'real' leaders in industry and elsewhere. At a time when more and more funding for such research was coming from industry and the military, researchers may have felt unconsciously pressured to shift research on leadership into applied contexts. Equally, however, as Korman (1968) was shown in a review of the literature dealing with 'those psychological characteristics which lead to effective leadership in the formal organization' (p. 295), researchers have not been overly successful in this respect either. Such research was much more concerned with the characteristics which distinguish effective from ineffective managers (i.e. leaders) and, as Yukl (1981) has observed, tended to expand the array of traits to include technical and administrative skills; hence the increase in attention devoted to these phenomena between Stogdill's 1948 and 1970 reviews. Three research programmes associated with the emphasis on the characteristics of effective leaders will be examined below. Thus, the reviews by Stogdill and others did not sound the deathknell for this area of study, though Korman's (1968) review suggests that the results emanating from it were somewhat equivocal. This equivocality, it will be argued below, is exacerbated by virtue of the questionable relevance of such research for the understanding of *leadership* in organizations.

Even if the leadership trait approach were completely discredited, which it is not, the study of the personal characteristics of leaders would still have a place, quite apart from the situational study of traits. One such area which can be detected in the literature is the considerable evidence that personal characteristics may affect leadership styles. In an experimental study which entailed a simulation of a production firm, Hinton and

Barrow (1976) sought to discern the personality correlates of the reinforcement strategies of 'leaders' in relation to their 'subordinates'. The subjects were university undergraduates in the USA. 'Leaders' who used positive reinforcement methods were, for example, more willing to take responsibility for, and have confidence in, their own actions, more prepared to make their own decisions, more relaxed, and more enthusiastic about life. Those using negative sanctions tended to be more socially bold, more suspicious and self-opinionated, more inclined to think in abstract terms, and more conscientious. Similarly, a study of US managers by Bass and Farrow (reported in Bass, 1981) suggests that leaders' authoritarianism (in personality terms) affected how consultative and manipulative they were in respect of their subordinates. Further, in a predominantly theoretical paper, House (1977) has sought to develop a theory about charismatic leadership, a category that is frequently found in classifications of types of leader (Bass, 1981, pp. 20-1). Many writers view the charismatic leader as referring to individuals with extraordinary powers who exert a powerful attraction in respect of their followers. House's approach is to suggest examining what such individuals do and the effects that they have on their followers. Based upon a review of the literature, he suggests that charismatic leaders differ from non-charismatic leaders in terms of 'dominance and self-confidence, need for influence, and a strong conviction in the moral righteousness of their beliefs' (House, 1977, p. 194).[2] In line with the work of researchers like Barrow and Hinton and Bass and Farrow, House seems to be recognizing the potency of personal traits as possible determinants of leader behaviour.

Finally, there is interest in the impact of personality variables which have only relatively recently been recognized outside leadership research on the behaviour of leaders. Two examples can be cited. The first is the 'locus of control' notion developed by Rotter (1966) which distinguishes between people in terms of whether they believe personal outcomes to be affected by their own actions. 'Internals' are people who see outcomes as a function of what they themselves do; 'externals' see them as a product of forces over which they have no control. The two terms pertain to a continuum rather than polar types. 'Locus of control' seems to influence the way leaders behave. A study by Durand and Nord (1976) of managers in a US textiles and plastics firm found that 'externals' were viewed by subordinates as exhibiting more 'initiation of structure' at work and consideration. Further evidence reviewed by Bass (1981, p. 132) suggests that 'internal' leaders are more task-oriented and employ rewards and respect as ways of influencing subordinates. 'External' leaders seem to be more coercive and threatening in their approach. There is also research which suggests that 'internal' leaders are more considerate, contrary to Durand and Nord. It would seem surprising if Durand and Nord were correct on this latter point, given the greater propensity of 'external' leaders for a coercive approach. A study of supervisors in a number of US organizations by Johnson, Luthans and Hennessey (1984) found that 'internal' supervisors were more likely to be seen as persuasive and influential with their own supervisors than 'external' supervisors. Miller and Friesen (1984) found that small, simple firms which had 'internal' leaders were much more likely to be entrepreneurial, in the sense of seeking to be innovative even in the face of hostile markets. In other organizational contexts the effect of the locus of control of leaders on the firm's entrepreneurship was either less evident or non-existent. Such findings imply that the idea of locus of control may have an effect on the behaviour of leaders, and possibly their effectiveness, but that its influence may be affected by the situation.

Secondly, Drory and Gluskinos (1980) examined the impact of Machiavellianism, which refers to 'cognitive agreement with the basic ideas of Nicollo Machiavelli, for example, mistrust in human nature, lack of conventional morality, opportunism, and lack of affect in interpersonal relationships' (p. 81). A laboratory experiment was designed on the basis of responses to a scale of Machiavellianism, as well as experimental manipulations of levels of task structure and of leader position power. Thus work groups (university undergraduates) were created such that some were led by high scoring Machiavellians, others by low scorers. Those leaders who scored high on the scale gave more orders, were more responsive to situational demands, but were less sensitive to group members' feelings than low scoring leaders. Variations in the Machiavellianism of leaders had no impact on the productivity of the work groups. This finding is somewhat unencouraging since the personal characteristics which distinguish effective from ineffective leaders have been of concern to many trait researchers. Nonetheless, it would seem that personality characteristics like the two just reviewed, which had not been fully explored in a leadership context at the time of the various seminal reviews like Stogdill's, may be found to have a role in future research. This is particularly so in the context of the examination of the personality determinants of leader behaviour which dovetails well with the preoccupations with leadership style exhibited by research discussed in later chapters.[3]

A great deal of the research which was assessed by the classic reviews of Stogdill, Bird, Gibb, and others was based upon the study of leadership in small group, leaderless contexts located either in the laboratory or in field contexts (e.g. school classrooms, or the study of an Antarctic station cited above). It was suggested that the fact that much of the research was not based on formal organizational contexts may have been a factor in some of the disillusionment with trait research. What of the possible role of personal factors in such milieux? Korman's (1968) conclusion, cited above, suggests that the bulk of trait research situated in formal organizations did not readily permit the prediction of leadership ability. We shall now turn to three research programmes which were in their infancy at the time of Korman's review and ask how far personal traits are important factors in distinguishing effective from less effective managers.

Studies of personal traits in relation to managerial performance

Ghiselli and the study of 'managerial talent'

Ghiselli (1971) was concerned to identify the 'totality of traits and abilities' (p. 16) which are required in the gamut of managerial jobs, that is 'managerial talent'. In particular, this entailed seeking to discern those traits and abilities which impinge upon successful or unsuccessful managerial careers. In order to distinguish success from failure in managers, Ghiselli relied upon superiors' assessments of the subjects of the investigation. The sample comprised 306 predominantly middle managers drawn non-randomly from a range of US firms. One feature of the research is that the managers were not aware of their participation in the research, in that they believed that the various personality inventories which they filled in were being used for their evaluation. A procedure of this kind is often regarded as unethical by social scientists as it transgresses the principle of 'informed consent' (Diener and Crandall, 1978). The superiors' assessments of the managers in the sample resulted in 57 per cent being identified as more successful, 43 per cent as less successful. Data were also collected on line supervisors and line workers.

From the total array of possible traits and abilities which might impinge upon managerial performance, thirteen were chosen, and grouped under three main headings. Each manager filled in a research instrument called the Self-Description Inventory in which individuals are presented with sixty-four pairs of traits and are asked to choose the item in each pair which best (in thirty-two pairs) and least (thirty-two pairs) describes them. Individuals are then scored in terms of the thirteen traits presented below. The correlation coefficient relating each trait to managerial ability is provided in brackets:

1 . *Abilities*
(a) Supervisory ability – as indicated by managers' abilities to direct, organize and integrate the work activities of their subordinates (.46).
(b) Intelligence – an assessment of cognitive abilities (.27).
(c) Initiative – a capacity for both initiating action and being inventive (.15).
2 *Personality traits*
(a) Self-assurance – how effective managers see themselves at dealing with work problems (.19).
(b) Decisiveness – the degree of hesitation involved in coming to a decision (.22).
(c) Masculinity-femininity – meant to denote forcibleness, lack of passivity (masculinity), and logical (a somewhat stereotypical and implicitly disparaging view of femininity!) (−.05).
(d) Maturity – the extent to which an individual appears older than his age (−.03).

(e) Working-class affinity – a preparedness to be associated with the work and problems of the working class (−.17).

3 *Motivations*

(a) Need for occupational status – a drive to achieve the prestige and responsibility associated with high occupational status (.34).

(b) Need for self-actualization – the extent to which an individual feels impelled to ensure that their talents are fully utilized. This notion owes a great deal to the ideas of Maslow (1943) whose work heavily influenced the work of later 'human relations' writers who viewed this need as being insufficiently fulfilled in many modern work situations (see, e.g., Bryman, 1976) (.26).

(c) Need for power over others – a drive for direction and control over the work of others. Research by McClelland (1975) has shown this drive to be a key motivational force in successful managers in organizations (.03).

(d) Need for high financial reward – to what extent narrow instrumental preoccupations motivate a manager (−.18).

(e) Need for job security – this factor denotes not just concern about tenure, but also about the implications of work arrangements for jobs and status at work (−.30).

In his assessment of the *relative* contribution of each of these factors to managerial talent, Ghiselli scored them not only in terms of their degree of correlation with it but also (a) the extent to which managers exceeded both line supervisors and workers on each attribute, and (b) whether each trait is equally or differentially associated with success in managers, supervisors and workers. If a particular trait were associated with success among the latter two groups as well, then it could hardly be predictive of managerial talent as such. The broad pattern which emerged on the basis of these rating criteria (Ghiselli, 1971, p. 165) is broadly consonant with the picture gleaned from the correlation coefficients indicated above.

This is an ambitious and suggestive piece of research. Some of the results are fairly congruent with findings from other studies which point to the relevance of traits such as assertiveness, need for accomplishment and esteem, and self-actualization for rapid managerial advancement (Bass, 1981, p. 133). The lack of an association between managerial talent and need for power is slightly surprising in the light of McClelland's (1975) research which indicates that this is an important variable. However, the latter research suggests that this power motivation is directed towards organizational ends rather than career enhancement among successful managers. It may be that Ghiselli's measure failed to encapsulate this distinction sufficiently.

Ghiselli's work is often taken as relevant to leadership by writers like Dessler (1982, p. 327) who sees it as establishing the 'traits that distinguish effective from ineffective leaders'. That Ghiselli's research is relevant to leadership studies is also suggested by Filley, House and Kerr (1976, pp. 218-19) and House and Baetz (1979, pp. 353-4). Such assertions imply a central problem for research of this kind in relation to leadership studies, namely that it is about managers. Whether managers are *ipso facto* leaders is undemonstrated. In the case of Ghiselli's research this difficulty is particularly pertinent in the light of the large contribution of 'supervisory ability' to managerial talent. The difficulty is that it is precisely 'supervisory ability' that many leadership researchers have sought to explain, in many cases employing a trait approach!

Miner and the role motivation theory of managerial effectiveness

In 1968 Korman reviewed a range of studies concerned with the prediction of what he vacillated between calling leadership or managerial effectiveness. One set of studies was one in which researchers sought to use tests of 'leadership ability' to predict effectiveness (Korman, 1968, pp. 302-7). He concluded this section by asserting that the approach developed by Miner was 'actually predictive of managerial behaviour in a formal organization' (Korman, 1968, p. 307). Since then, Miner's (1978) techniques have been used by himself and others in a range of contexts.

The theoretical starting point of Miner's work is that all organizations have general managerial role prescriptions. Affective endorsement of the principles underlying these prescriptions is likely to contribute to greater managerial effectiveness; a negative reaction to them will yield less effectiveness in managers. Miner identifies six managerial role prescriptions; a positive attitude to each of them is supposed to contribute to managerial effectiveness:

(a) Attitude to Authority – the manager must be prepared to accept that some individuals have authority over him and to react positively to them;
(b) Competitiveness – managers must be prepared to go to battle for themselves and their subordinates;
(c) Assertiveness – managers must be prepared to assert themselves over decisions, discipline, and the like;
(d) Exercise of Power – managers must be prepared to exercise power and direct others, employing positive and negative sanctions as necessary;
(e) Standing Out – managers must have high visibility;
(f) Performance of Administrative Routine – managers must be prepared to engage in the more routine, mundane aspects of their work, and feel positively about it.

Miner uses a projective test, the Miner Sentence Completion Scale (MSCS) to gauge managers' affective reactions to these six role prescriptions. The scale contains forty items, thirty-five of which are scored to form seven sub-scales (competitiveness is elaborated to produce two sub-scales – competitiveness in both games and situations – hence the extra measure). The test involves respondents completing sentences, responses to which are coded in terms of the subject's motivation in connection with the role prescriptions. Thus 'Making introductions . . .' elicits responses, relevant to Standing Out; 'Dictating letters . . .' to Performance of Administrative Routine, and the like.

Is there a positive correlation between the managerial motivation and managerial success? In a review of studies of managers in which the MSCS was employed, Miner (1978) found that high overall scores seem to be associated with managerial success, as measured by a variety of criteria, including organizational rank and ratings of performance or potential. In particular the two sub-scales concerned with competitiveness tended to be fairly consistently related to these criteria, as did positive attitudes toward authority and the exercise of power, albeit to a lesser degree. However, Miner's review also establishes that the scale does not have predictive power in some organizational contexts, such as schools, in which bureaucratic role descriptions are presumably either less important or less pronounced.

Miner also examined seventeen experimental studies in which managers had been trained in the principles which can be derived from the role motivation approach. This review suggests that people's orientation can be changed (sixteen out of the seventeen studies), and that assertiveness and the exercise of power are particularly responsive attributes in this respect.

Once again, the results of this research are suggestive. Indeed, there is some congruence between some of the Ghiselli traits and the MSCS sub-scales (Miner, 1978, pp. 754-5). Research of this kind, which is based in formal organizational contexts, differs from the studies of emergent leadership conducted by generations of trait researchers preoccupied with the personal characteristics of leaders who emerge in leaderless contexts. In this context, it is interesting to note that Miner (1982, pp. 300-2) reports research which suggests that the MSCS role motivation scale is unrelated to leadership emergence in small, leaderless groups. It may be that a finding such as this is due more to the fact that the role motivation approach is not really about leadership as some writers (e.g. Korman, 1968; Yukl, 1981) think it is. Miner seems implicitly to recognize this possibility when he observes that 'research bearing on the extent to which role-motivation theory and leadership formulations . . . deal with similar constructs is lacking' (Miner, 1978, p. 757). We are left with a well documented, fairly well supported, suggestive series of studies which are often viewed as manifesting a trait approach to the study of leadership, but which seem only to be on the margins of leadership research.

The assessment centre and the identification of managerial potential

Since the late 1950s an approach to the identification of managerial potential has gained a considerable following. Known as the 'assessment centre', the procedure involves subjecting prospective managers to a wide variety of tests and interviews in order to assess skills and traits which are deemed to be predictive of managerial ability. The assessment centre is often used as an important component of the development of existing managers too. One of the most exhaustive studies of the efficacy of the assessment centre approach is an eight-year study carried out at American Telephone and Telegraph Company (AT and T) reported by Bray, Campbell and Grant (1974).

During the years 1956, 1957, 1959 and 1960, 274 recruits to AT and T attended an assessment centre for a period of three-and-a-half days in small groups. The research design involves annual interviews with the respondents each year after the assessment, as well as data being collected about them from members of the subjects' companies (e.g. superiors). Eight years after the initial assessment, a reassessment takes place. The aim of the study and the centre itself is to 'determine as completely as possible the abilities, potential, motivation, attitudes, and personality character- istics of each subject at the time he started in the study' (Bray *et al.* 1974, p. 18). To this end twenty-five personal attributes were designated as likely to be important in future managerial success. They are summarized in Table 2.2.

In order to assess recruits in terms of these criteria a number of techniques were employed. Firstly, the 'Business Game' in which a group, for example, simulates a partnership involved in manufacture. The group is given a small amount of money to start the enterprise and must then buy parts for, assemble, and sell the commodity for profit. This exercise was meant to shed light on the following attributes for each individual: 3, 7, 9, 11, 19, 21, 23, 24 and 25. A second component, again a group-based exercise, is 'The Group Discussion Problem'. The example given in the Bray *et al.* report involves each of the six members of a group, supposedly in a middle management role, having to argue for the promotion of a foreman for a vacancy. Each member is given a brief description of a different foreman, and delivers a short presentation arguing the case for that particular person's promotion. There is then a one-hour free discussion to select and rank the foremen. This technique relates to the following criteria: 2, 3, 5, 7, 9, 11, 21, 23 and 24. The 'In-Basket' is a more individually-based test. The recruit has to imagine that he or she has recently been notified of the death of a plant manager whose position he assumes. He has only two or three hours to deal with the in-basket of his predecessor. Which of the myriad of problems and paper work in front of him does the assessee deal with, how and why? Candidates are interviewed to determine their rationales for their plans of action. The In-Basket is intended to shed light on: 2, 3, 6, 10, 12, 19, 21, 23, 24 and 25. Fourthly, projective psychological tests are used 'to discover important aspects of a man's motivational and personality characteristics by an analysis of his free responses to pictures and words' (Bray *et al.*, 1974, p. 26). Projective tests involve stimuli which can engender a range of responses (e.g. an incomplete sentence, such as 'To me, failure is ————'), responses to which supposedly reveal something about the respondent as a person. In addition, assessees are interviewed, take tests of mental ability, and fill out personality and attitude tests. Each recruit is then rated on a five-point continuum in respect of each of the traits.

To what extent were the recruits' assessment centre scores on each of the traits correlated with their progress in management (that is, the

Table 2.2 *Management progress traits*

1 Scholastic aptitude (.19)
2 Oral communication skills (.33). Written communication skills (correlation not given).
3 Human relations skills – ability 'to lead a group to accomplish a task without arousing hostility' (Bray *et al.*, 1974, p. 19) (.32).
4 Personal impact – the extent to which someone stamps his presence on others, but is likeable (.15).
5 Perception of threshold social cues – a person's sensitivity to behavioural cues offered by others (.17).
6 Creativity – ability to solve problems in an innovative manner (.25).
7 Self-objectivity – how far a person exhibits a realistic appraisal of his assets and liabilities, and an awareness of his motives (.04).
8 Social objectivity – degree of prejudices against social groups (race, socio-economic, etc.) (.13).
9 Behaviour flexibility – ability to modify behaviour in order to attain a goal (.21).
10 Need for approval of superiors – degree of emotional dependence on authority figures (−.14).
11 Need for approval of peers – degree of emotional dependence on peers and lower status associates (−.17).
12 Inner work standards – extent to which someone strives to do a better job than that required (.21).
13 Need for advancement – need to achieve promotion early in one's career (.31).
14 Need for security – extent to which a person needs a secure job (−.20).
15 Goal flexibility – ability to change 'life goals' in the light of new circumstances (−.18).
16 Primacy of work – extent to which satisfactions derived from work exceed those derived from non-work (.18).
17 Bell system value orientation – likely ability to imbibe Bell (i.e. AT and T) values (−.02).
18 Realism of expectations – how realistic a person's work life expectations are (.08).
19 Tolerance of uncertainty – a person's work performance under uncertain or unstructured circumstances (.30).
20 Ability to delay gratification – ability to defer immediate rewards for greater future ones (−.19).
21 Resistance to stress (.31)
22 Range of interests (i.e. in non-work areas) (.23).
23 Energy – ability to keep going even when working very hard (.28).
24 Organization and planning – ability to organize work and plan ahead (.28).
25 Decision-making – preparedness to make decisions, and their quality (.18).

N.B.   N = 123 due to subsequent movement from AT and T. Correlations (in brackets) at or in excess of .23 are significant at the .01 level; at or over .18 significant at .05 level.
Adapted from Bray *et al.* (1974, pp. 18-20 and 77).

managerial level attained), which Bray *et al.* take to be indicative of managerial success? Table 2.2 provides the correlation coefficients (in brackets) relating each trait to success in management. The correlations often achieve statistical significance though only nine are at or over the .01 level. The highest correlation, for oral communication skill, still leaves 90 per cent of the variation in management success unexplained. It would have been useful to see a multiple correlation coefficient in order to find out how far the twenty-five traits in total correlated with success. Huck (1977) reports an earlier AT and T study of the sample used in the Bray *et al.* research, which was based on trainees who had just graduated from university, and a second sample of non-college people who had been appointed to non-management positions but who had advanced rapidly into management. This second group underwent an assessment centre regime too. The correlations between overall assessment centre predictions and management level only five to seven years later were .44 and .71 for the university and non-university samples respectively. Such findings point to a good degree of predictive accuracy, though it is a good deal less impressive for the sample that was the chief focus of the Bray *et al.* (1974) study. Whether such correlations are deemed 'large' depends on one's interpretation, but for practical programmes of action it is a little disconcerting to see so much variance in performance being unexplained.

Nonetheless, 64 per cent of the university group predicted to reach middle management in ten years had done so after eight years, as against 32 per cent of those not so predicted or about whom assessors were unsure; for the non-university group the percentages were 40 per cent and 9 per cent respectively. By year sixteen, 89 per cent of the university group predicted to reach middle management had done so, as against 66 per cent of their peers who were not predicted to do so; in the non-university group the percentages were 63 per cent and 18 per cent respectively (Thornton and Byham, 1982, p. 256). This confirms that the ability to predict managerial potential is stronger in the non-university group. Furthermore, the assessment centre approach fares better at identifying people who will get to middle management swiftly (which in any case is its main aim), since a large percentage of the university group not predicted to reach middle management within ten years (66 per cent) had nonetheless done so within sixteen years.

It is also debatable whether the achievement of higher management levels is a sufficiently good criterion of performance. Not only has it been used by Bray *et al.*, but also in many of the managerial role motivation studies reported by Miner (1978) and in a study by Hall and Donnell (1979) mentioned in the next chapter. The achievement of higher positions in management is obviously related to how good a person is. But it is also very much related to a very individualistic striving for personal success. In the Bray *et al.* research, the third highest correlation with management success (.31) was 'need for advancement' which is indicative of a possibly selfish striving for personal advancement. Of course the organization may benefit as a result of such ambition, but it would be interesting to know whether a correlation between need for advancement and superiors' ratings of job performance would be quite as large. This point is particularly important in view of the possibility that a person's political skills may be instrumental to their organizational advancement. This variable was not measured by the AT and T researchers, though it may be highly potent in respect of managerial success as they define it. Nonetheless, while only one study of an assessment centre has been dealt with, albeit possibly the most important, literature reviews by Finkle (1976), Huck (1977) and Thornton and Byham (1982) generally point to observed traits having good predictive validity, though the studies diverge in the characteristics focused upon.

General implications

As with the research into personal traits reported earlier in this chapter, these three approaches to the study of the personal traits associated with managerial success – Ghiselli's research, Miner's theoretical and empirical investigations, and the Assessment Centre Approach – collectively posit a bewildering array of possible and actual correlates. The divergent approaches to the conceptualization and measurement of these traits (as well as of managerial success or performance) make stable comparisons exceedingly difficult. There are clearly some factors which seem to be similar across the studies and which appear to be predictive. Examples would be the importance of intelligence and a low need for security in the Bray and Ghiselli studies. Many of them are also borne out by a large piece of research into American, Australian, Indian, and Japanese managers (England, 1975), in which managerial success, defined as pay relative to age, was associated with an emphasis upon pragmatic, dynamic, achievement-oriented personal values. Less successful managers emphasize static and passive values. A study of managers from twelve nations by Bass *et al.* (1979) discerned a number of traits which affected their respondents' rate of advancement through management. While national differences were found to exist, the investigators were able in general to confirm the contribution of a pragmatic attitude to rate of advancement, as well as decisiveness, proactiveness and a desire for status, all of which are traits found to be of importance by other researchers. Bass *et al.* were also able to confirm the negative effect of a need for security on a manager's potential and career.

While the diversity of traits which nowadays are examined in relation to managerial ability (Bass, 1981) is somewhat overwhelming, there appear to be some convergent findings which suggest that Korman's (1968) pessimistic conclusion would require some revision. Clearly, those researchers who chose to maintain an interest in personal traits associated with leadership and managerial ability, in spite of the unencouraging reviews of Stogdill and Korman, have been able to deliver findings of considerable interest. Stogdill's re-assessment of the literature between 1948 and 1970 (cited above) – some of which include early versions of the

research concerned with management effectiveness reported in this chapter
– reflects this tendency.

What is disconcerting about the studies of managerial talent, effectiveness, and progress, quite apart from the problems associated with their
measurement, is precisely what they have to do with leadership. Reference
has already been made to the association in some writers' views of the
work of Ghiselli and Miner with the study of leadership. Writers such as
Yukl (1981) and Bass (1981) appear, at least by inference, to take
assessment centre studies, like that conducted at AT and T to be relevant
to the study of leadership. But in what sense are they relevant? Leadership
and management are not the same thing, as suggested in Chapter 1. Simply
because it may be possible to identify clusters of traits which can predict
managerial effectiveness (or talent) does not necessarily mean that they are
predictive of leadership effectiveness. This problem is confounded, as
suggested above, by the fact that in the Ghiselli study 'supervisory ability',
an idea which leadership trait researchers are often at pains to predict, is
itself the chief correlate of managerial talent. Similarly, in the AT and T
research the second highest correlate of managerial advancement was
'human relations skills' (see Table 2.2 for the definition). In terms of the
definitions of leadership reviewed in Chapter 1, what Bray *et al.* meant by
'human relations skills' is almost exactly the same as many of those
definitions. Yet human relations skills are apparently predictive of
managerial success, so the two ideas – leadership and managerial
effectiveness – cannot be the same. As with Ghiselli's 'supervisory ability',
the idea of 'human relations skills' is precisely what researchers into
personal traits in relation to leadership would be interested in explaining
or predicting.

An insight into this point is provided by a piece of research which seems
to have been conducted at an early stage in the AT and T programme
reported by Rychlak (1963). The research deals with eighty-four foremen
who attended the assessment centre. Assessments were made of the extent
of each person's leadership, defined as 'behaviour calculated to influence
the group members in acts relevant to the problem' (Rychlak, 1963, p. 48).
The assessments were based on the Business Game and Group Discussion.
On the basis of personality assessments filled in by the subjects, the
correlates of leadership were assessed. It was found that: 'Leaders were
typified by dominance and aggression needs, and achievement orientation,
and good mental and scholastic ability' (Rychlak, 1963, p. 51). Clearly,
this was a study of the personality correlates of what the AT and T
researchers later called human relations skills. Since the latter is an
important contributor to managerial success, it is clearly misleading to
identify such studies with leadership research. Such research shows that
leadership skills are, or may be, a factor in managerial success. However,
effectiveness as a leader is not necessarily the same as success as a
manager, hence the implications in the AT and T study that the former
contributes to the latter, while a number of other variables, commonly
employed to predict leadership ability, were examined as possible
predictors of managerial potential. Studies like the AT and T research, as

well as the work of Ghiselli, Miner, England and others, make no pretensions about studying leadership rather than management, so it is important not to fall into the trap of treating them as synonymous terms.

It may be asked why the studies of managerial success were included at all, in view of the foregoing reservations. The material was included for two reasons. Firstly, such studies are relevant insofar as leadership is a component of the managerial role and so may contribute to success in this sphere. Secondly, the research is often treated, albeit unquestioningly, as though it were part of the literature on leadership. Thus, while the studies of the personal factors associated with management effectiveness do have implications and ramifications for the study of leadership, it is misleading to assume that the two areas are identical or even similar. We are clearly witnessing in some of these confusions the problems associated with a 'fuzzy' concept like that of leadership.

Summary

The reviews of studies of the personal traits associated with leadership written in the late 1940s and early 1950s were generally pessimistic about this line of research. Stogdill's review in 1948 seems to have been particularly instrumental in turning many researchers away from the study of traits to the examination of what leaders do. In fact, his review merely asserted that greater sensitivity was required to situational circumstances, an emphasis which in 1974 he suggested may have been too great. Later reviews of trait studies, such as the latter, coupled with the research on managers in formal organizations (insofar as it has a bearing on leadership research) seem to point to a more consistent set of findings.

3
LEADERSHIP STYLE I:
EARLY APPROACHES AND
NORMATIVE PROGRAMMES

In the late 1940s the study of leadership in organizations shifted its emphasis away from the study of the 'traits' of leaders towards their 'style' or behaviour. Leadership style and behaviour are usually treated as synonyms, both pointing to what leaders do. At least three factors seem to have contributed to this change of emphasis. The chief one is undoubtedly the lack of consistent findings which Jenkins (1947), Stogdill (1948) and others had identified. As Shartle (1957, p. 1) and Fleishman (1973), both of whom are associated with the style approach, have observed there was a strong feeling that the emphasis upon traits had reached an impasse. Consequently there was a

> shift in emphasis during that period from thinking about leadership in terms of traits that someone 'has' to the conceptualization of leadership as a form of activity that certain individuals may engage in. (Fleishman, 1973, p. 3)

The second factor which may have contributed to this 'shift' is that general psychological work on leadership seemed to be moving in the direction of examining what leaders do. This emphasis is particularly evident in a group of studies occasionally referred to as the 'Iowa Childhood Studies' (see Lewin, Lippitt and White, 1939; White and Lippitt, 1960). The approach was to create experimentally different social climates which reflected leadership behaviour patterns. An early study involved organizing two clubs of ten-year-old children engaged in a work task over a three-month period. Each group had the same leader, but with one group he acted in an authoritarian manner; in the other group, democratically. This study suggested a number of hypotheses which were followed up in a similar but more detailed experiment. This second study added a third form of leadership, *laissez-faire*, to the earlier pairing. In the authoritarian treatments, the leader determined policy, work techniques and organization, remained aloof, and was 'personal' in his praise or criticism of group members. In the democratic conditions, policy matters were decided

36

on a group basis, only general procedures were suggested by the leader, work organization was relatively freely decided and the leader was objective in his praise or criticism. The *laissez-faire* leader allowed complete freedom to the group, was a non-participant in the group's activities, was reactive in terms of matters of work organization, and made few comments on group members' work. Four groups of ten-year-old boys were given these treatments, but in this second study, each group experienced all three leadership styles, but in different orders.[1] The boys' responses to these different treatments (including those in the earlier experiment) were gauged from observations, conversations, comments by leaders, and by a number of other techniques. The researchers found that authoritarian leadership generated aggression, hostility, in-group scape-goating, and more dependence on the leader. While authoritarian leaders tended to have more productive groups (they were engaged in 'hobby activities') in quantitative terms, democratic leaders' groups had greater work motivation. Groups under democratic leadership tended to have friendlier environments, to be more group-minded and less submissive to the leader. There was also evidence that there was much latent discontent in the authoritarian condition, as implied by the boys' preference for democratic leaders and the fact that four of them dropped out during autocratic 'periods'. In the *laissez-faire* condition, less work was done and it was of poorer quality.

Although not totally unambiguous and not in an applied context, results such as these pointed to the possible fruitfulness of examining the behaviour of leaders rather than their personal characteristics. The foregoing behavioural effects were of interest to researchers interested in organizational phenomena, and writers concerned with the effects of different styles of leadership in organizations often acknowledged their intellectual debt to these studies (e.g. Morse and Reimer, 1956, p. 120; Tannenbaum, 1966, pp. 85-7).

There is yet a third reason why leadership style emerged as a prominent focus, which relates to the emergence of the 'human relations' approach to the study of the firm. The human relations movement emerged in the wake of the Hawthorne Studies conducted at the Western Electric Company's Hawthorne plant in Chicago between the years 1927 and 1932. One of the principal findings of this research was that benign, friendly, loose supervision had a positive impact upon worker morale and productivity. In other words, it was what the supervisor/leader *did* which led to superior performance. This finding stimulated a major preoccupation of the subsequent human relations movement with supervisory style and its concomitants (Landsberger, 1958, pp. 101-3). Ironically, in spite of the fact that many writers treat as axiomatic the role of the Hawthorne Studies in establishing the importance of supervisory style for worker attitudes and productivity, the evidence was often at variance with the conclusions.

The first Relay Assembly Test Room study, which lasted over two years, is often taken to exhibit a clear demonstration of the importance of lenient supervision. A group of women were taken out of their normal department and placed in a special room. Over the entire length of this research, the group's production level increased by 30 per cent, in spite of numerous alterations to hours of work, rest pauses, incentive system, and the like. The view emerged that 'the girls' release from oppressive supervision as exercised in their regular department was a chief determinant of their favourable response to the experiment' (Landsberger, 1958, p. 53). A re-examination of the documents pertaining to the study by Carey (1967) would lead one to doubt this interpretation. During the early months of the study there was concern that some of the assembly operators were not showing the 'proper' attitude and were talking too much. Lack of cooperation was reported and there were threats of disciplinary action. Roughly ten months after the start of the study, during which output had been stationary or falling, two of the operators were dismissed and replaced. According to Carey's (1967) qualitative analysis of the documentation and Franke and Kaul's (1978) time-series analysis, it was the re-assertion of tight discipline which culminated in the dismissal of the two operators which led to a surge in the group output level. After a while, the more relaxed style of supervision was restored, though output does not appear to have increased very much from this point to the end of the study. Interviews, fifteen years later, with some of the test room participants indicate that periods of tight, disciplinarian supervision definitely existed (Greenwood, Bolton and Greenwood, 1983). The irony of such re-assessments, however, should not blind us to the very significant impact of the *belief* that the study demonstrated that supervisory practices significantly affect people's morale and productivity. Lenient, considerate supervision became a key ingredient of the emergent human relations approach with its interest in the role of social factors at the work place. Indeed, the preoccupation with leadership style which is revealed in the material dealt with in this chapter is part-and-parcel of the human relations tradition.

These three factors seem to account at least in part for the increased interest in leadership style which arose in the late 1940s. The central focus of this tradition is one which is implicit in both the Iowa studies and the post-Hawthorne human relations movement – namely, the impact of different types of leader behaviour upon group attitudes and performance. It should also be noted that the shift from 'trait' to 'style' approaches has, or is deemed to have, practical significance, since, as Adair (1983, p. 8) has observed: 'The assumption that leaders are born and not made favours an assumption upon *selection* rather than *training* for leadership.' If leadership is a matter of personal qualities, then ensuring a supply of good leaders for an organization is a matter of selecting those with the recognized attributes and weeding out those who do not exhibit them. On the assumption that personal qualities cannot be easily changed, the point of entry (or non-entry) is the critical area. If it was what leaders do, or rather what good leaders do, that is the important issue, then the chief practical implication is that they need to be trained in the proper manner. Certainly, as the emphasis shifted towards style and behaviour approaches, greater and greater attention was given to the development of leadership skills and abilities (e.g. Fleishman, Harris and Burtt, 1955). Adair's dictum is not perfect, however, for the view is also expressed by some writers that leadership style is a manifestation of an individual's personality and character. The writings of Fiedler, which will be examined in Chapter 5, often raise this possibility. If this were true, then the role of training in the conventional sense becomes somewhat problematic. This is, however, a minority view and most writers on leadership style and behaviour do not view these phenomena in terms of invariant personal characteristics.

The Ohio State Leadership studies

The title of this section refers to a highly influential series of studies conducted by an interdisciplinary team of researchers. Its main impact derives from its relatively early development of precise operational definitions of what people in leadership positions do. Two points are of immediate significance. The research team was genuinely interdisciplinary, in that although psychologists predominated, a sociologist, an economist and an educationalist were also members. In subsequent years, psychologists have dominated the field, and other disciplines have made infrequent contributions. Secondly, the focus was on the activities of leaders, i.e. people in positions of leadership, an emphasis which was a highly conscious shift from the 'trait' approach which seemed to be a less than fruitful line of research.[2] As Shartle (1957, p. 1), the research team's director, remarked:

> In the Ohio State Leadership Studies the approach to the topic of
> leadership has been that of examining and measuring performance or
> behaviour rather than human traits. The trait approach had reached an
> impasse before the beginning of World War II.

It is for the development of rigorous measures of leadership behaviour and their catchy descriptions of such behaviour – Consideration and Initiating Structure – that the Ohio researchers will be remembered. Having amassed a large number of possible descriptions of the behaviour of leaders, the group eventually reduced this accumulation to 130 questionnaire items. This research instrument was named the *Leader Behaviour Description Questionnaire* (LBDQ), and was supposed to reflect eight theoretical aspects of leader behaviour.

A central development in the Ohio programme was a factor analysis of the results of the administration of the LBDQ to 300 members of air crews who were asked to describe the behaviour of their leaders in terms of the 130 questionnaire descriptions (Halpin and Winer, 1957). The factor analysis was conducted to discern any 'clustering' or 'bunching' of the descriptions, i.e. to discern whether particular descriptions tended to be related to each other. The analysis revealed that four factors predominated in the depictions of leader behaviour:

(a) Factor I (49.6 per cent of Common Variance) was called *Consider-ation* which denoted camaraderie, mutual trust, liking and respect in the relationship between aircraft commanders and their crew. Questionnaire items which are predominant in this factor are

- Does personal favours for crew members
- Is friendly and approachable
- Refuses to explain his actions (negative association with the factor)
- Finds time to listen to crew members.

As Halpin and Winer (1957, p. 42) emphasized, the leader who scores high on this description is not lax in the performance of his duties, but is considerate towards his subordinates.

(b) Factor II (33.6 per cent of Common Variance) was named *Initiating Structure*. Leaders whose behavioural descriptions result in their receiving high scores on this dimension tend to organize work tightly, to structure the work context, to provide clear-cut definitions of role responsibility, and generally play a very active part in getting the work at hand fully scheduled. Questionnaire items which are supposed to denote this dimension are:

- Maintains definite standards of performance
- Makes his attitude clear to the crew
- Assigns crew members to particular tasks.

It was clear to Halpin and Winer (1957, p. 43) that Consideration and Initiating Structure were the central ingredients of the measurement of leader behaviour since it was possible to specify them and their constituents with such great precision. Their analysis suggested two other factors which, while they were recognized as being theoretically interest-ing, were not capable of specification with the same degree of certainty:

(c) *Production Emphasis* (9.8 per cent of Common Variance) was regarded as indicative of 'motivating the crew to greater activity by emphasizing the mission or job to be done' (Halpin and Winer, 1957, p. 43).

(d) *Sensitivity (Social Awareness)*, which accounted for 7 per cent of Common Variance, appeared to suggest 'the aircraft commander's sensitivity to and awareness of social interrelationships and pressures existing both inside and outside the crew' (Halpin and Winer, 1957, pp. 43-4).

While the Ohio researchers did not intend to belittle the empirical or theoretical significance of the latter two factors as plausible dimensions of leader behaviour, they were clearly impressed by the high percentages of Common Variance that Consideration and Initiating Structure revealed. While Production Emphasis and Sensitivity were not totally ignored in later writings, the emphasis by both proponents and critics (e.g. Korman,

1966) of the Ohio research was placed upon Consideration and Initiating Structure. This emphasis revealed itself at an early stage when an eighty-item LBDQ was devised. While all eighty items were administered to respondents, only the thirty questions which reflected Consideration and Initiating Structure (i.e. fifteen items each) were scored and used. A slightly later edition comprised only forty items, thirty of which were indicators of Consideration and Initiating Structure, the remainder not being employed in the subsequent analysis (Halpin and Winer, 1957, p. 47).

The most frequently used version of the LBDQ is that devised by Stogdill (1963) and known as LBDQ-X11. In contrast to the apparently growing emphasis of Consideration and Initiating Structure, this new version was a 100-item questionnaire which included ten additional categories of leader behaviour. In spite of the LBDQ-X11 emphasis upon twelve theoretical dimensions of leader behaviour the bulk of researchers, particularly the more recent investigators, have concentrated upon or stressed the Consideration and Initiating Structure sub-scales, each being represented by ten items. The questions were either identical or similar to those provided above as examples of the early LBDQ, the scoring being on a five-point metric: Always; Often; Occasionally; Seldom; Never.

Developments in questionnaire instruments by the Ohio researchers do not rest here. In tandem with the various metamorphoses in the LBDQ was the development of the *Supervisory Behaviour Description Questionnaire* (SBDQ). Whereas the LBDQ comprised theoretical dimensions other than Consideration and Initiating Structure, the SBDQ emphasized these two alone with twenty-eight items measuring the former and twenty for the latter. Like the LBDQ, the SBDQ was administered to the subordinates' designated leaders and was meant to be applicable to a variety of work contexts but with particular emphasis on industrial settings. The items which make up the questionnaire are similar to the LBDQ.

Examples of Consideration items are:

– He stresses the importance of high morale for those under him
– He treats people under him without considering their feelings (Reverse)[3]
– He helps his foremen with their personal problems
– He expresses appreciation when one of us does a good job.

Examples of Initiating Structure items are:

– He rules with an iron hand
– He talks about how much should be done
– He sees to it that people under him are working to their limits
– He assigns people under him to particular tasks.

The scoring system was similar, though not identical, to that associated with the LBDQ. Respondents are asked to indicate either their degree of agreement with each statement or the frequency with which a particular pattern of behaviour occurs. Readers will recognize that the items are imbued with sexism.

There is yet a third prominent measuring instrument which derives from the Ohio Research, the *Leadership Opinion Questionnaire* (LOQ). Like the SBDQ it comprises only Consideration and Initiating Structure questions (twenty each), but unlike both the LBDQ and SBDQ, responses are gleaned from leaders themselves. It asks respondents, who will obviously be in leadership positions, how they should act as supervisors. Examples of Consideration questions, to which respondents would indicate how often they feel that they should behave in the way described, are as follows:

— Do personal favours for people in the work group
— Treat all people in the work group as your equal
— Be willing to make changes
— Refuse to explain your actions (Reverse).

Examples of Initiating Structure items are:

— Criticize poor work
— Assign people in the work group to particular tasks
— Let others do their work the way they think best (Reverse)
— Emphasize meeting of deadlines.

The presentation of the three main Ohio instruments has not been undertaken to provide a pedantic social history of the work of this research programme. Not only does it give an indication of their commitment to a continuous refining of research instruments, the above exegesis is necessary since in later years it was apparent that the questionnaires often fail to give identical – even similar – results. This latter point will be dealt with in greater detail below.

Some general observations about the Ohio studies

The general methodology of the Ohio studies is worth pointing to. The approach is to focus upon putative leaders in an organization, i.e. those who are in *prima facie* positions of leadership. When the LBDQ and SBDQ are used, the questionnaires are administered to their subordinates in order to gauge the behaviour of these leaders. The questionnaires invariably comprise additional scales to examine various aspects of the climate or morale of the work group attached to leaders. The scores of the respondents in each group are then aggregated to discern that leader's leadership profile and the general climate or morale, for example by means of an index of job satisfaction, of that group. The superiors of the leader were sometimes questioned, particularly when indicators of the focal leader's effectiveness were required. The LOQ studies follow a similar methodological path, except that they are based upon leaders' opinions regarding proper leadership.

This cluster of methodological procedures reflects three important characteristics which underpin much of the research considered in this chapter, not just the Ohio research. First, the work group is the level of analysis. This emphasis is consistent with many of the definitions and general accounts of the phenomenon of leadership discussed in Chapter 1. Leadership is thus conceptualized at the social psychological level, as something manifesting itself through the medium of the group. Second, the focus is upon what have been called designated or putative leaders, that is on individuals in supervisory positions within a broader hierarchy. That such people are leaders is taken as given; whether they exhibit leadership is very much subordinate to the question of what leadership characteristics are in evidence as measured by the Ohio instruments. The discussion of what precisely leadership is or how to recognize it tends to be of subsidiary interest. Further, whether leadership, however defined or measured, can be said to exist outside the formal allocation of responsibility, control and authority is given scant attention. Third, the Ohio studies and most leadership research seeks to relate descriptions of leadership to measures of outcome (e.g. performance, job satisfaction, absenteeism). These empirical relationships generally have been examined by concurrent assessments of leadership and outcome, thereby tending to assign a somewhat static quality to a great deal of the research.

It is now appropriate to turn to a consideration of some of the Ohio State findings.

Some findings of the Ohio studies

(a) Consideration and Initiating Structure

One of the most interesting findings of the Ohio researchers, and one about which there was much excitement (Fleishman, 1973), is that Consideration and Initiating Structure are independent dimensions of leader behaviour. Contemporary research at Michigan (see below), which seemed to follow a similar conceptual approach, appeared to be conceptualizing leadership behaviour along a single continuum of Employee-centred versus Production-centred supervision (Fleishman, 1973). According to the Ohio researchers, Consideration and Initiating Structure seem to be independent dimensions, so that various leadership 'profiles' could be envisaged.

As Figure 3.1 suggests, a leader could be conceptualized as scoring high or low in respect of both dimensions. The closer a leader is to the cross-over point in the middle, the more average he is in respect of both dimensions. If such a model of the relationship between the two dimensions had empirical validity, only a small correlation between them would be expected. In reality, studies employing the Ohio concepts and indices have differed considerably over whether there is a sizeable correlation between them. That there is a correlation of some magnitude between them was evident at an early stage. The Halpin and Winer (1957) study of twenty-nine air crew members on the basis of the early LBDQ found a correlation of .52. A similar study of aircraft commanders by Halpin (1957) revealed a correlation of .51. A review of the relevant literature by Weissenberg and Kavenagh (1972) established that researchers using the Ohio instruments

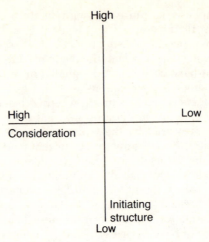

Figure 3.1 *Spatial representation of consideration and initiating structure*

tend to find the two dimensions to be relatively uncorrelated (i.e. independent) when the LOQ is employed, but that studies in which the LBDQ was used tend to exhibit clear positive correlations. This finding is of substantive, as well as methodological, interest, as it implies that leaders believe that they should behave as though Consideration and Structure are independent, but that their subordinates do not perceive them as acting in this way. A discrepancy of this kind points to some of the problems which a reliance on perceptual measures of behaviour may engender.

In a further review of the literature, Schriesheim, House and Kerr (1976) found that Structure and Consideration tend to correlate negatively in studies using the SBDQ. This occurred in eleven of the fifteen studies reviewed though the negative correlations tended to be small with only two instances being in excess of −.3. LBDQ studies always produce positive correlations, which tend to be higher when the later LBDQ is used. The reason for the difference between SBDQ and LBDQ findings seems to be the greater prominence of 'punitive, autocratic, and production-oriented' (Schriesheim *et al.*, 1976, p. 303) items in the former. They argue that when the Initiating Structure scales contain items which indicate punitive, autocratic leadership, leaders exhibiting such behaviour are simultaneously less likely to be viewed as considerate; hence a tendency to a negative correlation when such items are included. Further, such punitive items are likely to distort those components of the scale which are more clearly indicative of Initiating Structure, thereby creating unintended effects in the relationship to both Consideration and various outcome measures. An example of a punitive SBDQ item is

– He 'needles' people under him for greater effort.

An example of an autocratic item is

– He rules with an iron hand.

This latter statement exists in the early LBDQ as well as the SBDQ, but has been purged from the later LBDQ.

The fact that Consideration and Initiating Structure appear to achieve sizeable correlations with each other suggests that they are not totally independent. One would expect, accordingly, that a highly Considerate leader is likely to have a fairly high score on Initiating Structure and *vice versa*, thereby calling into doubt the kind of scheme depicted by Figure 3.1. It also suggests that in examining the relationship between one of the two dimensions and an outcome measure it would be necessary to control for the other dimension in order to search for its unique effect.

(b) Consideration, Initiating Structure and outcomes
In the early Halpin and Winer (1957) LBDQ study of air crew commanders Consideration was clearly positively related to the crew's satisfaction but negatively (albeit weakly) to various measures of effectiveness, based upon the responses of superiors. These negative correlations were enhanced when Initiating Structure was controlled; in other words Considerate leaders have a deleterious effect on effectiveness. By contrast, Initiating Structure was modestly associated in a positive direction with all of the measures of effectiveness as well as the crew's overall satisfaction, but the correlations were greatly enhanced by controlling for Consideration. The similar study by Halpin (1957) of aircraft commanders achieved congruent results, though this study did not control for the contaminating effects of either dimension of leadership. Initiating Structure tended to be positively associated with various ratings by superiors (e.g. technical competence, performance under stress) as well as the satisfaction of the crew. Consideration tended to exhibit mildly positive (rather than negative, as in the earlier study) correlations with superiors' ratings, and strong positive correlations with crew ratings (e.g. satisfaction, friendship and cooperation). However, Consideration and Initiating Structure were scarcely different in the magnitude of their correlations with crew assessments of Confidence and Proficiency and Morale. Such findings were broadly in line with findings in an industrial context by Fleishman, Harris and Burtt (1955). Interestingly, this study acknowledged the possibility of informal leadership in that the focal leaders were those production foremen nominated by their work groups as the ones from whom they took most of their orders. This strategy only partially deals with the possibility of informal leadership processes since it precludes the possibility of emergent leadership from within the work group itself. In line with the research on air crews, Fleishman *et al.* (1955) found that workers tended to prefer Considerate foremen, whereas high Structuring foremen often engendered grievances but were more likely to be regarded as proficient by their superiors.

Such results seemed to suggest a tension between Consideration and Initiating Structure. At first blush, Considerate leaders seem to provide a pleasant work environment for their subordinates, but are regarded as less effective. Leaders who emphasize Structuring work activities often reduce the levels of job satisfaction experienced by the work group, but are regarded as more effective by their superiors. At an early stage in the development of the Ohio research programme, it was clear to the investigators that their results often indicated a greater complexity in the relationships among the main variables. Two such studies serve as useful examples of the manner in which the Ohio researchers elaborated their work.

The first study is Halpin's (1957) aforementioned one of aircraft commanders. Following the initial analysis of Consideration and Structure in relation to various outcome measures, Halpin looked at commanders with high and low scores on both of these dimensions. Initially, commanders were divided into two groups in terms of superiors' ratings of 'Overall Effectiveness in Combat'. One group (N = 13) was made up of the top 15 per cent in terms of this measure; the second group (N = 12) the lower 15 per cent. Halpin found that among the first group, eight scored above the mean on *both* Consideration and Initiating Structure, whereas only one commander scored below the mean on both dimensions. One assumes that the other four commanders were 'mixed' leadership types. When Halpin examined the second (i.e. poor performing) group, six scored below the mean on both leadership dimensions, and only two above the mean. This finding led Halpin (1957, p. 64) to conclude that the optimal leadership behaviour is that which achieves high scores on both dimensions, and not that which involves a trade-off between the two. Further, since Considerate leaders tend to have more satisfied subordinates, both crew and superiors will prefer leaders who score high on both dimensions. Almost identical results had been noted in Hemphill's (1955) study of university department heads, which showed those scoring high on both dimensions to have above average administrative reputations. In later years, the sobriquet of the 'Hi-Hi leader' was employed to describe the leader who exhibits high scores on both dimensions.

A second, and indeed often quoted, study which pointed to a more complicated set of relationships is a study of fifty-seven production foremen and their work groups in a motor truck manufacturing plant by Fleishman and Harris (1962) using the SBDQ. When Consideration was related to both grievances and turnover, the relationship was found to be negatively curvilinear as in Figure 3.2; for Initiating Structure the relationships were positively curvilinear as in Figure 3.3. Such findings are crucial, for they imply that at particular sections of the relationship neither Consideration nor Initiating Structure make much difference to observed variation in either of the outcome measures, grievance rates and turnover. At a certain juncture higher levels of Consideration do not greatly reduce grievances or turnover; similarly, up to a particular juncture levels of Structure have little impact on these variables. Fleishman and Harris then examined the way in which different combinations of leader behaviour impinged upon the two outcome measures. Their findings suggest that Initiating Structure has little effect upon grievances or turnover, and that Consideration is the crucial variable. Turnover and grievances tend to be high when foremen score low on Consideration, regardless of their levels of Initiating Structure; they were at their lowest when Consideration was

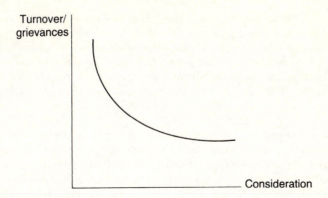

Figure 3.2 *Diagrammatic presentation of findings for Consideration in Fleishman and Harris's (1962) study*

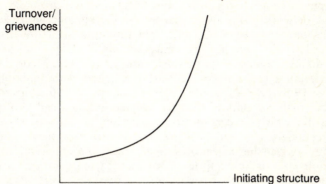

Figure 3.3 *Diagrammatic presentation of findings for Initiating Structure in Fleishman and Harris's (1962) study*

medium to high and Structure was low. However, larger increments of Structure had little or no impact on grievances and turnover when Consideration was medium to high. Such a finding is crucial in the light of other Ohio findings suggesting that leaders who provide Structure are more proficient, since they may be able to compensate for the interpersonally deleterious effects of their behaviour by enhancing Consideration. Such a finding, of course, provides further confirmation of the benefits of leadership behaviour which emphasizes both dimensions. Results such as these, coupled with Halpin's (1957), suggested that the empirical relationship may not be linear, and that there may be an interaction between Consideration and Initiating Structure in terms of their effects on various outcomes.

Criticisms of the Ohio studies

The foregoing summary cannot do full justice to the wide range of studies which the Ohio programme spawned, but it is hoped that the reader will have grasped the basic tenor of the approach. The studies have received many criticisms over the years, many of which are not peculiar to the Ohio research as such. It is the purpose of this section briefly to summarize the more fundamental issues that have been raised. The responses to some of the problems raised by later researchers will then be addressed.

1 Discrepant findings

A detailed analysis by Korman in 1966 of virtually every study in which Consideration and Initiating Structure figured prominently revealed that the magnitude and direction of correlations both between each of them and also with various outcome measures were highly variable. The vast majority of the correlations failed to achieve statistical significance. Korman broke his analysis down into various groups depending on the kind of Ohio schedule used and the nature of the outcome measures. For example, among studies using the LOQ and which employed superior ratings of work group performance, the correlations with Consideration range from −.06 to +.32, and with Initiating Structure from −.39 to +.13. To take another example, among LBDQ studies which use subordinate ratings (e.g. morale, satisfaction, etc.), correlations with Consideration range from −.52 to +.84, and with Initiating Structure from −.19 to +.68. Not only is the fact of divergent findings troublesome, but the small correlations that are frequently found call into question the extent to which leadership (or leadership as measured by the Ohio researchers) is a genuinely important predictor of the various outcome measures which have been examined. Even the apparently more robust assertion that it is high levels of both Consideration and Initiating Structure that promotes work group effectiveness, job satisfaction, morale, and the like, has been found empirically wanting. Research by both Larson, Hunt and Osborn (1976) and Nystrom (1978) strongly suggests that knowledge of a leader's combined Consideration and Initiating Structure scores fared little better than examining the effects of either dimension on subordinate satisfaction and performance on its own. These researchers tend to prefer a more parsimonious model which examines the effects of Consideration and Initiating Structure singly rather than together.

However, a laboratory study involving Canadian undergraduates was much more supportive of the Hi-Hi notion (Tjosvold, 1984). The investigation involved creating experimental conditions for directive and non-directive leadership, and also for warmth or coldness in a leader. In Tjosvold's view the two independent variables − leader directiveness and warmth − correspond to the Initiating Structure/Consideration pairing. Leader warmth tended to engender very positive affective responses on the part of subordinates. However, the type of leader behaviour that had the most pronounced impact on task performance was that involving a combination of both warmth and directiveness. The least effective pattern was the non-directive/warm combination. These findings provide strong support for the benefits of the Hi-Hi combination from a study in which the direction of causality is fairly clear. The research raises an interesting methodological point in that a large component of the operationalization of the warm/cold conditions involved the non-verbal transmission of these feelings, e.g. through voice tone and smiling. It may be that the measurement of Consideration and adjacent concepts by questionnaires does not adequately capture this component.

On the face of it, the early promise of the Ohio research seems to have waned. However, in considering some of the criticisms which will be examined below, many writers have been able to show that many of the discrepant results are capable of elaboration. This is particularly the case in the context of the second of the criticisms to be explicated.

2   Absence of situational analysis

Korman (1966) took many of the Ohio studies to task for failing to include situational variables in their analysis, that is, variables which moderate the relationship between leader behaviour and various outcomes.

That it is necessary to accuse the Ohio researchers of failing to be sensitive to contextual variables is surprising in view of Fleishman's (1953) awareness of their importance, and Stogdill's (1948) recognition that the importance of particular leadership traits is likely to vary from situation to situation. Further, the relevance of contextual factors had been recognized, albeit not within an Ohio framework, by Pelz (1951), for example, when he found that the effectiveness of a supervisor in promoting satisfaction within the work group depended upon his ability to influence his own superiors. Supervisors who have such upward influence tend to be seen by their subordinates as likely to help them achieve their own work-related goals. As it stands, the Ohio output implicitly generates universalistic leadership recommendations which take little account of broader contexts, such as those examined by Pelz.

In an influential paper, Kerr, Schriesheim, Murphy and Stogdill (1974) have sought to instil a situational interpretation into many of the Ohio studies. As a consequence, they are able to point to some possible causes of the discrepant evidence that abounds. It is only possible to deal with a few instances. They point to existing studies which suggest that *pressure* on the work group (e.g. due to time urgency, external threat) moderates the relationship between Initiating Structure and both satisfaction and performance in a positive direction. The latter was confirmed in a study by Schriesheim and Murphy (1976) of a social services organization using the LBDQ-X11, in that when jobs are stressful greater Initiating Structure enhances subordinate performance; but when they are not stressful it reduces performance. These researchers also found that job stress moderated the effects of Consideration. In high job stress conditions the correlations with both performance and job satisfaction were negative; in low stress conditions they were positive. Failure to take into account this variable may in part be the reason for some contradictory findings. The Kerr *et al.* (1974) review points to intrinsic task satisfaction as a moderating variable, such that higher levels of intrinsic satisfaction reduce the positive relationships between Consideration and both job satisfaction and performance, and render less negative the former variable's relationship with Structure.

The role and significance of such moderating variables is clearly a sensible line of enquiry which various researchers have found often produces interesting findings. Thus, in a field study, Katz (1977) found that the relationship between Initiating Structure and group performance was affected by the amount of conflict within the group. When affective conflict within the group is high, there is a stronger positive relationship between Initiating Structure and performance. Research on foremen by Cummins (1972) suggests that when leader-member relations are poor, Initiating Structure tends to have an adverse effect on the quantity and quality of work group productivity. Schriesheim's (1980) research on managerial and clerical employees in a US public utility indicated that group cohesiveness strongly moderated the consequences of leadership style. For example, when cohesiveness was low greater Initiating Structure enhanced both subordinate satisfaction with supervision and performance; but when cohesiveness was medium or high, these relationships were absent. She also found Consideration to be positively correlated with performance only in the highly cohesive work groups. Group cohesiveness did not moderate the effect of Consideration on satisfaction. Clearly, the work of these writers points to the importance of group-level attributes as moderators of empirical relationships involving leadership behaviour.

The role of the nature of the task and subordinate personality as possible moderators can be inferred from a laboratory experiment involving US undergraduates (Weed, Mitchell and Moffitt, 1976). This study involved the manipulation of three variables: leader's style (task or human relations orientation); the nature of the task (easy or difficult and structured or ambiguous); and subordinate personality (high or low dogmatism). While the symmetry between task/human relations orientation and Initiating Structure/Consideration is not perfect, the results are nonetheless suggestive. Weed *et al.* found that both task attributes and subordinate personality moderated the effect of leadership style on group performance. For example, dogmatic subordinates perform better with task-oriented leaders, irrespective of both the leader's level of human relations orientation and the nature of the task. Less dogmatic subordinates performed better under a human relations approach to leadership.

There are two other factors relevant to the Ohio tradition which many writers have found to be of relevance and which are implicit in the preceding discussion. These two factors affect directly findings within the Ohio tradition but are a different class of moderating variable from those dealt with so far. One of these is the suggestion that Consideration may be a moderating variable in the context of the relationship between Structure and outcome measures. Such a suggestion is prompted in large part from the aforementioned discrepancies in the relationships between Consideration and Initiating Structure. The notion of Consideration as a situational moderator is implicit in Fleishman and Harris's (1962) work and has been confirmed by writers like Schriesheim and Murphy (1976) who, in the study cited above, found that high levels of Structure among supervisors led to lower performance only when they exhibited low levels of Consideration. The second situational moderator, occasionally mentioned in the literature, is the particular Ohio schedule employed in various studies. Earlier it was noted that the type of questionnaire used (i.e. LOQ or LBDQ, etc.) affects the correlation between Consideration and Initiating Structure. Schriesheim, House and Kerr (1976) found that, for example, the relationship between Structure and both job satisfaction and role clarity is more strongly positive when the LBDQ (early or revised) is used than the SBDQ. A comparable study by Szilagyi and Keller (1976) found Initiating Structure, when measured by the LBDQ-X11, to be positively correlated with outcomes such as satisfaction with supervision and general satisfaction; when measured by the SBDQ, however, these correlations were negative. Like Schriesheim *et al.* (1976), these writers blame the presence in the SBDQ Initiating Structure scale of questions which inadvertently indicate that the leader is punitive for these discrepant findings. Consequently, it appears that close attention to the nature of the Ohio measures employed has to be paid when interpreting the various inconsistent findings.

Clearly, an increasing number of writers have become conscious of the need to take into account situational moderators in employing the Ohio approach. The outcome of this tendency is a loss of the neatness of the early Ohio research and a necessity for more complex ways of handling the data. There is also the problem that there is often little theoretical (or even practical) justification for the various situational factors examined by various researchers. To rely on what occurs to particular students of leadership as a potential moderator is unlikely to have a positive, cumulative impact on research in this tradition. To some extent the path-goal approach (discussed in Chapter 5) mitigates this tendency, but it too has a tendency for atheoretical investigations of particular moderating variables. Any notion of a grand synthesis of work in the Ohio tradition becomes more difficult to envisage while researchers proceed with their investigations in this manner.

3   The problem of causality

Like the two criticisms developed thus far, the problem of causality applies equally to other approaches to the study of leadership style (and 'traits' too), and by no means solely to the output of researchers in the Ohio tradition. The assumption in such research tends to be that style of leadership influences various outcomes, so that the direction of causal influence is:

LEADERSHIP STYLE ─────────────▶ Group performance, job satisfaction, role clarity, etc.

However, the overwhelming majority of research mentioned thus far is cross-sectional, i.e. the observations of both the presumed causal variable (leadership style) and dependent variable (e.g. job satisfaction) are gleaned more or less simultaneously. The notion that leadership style constitutes the causal or independent variable is an assumption rather than the consequence of investigations designed to establish such a view. As Korman (1966) observed, it is extremely risky to deduce a cause-effect relationship from the correlation of two variables. Indeed, such a deduction has quite a strong *prima facie* set of reasons for being incorrect, for it would not seem in the least unlikely to suppose that leaders adjust their styles in response to group performance or climate:

Group performance

Job satisfaction   ⎯⎯⎯⎯⎯⎯⟶   LEADERSHIP STYLE

Role clarity, etc.

It is not possible to choose between these competing explanations of a correlation between two variables. Nor can empirical investigation of the situational factors which impinge upon such two-variable designs in any way improve one's ability to impute causality to one variable or the other. Further, the problem of the *direction* of causality does not exhaust the full range of difficulties which may be subsumed under this general umbrella. At least one other difficulty is that a third variable may impinge on the relationship:

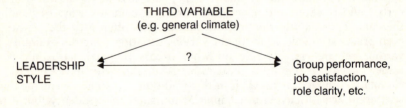

It may be that the apparent relationship between the two variables is an artefact of variations in the general climate across particular sections of an organization or across organizations. Harmonious climates, which may have nothing at all to do with the style of each focal leader in an investigation may have a tendency to produce particular styles of leadership *and* group response.

Two kinds of research design can be envisaged (and, indeed, on occasions employed) to go some way towards dealing with such issues. One is an experimental design, in which the leadership style would be manipulated and its effects estimated. The second is a longitudinal design in which observations of the relevant variables are made at different points in time. Both of these designs were briefly explicated in Chapter 1.

There has been only a small number of experimental designs dealing solely with the implications of Consideration and Initiating Structure for group performance. From the point of view of this section, a difficulty that one encounters is that Consideration and Initiating Structure are not always the only aspects of leadership style considered. One of the most frequently quoted studies is that of Lowin and Craig (1968), a laboratory study in which variations in subordinate competence, in terms of quantity and quality of work, were experimentally created. The question then was: did the people who were allocated the role of leader in the study vary their leadership style in response to good or poor performance? The results suggest that when faced with subordinates who perform poorly, leaders exhibit greater Initiating Structure and closeness of supervision (a term used by researchers in the Michigan tradition – see below), but less Consideration. Evidence such as this is important for two reasons. First, it points to the likelihood that a leader's style is not an inert entity, or an ingredient of his or her personality, but something which can react to the circumstances of his or her subordinates. Second, it challenges the leadership style-causes-outcome paradigm, by pointing to the possibility of causation being the other way around. Of course, it does not disprove the paradigm, for performance may also be responsive to leadership style, and this was the chief focus of another laboratory investigation by Lowin (Lowin, Hrapchak and Kavanagh, 1969) which sought to examine the effects of Consideration and Initiating Structure by modifying them such that they became experimental treatments. By observing experimental subjects under conditions of experimentally induced 'high' or 'low' Consideration or Initiating Structure their effects can readily be gauged. Lowin *et al.* (1969) found that Consideration among undergraduates acting as foremen resulted in greater productivity, quality and job satisfaction; but that the effects of Structure on these variables were not as pronounced as those for Consideration. The findings for Structure, therefore, were much less consistent with those that the Ohio tradition would lead one to expect.

A very detailed study by Barrow (1976) conceptualized and measured four leader behaviour patterns – Task-emphasis; Supportive-Consideration; Punitive-Performance emphasis; and Autocratic emphasis. The first two types are more or less synonymous with Initiating Structure and Consideration respectively; Punitive-Performance emphasis denotes a punitive approach to poor subordinate performance in order to enhance compliance; and an Autocratic emphasis indicates the maintenance of strict control coupled with a resistance to suggestions by subordinates. Experimental treatments were varied in terms of both whether each 'leader's' subordinates were good or poor performers and the complexity of the task, the latter being a variable found to be of significance in another experimental study (Hill and Hughes, 1974). Like Lowin and Craig, Barrow found that subordinate performance affected leader behaviour. Poor subordinate performance tended to result in a more punitive, autocratic style with greater emphasis on production, but little consideration. Good performance had the opposite effects. Further, Barrow found that task complexity tended to result in an Initiating Structure style on the part of 'leaders'. Of particular interest is that as subordinate performance improved, 'leaders' became more supportive and considerate; by contrast, a deterioration led to more autocratic and punitive patterns of behaviour.

These experimental results strongly suggest that leaders can and do adjust their behaviour and style in line with subordinate performance and characteristics, as well as to the nature of the task at hand. Leadership style can be, and is, both a dependent and an independent variable. Such findings shed doubt on the interpretation of much of the cross-sectional, correlational research conducted in the Ohio tradition. Moreover, it is clear that leadership style is not inert – leaders may alter their behaviour as circumstances change – so that cross-sectional studies are as a frozen frame is to motion picture film.

Experimental research is not without its problems, however, in that the studies cited above are all laboratory simulations, invariably relying on undergraduates for their subjects. While strong on internal validity, such work is often criticized for its external validity, the latter being a very real problem for a topic such as leadership which is often supposed to be capable of a practical pay-off. A longitudinal investigation of first-line managers from a number of firms by Greene (1975) provides some confirmation of the experimental findings. Observations were conducted at three one-month intervals to allow for 'lagged' effects of leader behaviour. The LBDQ-X11 was employed. His research suggests that higher Consideration leads to greater subordinate satisfaction, a causal interpretation very much in line with conventional reasoning, as well as some of the experimental evidence. Greene also found that subordinate performance (both quantity and quality as rated by each subordinate's peers) affected Initiating Structure; poor subordinate performance led to more Structuring behaviour on the part of leaders. This finding, which is highly consistent with the work of Lowin *et al.* (1969), Lowin and Craig (1968), and Barrow (1976), strongly suggests that Initiating Structure is best thought of as *a response to* subordinate performance levels rather than *a cause of* them. However, Greene also found that Consideration moderated the direction of the relationship. Among highly Considerate leaders, greater Structure makes for better performance; when they are low in Consideration, performance is the causal variable in that better performance leads to a lesser emphasis on Structure. These findings confirm that the causal direction is often not of the leadership style-influences-outcome kind, but in the other direction. In passing, Greene's work adds to the afore-mentioned suggestion that Consideration often acts as a mediator of empirical relationships involving Initiating Structure.

Both experimental and longitudinal investigations imply that the pattern of causal relationships between leadership style and various outcome measures is more complicated than is often assumed and presented in textbooks on Organizational Behaviour. We may also get an inkling of a clue as to why the results concerning the 'Hi-Hi' pattern are so inconsistent. It may be that when considering the combined effects of Considerating and Initiating Structure, the analyst is adding (or multiplying) two variables which are dissimilar, one being an independent variable, the other often a dependent one. In any event, there are strong grounds for suggesting that Korman's (1966) strident castigation of Ohio-style research for imputing causal effects from static, cross-sectional research designs was somewhat warranted.

4   The problem of the group

The point has repeatedly been made in the course of this book, that the predominant focus in leadership theory and research is the leader in relation to the group. The Ohio tradition is no exception to this approach, and indeed exhibits its quintessential ingredients. There has been a growing recognition that the group-level emphasis imposes something of a dilemma on leadership researchers. The Ohio approach, and that of a number of other researchers, involves averaging individual subordinates' descriptions of their leader (when instruments such as the LBDQ or SBDQ are used) to form a *group*-level description of their leader. But as researchers such as Lowin and Craig (1968) have observed, leaders often behave in different ways to different group members so that the procedure of averaging individual descriptions may mask important divergences in the style(s) of a leader in respect of particular subordinates. In a series of papers advocating a *Vertical Dyad Linkage* (VDL) approach to the study of leadership, the averaging approach has been criticized by Graen and Cashman (1975) and Danserau, Graen and Haga (1975). Their approach involves much closer attention to the exchange and negotiation practices and processes which underpin the formulation of the leader-subordinate dyad. It is the leader in relation to the subordinate, not to a work group or unit, which is the focus of their attention.

Approaches, like that of the Ohio State studies, which average subordinates' accounts of a leader and, for that matter, of job satisfaction, absenteeism, turnover, and the like, ride roughshod over the variations within the group in respect of how the leader behaves or is deemed to behave. While writers such as Schriesheim (1979) have noted a drift away from the averaging method, and a consequent recognition of the need to focus on dyadic relationships, a problem still remains because the questions embedded in schedules like that of the Ohio school are *group* directed, i.e. the content of the questions is focused on the group not the individual. This effectively means that individual respondents are being forced to carry out their own averaging procedures when answering questions. Very often, the group directedness of the questions is very explicit as the following LBDQ-X11 questions indicate:

- Lets group members know what is expected of them (Initiating Structure)
- Puts suggestions made by the group into operation (Consideration).

In other words, not only is there a problem with the analysis of data used by many researchers (i.e. the use of averages of subordinates' descriptions), but even when this difficulty is dealt with, there is a further problem with the wording of questions. The VDL ideas have not gone unchallenged, however. Cummings (1975) has strongly indicated that he feels that the approach exaggerates the variability in subordinates' reports. For example, he points out that the need to behave equitably to subordinates, thereby not discriminating or displaying preferences, constrains the leader to limit the variability of his behaviour in respect of subordinates. Against such a view are some of the findings deriving from the VDL approach. An example would be a study of managers (Danserau, Cashman and Graen, 1973) which found that whereas averaged LBDQ measures were virtually unrelated to turnover, individual level scores were related to this variable. It would seem that the case for VDL or averaging approaches is not clear-cut so it is proposed to turn to two studies which explicitly investigate these issues.

The first study is an investigation by Schriesheim (1979) of managerial and clerical personnel in a large US public utility. In order to address the problem of the level of analysis at which questions are directed, Schriesheim altered the LBDQ-X11 questions so that they were either group-directed or individual-directed. Each respondent was given both forms as well as a number of outcome measures. Schriesheim found a very strong relationship between the two types of leader behaviour description. In addition, very similar correlations between both individual and group descriptions and a wide range of outcome measures (job satisfaction, group productivity, anxiety, role clarity, etc.) were discerned. Such findings strongly imply that the level at which questions are directed (i.e. group or individual) makes little difference. However, Schriesheim only used a dyadic analysis in handling his data, not an averaging method for descriptions of leader behaviour, so that it is not possible to discern whether averaging makes a difference as indicated by proponents of the VDL approach.

The second study, a survey of commanders, sergeants and their respective subordinates in the US Army National Guard by Katerberg and Hom (1981) is of interest in this respect. This research did not take into account Schriesheim's (1979) observations about the level at which questions are posed, but allowed the authors to examine whether average army unit depictions of leader behaviour or individual accounts were more strongly related to various outcomes. Katerberg and Hom found that variations in leadership behaviour using the LBDQ-X11 analysed at the individual level (called within-unit leadership variance by the authors) tended to display strong relationships with various measures of satisfaction, as well as role clarity and conflict. This was the case more or less irrespective of whether the leader was a commander or first sergeant. Some evidence was also found to suggest that averaged depictions of leaders by their subordinates (between-unit leadership variance) also had an impact – albeit a lesser one – on various measures, particularly those associated with satisfaction. A rather disconcerting finding was a low correspondence between individuals' and averaged group descriptions of leaders, suggesting that individuals perceive their leaders' pattern of behaviour differently from how their work group as a whole sees them. This finding would confirm the suggestion that averaging respondents' descriptions rides roughshod over the differences within a work group regarding how the leader is viewed as behaving.

Both studies point to the need to take both levels of analysis into account, confirming Cummings's (1975) implicit argument that it is far too early to confirm that the VDL approach should become the prevailing paradigm. It would also seem that we know far too little about how group level consensus relating to leadership behaviour emerges, and its significance relative to individual variations in how a leader is perceived.

5 Informal leadership

The literature on leadership in organizations addresses the question of informal leadership surprisingly rarely. The vast majority of studies employing the Ohio instruments direct their questioning to designated leaders, that is, people in positions of leadership. In this sense, leadership has to do with the incumbent of an office or position in a hierarchy, and the focus of empirical enquiry is upon what he or she does and its effects. Yet social scientists have long been aware that individuals often assume, or are ascribed, leadership even when the group in question does not have a formal structure. Whyte's (1943) classic study of a street corner gang in the USA is an example of such a process. In an apparently egalitarian group, Whyte (1943, pp. 258-60) was able to show how leadership emerges, who seems to become a leader, and how the leader retains his status. Such processes point to *informal* leadership which does not occur within a formalized and hierarchical system of right and obligations in which individuals are appointed to positions of putative leadership. If the emergence of leadership can be demonstrated in contexts such as these, it may be hypothesized that informal leadership may arise outside a formal system within work organizations. Indeed, there is every reason to expect the emergence of informal leaders in work groups in view of the recognition of the importance of the so-called 'informal organization' which arises in the context of the formal organization. This term refers to a cluster of unofficial practices and structures, which, it is often suggested, arise in all work environments (see, e.g., Selznick, 1943; Blau, 1956). The informal leaders may well emerge as part of the phenomenon of informal organization, such that a group of peers have their own, rather than a bureaucratically conferred, leader. The emergence of 'natural leaders' is documented by Page (1946), for example, as but one aspect of the informal structure of the US Navy.

Occasionally one finds in the literature instances of an acknowledgment of the possible importance of a distinction between formal and informal leadership. Indeed, it is one of the classic Ohio State studies that furnishes just such a recognition. In their examination of foremen at International Harvester in the USA, Fleishman, Harris and Burtt (1955, Chap. 6) sought to examine how far their leadership styles, in terms of Consideration and Initiating Structure, were similar to those of their own superiors. The authors introduced the notion of 'leadership climate' to denote the possibility that the foreman's leadership style is affected and conditioned by that of his own boss. In deciding who should be taken to be each foreman's superior, Fleishman *et al.* chose not to follow the formal organizational chart because 'occasionally the person actually acting as leader might not be the one assigned' (Fleishman *et al.* 1955, p. 53). The methodological consequence of this recognition was that foremen's superiors were those who were *nominated* by them as such. In fact the authors found that both formal and informal leadership positions were roughly the same. Parenthetically, this study found that nominated supervisors' leadership styles were related to those of the foremen. Indeed, so powerful was the influence of leadership climate that it tended to override the influence of training programmes attended by the foremen which emphasized 'human relations' components in supervisory practice.

Fleishman *et al.* (1955, ch. 8) took the formal-informal distinction even further in examining the effects of the foreman's leadership style on his/her subordinates. Each worker was asked to designate the foreman 'from whom he took most of his orders' (p. 76). Clear instances were found of formally designated foremen who were consistently by-passed by subordinates such that they turned to another person as 'leader' either sometimes someone higher in the managerial hierarchy or another foreman. While necessarily based upon a very small sample, the authors compared foremen who were consistently by-passed with those who tended not to be. Only ten comparisions were possible due to the relatively few departures from the formal system and also the need to make valid comparisons. They concluded that:

> a favoured foreman might be described as standing behind his workers when they are in trouble; taking an active leadership role by instituting his own ideas and encouraging both quantity and quality of output; maintaining, nevertheless, a certain flexibility in his dealings with his work group in that he explains the reasons behind his actions and institutes ideas presented by members of his work group. (Fleishman *et al.*, 1955, p. 77)

Findings such as these are highly tentative, but have clear potential in furthering the understanding of leadership in organizations. There is the implication, for example, that leadership styles of informal leaders may differ from those of formal leaders. Yet the bulk of research on leadership in organizations examines the activities of putative (i.e. designated) leaders and their immediate subordinates. Findings such as those examined point to the possibility that in some instances, when subordinates are asked about their designated leaders, inappropriate people are the referents of the questions. Insofar as Fleishman *et al.* found relatively few nominations which departed from the formal system, the impact upon findings in this field of study may not be too great. However, this research is concerned with formally designated leaders who act as informal leaders in respect of subordinates for whom they are not officially responsible. Informal leadership may also materialize among putative peers, as students of informal organization have long recognized. Moreover, informal leadership that arises within the work group may exhibit different attributes from those of formally designated leadership. Experimental evidence suggests that elected as against appointed leaders perceive themselves, and are perceived, differently by followers. Also, they differ in the amount of influence they have over their followers (Hollander and Julian, 1978a, b). While the appointed/elected distinction differs from formal/informal, they do share some common ingredients, so that the suggestion that the impact of informal leadership needs to be taken into account receives some reinforcement from these findings.

Why is there so little attention paid to informal leadership and the possibility that its existence may contaminate some research findings? Two possibilities may be proffered. One reason is methodological: it is much easier to enter an organization and investigate the activities of designated leaders. Finding out who are the *de facto* leaders is time-consuming and costly, as it was in the case of the International Harvester study. A second reason is epistemological: by and large, research into 'informal organization' has derived from sociologists of organizations such as Blau, Dalton, Gouldner and Selznick (Mouzelis, 1967). While the formal/informal dichotomy has been shown to be conceptually and empirically problematic by these and other researchers, nonetheless the case studies of organizations were carried out by sociologists with a strong sense of informal processes in organizations. The study of leadership in organizations has tended to be dominated by social, organizational and industrial psychologists whose preferred methodological tools tend not to include the case study approach, based usually on participant observation and informal interviewing, that sociologists in the 1940s and 1950s were employing. Consequently, many psychologists do not 'see' informal leadership, or are not sensitive to it, as a consequence of the methodological dictates of their discipline. Thus in neither Yukl's (1981) textbook, nor Bass's (1981) handbook is there more than passing interest in such phenomena. To be sure, psychologists have been very interested in 'emergent leadership' – how leaders emerge and the skills and characteristics they exhibit usually in small group, laboratory contexts – but such studies shed little light on the continuities and discontinuities between formal and informal leadership in organizations.

6 *The non-observation of leadership behaviour*

A major problem with the Ohio scales and many other measures of leadership behaviour is that they rely predominantly on subordinates' accounts of what particular leaders do (as with the LBDQ and SBDQ) or on leaders' accounts of what they do or feel they should do (as with the LOQ). As such, these research instruments are perceptual or, as in the case of the LOQ, attitudinal. Consequently, when authors write about the observation of leader behaviour, as has been the case in this book, 'observation' has to be construed in a figurative rather than literal sense. In fact, leadership in organizations is not being observed at all. Occasionally, there are approximations to observations as in the laboratory studies cited above by writers such as Barrow (1976) and Lowin and Craig (1968). But these 'observations' are in fact observations of the effects of scripted experimental manipulations, the latter being derived from questionnaire-based research such as that of the Ohio State tradition. A difficulty with such research is that it is usually based on university students and so is not necessarily a reflection of the behaviour of 'real' leaders. What is perhaps surprisingly absent from the study of leadership in organizations are systematic observational studies of leadership in organizations.

Research exists which comes close to such a description. There are some excellent studies, for example of the world of management concentrating on what managers do, rather than what they say they do when confronted with a questionnaire schedule (e.g. Stewart, 1967; Mintzberg, 1973). The difficulty that is faced when confronting this research from the perspective of the study of leadership, is that of disentangling the leadership element in the real work of managers from all the other components of their work lives. As noted in Chapter 1, the 'Manager as Leader' is but one of a number of roles within the cluster of managerial activities distinguished by Mintzberg (1973) and, as he suggests, 'leadership permeates all activities' (p. 61). This attribute of leadership makes it particularly difficult to study directly through more observational techniques, such as structured observation, activity sampling, diaries, etc. Perhaps this is why it has been suggested by Schriesheim, Hunt and Sekaran (1982) that leadership and management research have developed into distinct and separate fields with divergent aims and techniques.

However, questionnaire-based studies do pose problems of interpretation, for as research methodologists often point out, there is often a disjuncture between attitudes and people's account of what they or others do, and their behaviour (e.g. La Piere, 1934; Deutscher, 1966). One particularly troublesome area for such studies of leaders is the broad problem of 'implicit' leadership theories. There is a complex pool of methodological work in this area, into which it will only be possible to dip one's toes. The study by Rush, Thomas and Lord (1977) will provide an example of this approach. Initially, undergraduates were given a brief description of a person in a supervisory position, which was varied slightly to convey different impressions of the supervisor's level of performance, level of accomplishment, and sex. No account was provided of the person's behaviour *qua* leader. The LBDQ-X11 was administered to the experimental subjects in a slightly altered form to reflect the fact that LBDQ statements about leaders for whom they have had little information would be assessed. Rush *et al.* found that the LBDQ descriptions provided were broadly similar to those which were typically provided in descriptions of actual leaders whose behaviour was being rated by real subordinates. The authors then assessed the effects of the manipulated performance cues (i.e. high, average or low departmental performance). The evidence suggests that respondents downgrade their assessments of both Consideration and Initiating Structure of a leader when the cue indicates poor performance. When provided with cues indicative of good performance, leaders tended to be evaluated in 'Hi-Hi' terms. These findings suggest that people carry around with them implicit theories about the nature of leadership which correspond closely to the central conceptual categories of leadership theorists. Such findings, which have been elaborated considerably in recent years, clearly raise questions about whether questionnaire approaches like that of the Ohio tradition are based on subordinates' depictions of a particular leader or reflect broad, implicit categorizations of leaders. To be fair to questionnaire approaches, recent research which has examined the operation of implicit leadership theories confirms that observers of leader behaviour can and do absorb information about leaders over and above these theories (Phillips and Lord, 1982; Phillips, 1984). As a result, as one of these researchers has put it, albeit somewhat opaquely:

> it is essential for researchers and practitioners to understand the difference between accuracy that stems from recall of specific behavioural incidents and inferential accuracy that coincides with an information-simplification heuristic. (Phillips, 1984, p. 136)

In other words, it is necessary to sort out the extent to which subordinates' descriptions of leader behaviour are based on 'accurate' reflections, as against being manifestations of fairly universal cognitions of such behaviour.

There is a definite awareness among some leadership researchers that techniques of investigation which are based less on questionnaires need to be developed. Bussom, Larson and Vicars (1982), for example, have sought to develop unstructured, non-participant observation in the context of leadership research. These researchers observed the work of police executives and focused in particular upon the nature and range of interpersonal contacts they engendered. Whether this is what 'leadership', as against 'management', denotes is questionable, but the methodology may open doors to further possibilities. However, like the research of many management researchers, it indicates what executives do, whereas the question which has preoccupied students of leadership in organizations is whether variations in what leaders do has implications for the attitudes and performance of their subordinates. Thus, while there may be a *prima facie* case for moving towards the less perceptual approaches of management researchers, it should also be recognized that their research designs and techniques may not be suited to the sorts of empirical question that leadership researchers are prone to ask. That, of course, may be a reason for changing the questions (cf. Mintzberg, 1982).

The Michigan Studies

It is preferable to distinguish two phases to the research output invariably referred to as the 'Michigan Studies'. The early period started in the late 1940s with a series of projects 'designed to discover the principles governing group performance and group motivation with specific reference to organizational structure and leadership practices' (Katz, 1951, p. 68). The research was under the general directorship of Rensis Likert, at the Survey Research Centre, University of Michigan, though he seems rarely to have been involved in the authorship of the early findings. There are a number of similarities between the early Michigan and Ohio research programmes, but they should not be over-emphasized. Whereas the Ohio team was (particularly in the early years) multidisciplinary, the Michigan researchers were mainly psychologists. While writers often see a consistency in the basic ideas about leadership (e.g. Schein, 1980), there are important dissimilarities too. Methodologically they are fairly dissimilar as the discussion below should reveal. Further, whereas the Ohio findings about leadership undoubtedly had a general impact upon practical schemes for training leaders, they do not seem to have been developed into a specific approach to such training. The early Michigan research was a major influence, by contrast, in Likert's (1961, 1967, 1979) programmatic development of ideas about how organizations should develop both their managers and their structures. The 'break' between the early and later Michigan approaches effectively occurred in 1966 with the publication by Bowers and Seashore of their four-factor approach which revised most of the early Michigan concepts. In a sense there are two 'later' Michigan approaches: the development of the Bowers and Seashore's ideas and Likert's somewhat more applied development of the early Michigan research. The latter is, however, an extension of the early research (Likert, 1979, pp. 153-4), whereas the four-factor approach involved a substantial revision of the early research. To that extent, the development of the Bowers and Seashore ideas more obviously warrants the 'later Michigan' label.

The early Michigan studies

Two early, and often quoted, studies provide most of the concepts with which the early Michigan approach is associated. The first was a study of clerical workers and their supervisors in the Prudential insurance company reported by Katz, Maccoby and Morse (1950); the second a study of railroad foremen and section gangs reported by Katz, Maccoby, Gurin and Floor (1951). These will be referred to in the text as *Clerical* and *Railroad* respectively. The fact that the two settings were so different was taken to be important by the researchers, as it would provide a stronger test of many of the human relations ideas which underpinned their investigations.

In the clerical study the research design involved selecting, on the basis of company records, twelve high and low productivity pairs of sections. The sections in each matched pair differed in terms of productivity, but were similar on a number of other accounts such as size and the nature of the task. A similar design guided the railroad study where thirty-six pairs of sections were selected on the basis of judgments by the Division Engineer and Track Supervisor. In both instances the research design was supposed to lead to an identification of the behavioural and organizational factors which distinguished high and low productivity sections.

Some differences from the Ohio approach are evident even at this early stage. The Michigan researchers seem to have exhibited a greater preoccupation with productivity, which was treated as a dichotomy rather than as a continuous variable as was usually the case with Ohio research. Also, the matched pairs approach is very different from the rather 'survey-style' approach of the Ohio researchers in which samples of leaders and their subordinates were the foci of investigation.

But it is over the elucidation and measurement of leadership practices that the Michigan researchers most obviously depart from their Ohio counterparts. Firstly, descriptions of leader behaviour were derived in large part from supervisors' own reports, whereas the Ohio researchers tended to use subordinates' accounts of leadership behaviour, except in the relatively small group of studies which employed the LOQ. Secondly, and more significantly, the questioning was through structured interviews (whereas the Ohio schedules are self-administered) and by means of open questions (as against the fixed-choice response format of the SBDQ, LBDQ and LOQ). Consequently, the characterization of leadership behaviour was rather more intuitive than the approach of the Ohio school. Examples of how the leadership practices of foremen and supervisors were crystallized from this style of questioning will be given *en passant*. In their early, more general writings on the fruits of their investigation of supervisory practices, the Michigan researchers tended to subsume their findings under four general rubrics which provides a framework which can usefully be followed here (see Kahn and Katz, 1953; Katz and Kahn, 1951).

1 Differentiation of supervisory role

The more productive supervisors tended to be those who spent *less* time doing the same work that their subordinates were carrying out. In the clerical study, of the twelve high productivity sections nine supervisors spent 50 per cent of their time in supervision, whereas only four of the low productivity section supervisors did so (*Clerical*, p. 17). In the railroad study the corresponding figures can be derived as being twenty out of thirty-six, and nine out of thirty-six respectively (*Railroad*, p. 12). In the latter study, confirmation of this point was evident from a table which suggested that high producing foremen are more likely to mention spending their working day doing 'more specifically supervisory duties such as planning and performing special skilled tasks' (*Railroad*, p. 14). Further, railroad gangs with high productivity foremen were more likely to perceive them as very good at planning work ahead of time, though the high-low difference was not great (38 per cent against 27 per cent). Interestingly, the railroad study found that informal leaders (based on the question 'Is there some one in the section who speaks up for the men when they want something?') were more likely to arise in low productivity sections, implying that there was insufficiently clear leadership in these groups. This awareness of the possible importance of informal leadership is a fairly enduring and distinctive feature of the Michigan tradition. However, not only was the percentage difference between high and low producing sections tiny (9 per cent against 17 per cent having informal leaders) but also there was an enormous amount of non-response (44 per cent and 46 per cent). Non-response is a recurring feature of the early Michigan research which renders many tables, which was their preferred mode of presenting data, difficult to interpret. A later study of a tractor factory confirmed the tendency for foremen who spent more of their time supervising to have more productive sections (Kahn and Katz, 1953, p. 557).

'Differentiation of supervisory role', then, denotes whether foremen distinguish, in their work activities, their position *qua* supervisor from the fact of their membership of a work group. According to Kahn and Katz (1953) this is important on two accounts. First, supervisors who have differentiated roles will be better at the technical aspects of their work – such as planning, organizing, etc. Second, he or she is more likely to have an effect on the motivation of his or her employees. This is a rather problematic contention. As Kahn and Katz admit, strong technical and motivational skills are unlikely always to be equally present in the same supervisor. It is not possible from their data to disaggregate these two components and their respective implications for productivity. 'Differentiation of supervisory role' is, then, a rather broad idea, encapsulating two potentially distinct aspects. What is particularly troublesome for students of leadership, like the Michigan researchers, is that it is only the second of the components – motivational skills – which really has any bearing on leadership as the term is generally understood. We see here a problem that arises when leadership is all too readily deemed to be synonymous with supervision, a term which will obviously include technical aspects.

2   Closeness of supervision

In the clerical study it was found that there was an association between the extent to which workers were closely supervised and productivity. The term 'general supervision' was coined to denote a cluster of practices which do not entail constantly checking subordinates, so that they are allowed considerable latitude. General supervision seemed to enhance productivity, but the picture is slightly unclear since only six of the twenty-four supervisors exhibited this style. Of the six, five were in high productivity groups, and only one in a low section. The remaining seven supervisors in the high productivity group were made up of six who adopted 'close' supervision (the obverse of general supervision) and one missing case. On the basis of such data, close supervision is not a barrier to high productivity, but general supervision is clearly superior. To give a flavour of how such results were ascertained, we are told that data on closeness of supervision are gleaned from:

> an overall code which defines closeness of supervision as the degree to which the supervisor checks up on his employees frequently, gives them detailed and frequent instructions and in general, limits the employees' freedom to do the work in their own way. (*Clerical*, p. 17)

Supervisors were classified in terms of their responses to open questions relating to these attributes.

No link seems to have been discerned between group productivity and whether supervisors adopted close or general styles in the railroad investigation. In the tractor factory study, foremen exhibiting general supervision (as perceived by subordinates) seem to have had subordinates who were happier with their job and the company (Kahn and Katz, 1953, p. 560). In particular, close supervision seemed to lead to dissatisfaction with jobs and company, largely due to a felt need for more autonomy.

Nonetheless, the findings suggesting that close supervision has a deleterious effect on the productivity of both foremen and their own subordinates is clearly an interesting finding. Later research in the shape of an experimental study on undergraduates by Day and Hamblin (1964) found that close supervision may increase aggression to both co-workers and supervisors and reduce productivity. No impact on dissatisfaction with the task was discerned. The finding that general, rather than close, supervision enhances productivity is broadly congruent with the precepts of human relations thinkers as well as some of the supposed ramifications of the Hawthorne Studies (Carey, 1967).

3   Employee-centredness

We now arrive at a notion which is often taken as the *leitmotif* of the early Michigan research. On the basis of responses to their interview questions in the clerical study, Katz *et al.* (1950) drew a distinction between 'employee-centred' and 'production-centred' (later the latter was sometimes called 'institution-centred') supervision. The former emphasize the 'human "relations" component of their jobs – that is, the motivating and training of employees' (*Clerical*, p. 20). They emphasize supportive personal relationships with their work group. Production-centred supervisors emphasize the technical and production aspects of the job in their relationships with subordinates, are work-oriented and treat subordinates as people who get work done.

In the clerical study, of the twelve high productivity leaders six were employee-centred, only one was production-centred, and the attitudes of the other five were not ascertained. In the twelve low productivity groups, seven were production-centred and only three employee-centred. The missing data are once again rather irksome as it is difficult to estimate their impact. Occasionally these data are presented without any reference to the missing cases which are disproportionately found in the high productivity group (e.g. Likert, 1961, p. 7).

In the railroad study, the foremen with high productivity gangs tended to: (a) take more interest in how their subordinates got along outside work; (b) be more helpful in training their men for better jobs; (c) react non-punitively to the men when their work was bad; and (d) be primarily concerned with their men, unlike production-oriented foremen who were more concerned with the work or the personal advantages of being a foreman. These indicators of 'employee-centredness', it should be noted, are based upon subordinates' accounts of supervisory behaviour. In the clerical study they were gleaned from supervisors' answers to one particular question and general impressions from the interview responses as a whole.

The tractor study confirmed many of these findings. Employees with better productivity records tended to report better relationships with their foremen, who tended to take more interest in them. These foremen also exhibited good communications in that they kept their men informed, were easy to talk to, helped with problems, and so on. Such employee-centred foremen were also found to contribute to greater subordinate satisfaction with the job, supervision and the company (Kahn and Katz, 1953, pp. 563-5). The tractor study also confirmed that the supervisory practices of foremen were often the same as those of their superiors.

The finding that employee-centredness leads to both enhanced productivity and satisfaction in the tractor study is obviously important. But it is questionable whether this is the case in the clerical and railroad studies in which productivity seems to be somewhat *negatively* related to intrinsic job satisfaction (*Clerical*, p. 51; *Railroad*, p. 28). This sheds some doubt on whether employee-centredness enhances job satisfaction, but this possibility was not directly addressed.

One frequently recurring difficulty with the production-centredness/ employee-centredness distinction resides in its interpretation. The confusion is twofold: what 'employee-centred' really means and whether it is a polar opposite to 'production-centred'. The first issue derives from an assertion by Likert as follows:

> Employee-centred supervisors were defined as those who focus on the human aspects of their subordinates' problems *and* build effective work groups with high performance goals. (Likert, 1979, p. 152 – author's emphasis)

He then asserts that 'other persons' ignored the high performance element. The definition that Likert provides here is almost identical to the earlier one in *New Patterns of Management* (1961, p. 7). The problem is that it is easy to see why 'other persons' may have mistakenly ignored the performance element as there is virtually no mention of it in the studies which have been cited. In the various definitions or near-definitions (Kahn and Katz, 1953, p. 562; Katz and Kahn, 1951, pp. 159-60; *Clerical*, p. 20; *Railroad*, p. 33), the building of groups with high performance goals seems to be absent. Indeed, we are told that a supervisor in the clerical study who, when asked about the most important part of his job, replies that it is getting the reports out (p. 21), is classified as production-centred. Of course, his other replies may have contributed to this assignment, but since this example was supposed to have been an illustration, it hardly enhances one's confidence that the performance component was at the front of the early Michigan researchers' thinking, thereby rendering Likert's (1961; 1979) account a little questionable.

What actually seems to have happened is that the early Michigan writers moved away from the idea that production- and employee-centredness were polar opposites to a view that supervisors can exhibit both styles. In a general article by Kahn (1956), in which some of the tractor research data were discussed, he suggests that the results showed that foremen with the best production records exhibited both styles (Kahn, 1956, p. 45). This view is much closer to that of the Ohio researchers who tended to conceptualize the kindred notions of Consideration and Initiating Structure as separate dimensions of leader behaviour. The metamorphosis of the Michigan thinking in this respect is ironic in view of

Fleishman's (1973, p 8) reflections on the excitement of the early Ohio researchers that their conceptualization differed from that of Michigan in not portraying leadership styles as polar opposites. It would seem that there is some confusion over whether employee-centredness as a leadership style comprises high performance goals or not; or whether good, employee-centred supervisors have high performance goals because they are *additionally* production-centred. The first interpretation seems to be that of Likert (1961, pp. 6-7); the second that of Kahn (1956). Either of these interpretations departs substantially from those implicit in the early formulations in the clerical and railroad studies. Indeed, even the nomenclature changes with Likert (1961) transforming production-centred into 'job-centred'.

4 Group relationships

This element has to do with the extent to which the leader inculcates a sense of group cohesiveness, pride in the group and the individual's membership of it, and mutual help. Conceptually, this attribute differs from the other three in that it seems to refer to a consequence of what leaders do, rather than an aspect of it. Nevertheless, in the high productivity sections of the insurance study, the researchers were more likely to find a high percentage of employees with considerable pride in their work groups (*Clerical*, pp. 48-9). This relationship was also demonstrated in the railroad study (*Railroad*, p. 15), but was much weaker. In the tractor factory study, however, the relationship was fairly well established once again (Kahn and Katz, 1953).

It would be grossly misleading to assume that these four foci can subsume all of the early Michigan interest in leadership. For example, one of the most frequently referenced Michigan studies of this period is the field experiment conducted by Morse and Reimer (1956). The experimental manipulation involved in this study comprised ideas which were derived from the early survey studies. In a large business firm, two large experimental groups were created, based on four divisions within the organisation. One group, the autonomy programme, received enhanced participative decision-making; the second group, the hierarchically controlled programme, received tighter managerial control. These manipulations comprise elements of both general/close and employee-centred/production-centred contrasts. The time-span was one and a half years and measurements were taken at a number of junctures. The groups were matched to ensure comparability and supervisors were trained in accordance with the underlying aims of each condition. In conformity with what one would predict from the survey studies, the autonomy programme enhanced the satisfaction of the employees (clerical workers), while the other programme produced a decrease. Both conditions resulted in an increase in productivity, but the hierarchical control programme produced the larger increase. Such findings, once again, point to the problem of assuming a positive linear relationship between satisfaction and productivity and, as Likert (1961, pp. 75-6) has observed, presents a dilemma to those seeking to draw practical implications from such studies.

A second reason for being cautious in assuming that these four aspects of leadership practices subsume all of the early Michigan interest is simply that alternative conceptualizations of leader behaviour were offered (e.g. Kahn, 1958; Likert, 1961; Mann, 1965). The approach of Mann (1965), for example, proposed the term 'human relations' skills, which roughly corresponds to employee-centredness (Mann, 1965, pp. 79-80) and denotes a sensitivity to the underlying principles of human behaviour, relationships, and motivation. He further distinguished 'technical' skills, that is the ability to use relevant knowledge, methods, techniques, equipment in order to achieve specific tasks, and 'administrative' skills which refer to an awareness of the broader organizational context and its goals, as well as organizing, planning, coordinating, and personnel deployment abilities. Mann's findings were based on studies from a numbr of contexts and led him to conclude that there was no 'best' style, since particular skills or combinations of skills were required at different times and levels in a firm. This rather relativist interpretation of leadership skills, which acknowledges the role of moderating variables, stands in stark contrast to the rather universalistic propositions which emanated from the early Michigan research.

The early Michigan research produced a number of often divergent conceptualizations of the phenomenon of leadership which contrast sharply with the fairly consistent Ohio preoccupations. Bowers and Seashore's (1966) paper presented a new formulation and ushered in a new Michigan approach to the study of leadership in organizations.

The later Michigan Studies

The Bowers and Seashore (1966) paper summarized and synthesized the conceptual classifications of leadership style developed not only by the early Michigan work, but also by the Ohio school and those developed at the Research Centre for Group Dynamics by Cartwright and Zander (1960). Their approach was to point to the substantial overlap between many of the notions, from which four underlying dimensions of leadership seemed to emerge:

1 *Support* – behaviour that enhances the subordinate's sense of personal worth.
2 *Interaction facilitation* – the engendering of close, mutually satisfying group relationships.
3 *Goal emphasis* – the stimulation of enthusiasm, without pressure, for the achievement of high performance levels.
4 *Work facilitation* – providing the technical and organizational means for goal accomplishment, i.e. scheduling, coordinating, planning.

Bowers and Seashore went beyond this classification by noting that such practices may be carried out or performed from within the group, in addition to being carried out by a formally designated supervisor. In this way, the fourfold classification of leadership behaviour is in effect a taxonomy of group needs, which can be met by both formal leaders and mutually by work group members. The first was called 'Managerial' or 'Supervisory Leadership' and the second 'Peer Leadership'. In large part, this second construct acknowledges the possibility of informal leadership though they are by no means synonymous. Consequently, the later Michigan research focuses upon eight dimensions of leadership.

An early study was carried out by Bowers and Seashore (1966) on forty agencies of a life insurance company, employing postal questionnaires sent to managers, supervisory personnel and sales agents. The questions on leadership were based on items drawn from the Ohio and early Michigan studies, so that descriptions are based on each respondent's assessments of his or her superior and peers. High correlations were found between both managerial and peer leadership dimensions, which were also correlated with a battery of measures of satisfaction and performance. Only peer interaction facilitation displayed consistently weak relationships with the various dependent variables.

As part of a general research questionnaire dealing with organizational characteristics, Taylor and Bowers (1972) developed a series of questions out of which the eight necessary measures can be fashioned. Each question is answered on a five-point scale on which respondents indicate degrees of agreement with a statement or how frequently it occurs. Two examples of each dimension are given below with the Supervisory Leadership (S) question first, followed by its Peer Leadership (P) counterpart:

Support
- How friendly and easy to approach is your supervisor? (S)
- How friendly or easy to approach are the persons in your work group? (P)

Goal emphasis
- How much does your supervisor encourage people to give their best effort?(S)
- How much do persons in your work group encourage each other to give their best effort? (P)

Work facilitation
- To what extent does your supervisor show you how to improve your performance? (S)
- To what extent do persons in your work group help you find ways to do a better job?(P)

Interaction facilitation
- To what extent does your supervisor encourage the persons who work for him to work as a team? (S)
- How much do persons in your work group encourage each other to work as a team?(P)

This instrument was employed in studies of a number of organizations, the overall results of which are reported in Taylor and Bowers (1972). In order to identify focal work groups and their supervisors, a grid was employed to discern who each person believed his supervisor to be. A somewhat disconcerting feature of the scales, particularly those relating to supervisory leadership, was a high correlation between them, thereby suggesting a considerable degree of overlap in empirical content. Also test-retest reliabilities (correlating measures of leadership at two different points in time) are often low (see Schriesheim and Kerr, 1977). Quite apart from the statistical problems of the scales, the ability of the four-factor schema to predict various outcomes is not all that it might be. In an analysis of data drawn from 284 work groups, Taylor and Bowers presented cross-sectional correlations between leadership and both satisfaction (with group, company, job, and supervisor) and group processes (group coordination, confidence and trust, desire to meet objectives, etc.). Correlations between these variables at two different junctures were also presented. Unfortunately, Taylor and Bowers present the correlations for Managerial and Peer Leadership *in toto*, i.e. the data for the four factors are summed. This procedure renders it impossible to indicate what aspect or component of either Managerial or Peer leadership is instrumental in contributing (or not contributing) to the various empirical relationships. It becomes difficult at an intuitive level to interpret what a correlation of any magnitude between Managerial Leadership and satisfaction means. Managerial Leadership was found to have a fairly strong positive relationship, both cross-sectionally and over time, with both group process and satisfaction. Peer Leadership had very high cross-sectional correlations in both time periods with group process (.81 and .83), but the lagged correlation fell markedly to .32. It may be that a large part of the cross-sectional correlation is due to the fact that they measure similar constructs. The cross-sectional correlations with satisfaction were fairly high, but the lagged correlation was only .22.

A similar analysis was conducted by Franklin (1975) who took from the Taylor and Bowers sample those work groups which had been examined at both points in time and which had the same supervisor. The model suggested by both his data and that of Taylor and Bowers is outlined in Figure 3.4.

The figure distinguishes between strong effects and a weaker effect, denoted by the broken arrow. It suggests that the nature of Managerial Leadership is strongly affected by the climate of the organization, as measured by a composite index which includes: decision-making practices, concern for people, how conflict is handled and hard work is induced, and communication flow. However, Franklin observed, confirming the Taylor and Bowers experience, that these relationships tended to pertain at the cross-sectional level, not longitudinally.

Further analyses presented in the Taylor and Bowers report point to the tendency for both Managerial and Peer Leadership to be associated with: lower direct labour costs, lower variable expenses, greater product quality (ML only), lower absenteeism, and fewer grievances. Many of the data are

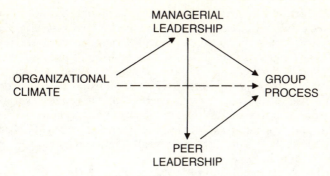

Figure 3.4 *Key empirical relationships in later Michigan research*

Reprinted from 'Relations among four social psychological aspects of organiz-ations' by J. L. Franklin, published in *Administrative Science Quarterly* (Vol. 20, September) by permission of *The Administrative Science Quarterly*.

difficult to interpret because only average correlations are presented for each relationship, the magnitude and often direction of the relationship vary according to the degree of time lag involved, as well as from one organization to the next. The latter problem arises from the tendency for data to be presented for each organization, rather than for all of the oranizations investigated. One of the only instances where the leadership measures were not presented as composite indices is an analysis of six very large firms in the Survey of Organizations sample. Six of the eight leadership measures exhibited high cross-sectional correlations with profit as a percentage of invested capital, the missing ones being Peer Work Facilitation and Interaction Facilitation. When a lag of two years was taken, these correlations declined markedly. With a one-year lag, the size of correlation coefficients was still quite large.

Research by Bowers (1975) sought to introduce possible moderating variables into the four-factor approach. A study of 1,683 workgroups in twenty-one organizations was conducted to assess the extent to which the type of industry and the hierarchical level of a group moderated the effects of Supervisory and Peer Leadership. While there was some evidence of rather weak associations between the leadership and outcome measures, Bowers confidently concluded:

> leadership which contains *more* support, interaction facilitation, goal emphasis, and work facilitation is associated in general with *greater* member satisfaction and *better* group processes, pretty much regardless of hierarchical level and type of industry. (Bowers, 1975, p. 177)

Nonetheless, significant mediating effects were discerned. For example, none of the leadership variables – supervisory or peer – correlated with satisfaction among top management groups. When type of industry was taken into account, only Supervisory and Peer Goal Emphasis had any effect on satisfaction in research and administration organizations. Each of the industries exhibited different profiles. Bowers's bold assertion is based on the fact that virtually all of the coefficients examined are positive, but it should also be recognized that quite a lot are non-significant and many are exceedingly small. Further, not only do the two mediating variables have an effect, but also they have differential implications (as do the leadership measures themselves), according to whether the dependent variable is satisfaction or an index of the quality of group functioning. When the effects of eight leadership variables are being assessed, it becomes exceedingly difficult to present an overall picture beyond the rather sanitized one quoted above.

A study by Yunker and Hunt (1976) of chapters in a large national business fraternity used both Ohio and Michigan four-factor approaches in order to discern their relative potential. Only the supervisory dimensions from the Michigan instrument were employed. While the Michigan styles were generally positively correlated with a range of measures of satisfaction, in line with Bowers's (1975) findings, the pattern was such as to suggest that the Ohio dimensions were more strongly and more consistently correlated in a positive direction with the satisfaction indices. Supervisory Support was the dimension which was most poorly correlated with satisfaction. Neither the Ohio nor the Michigan dimensions correlated well with a performance measure, but the former were considerably stronger. Indeed, two of the Michigan supervisory leadership dimensions correlated negatively with performance, and a third was a correlation of 0.

Criticisms of the Michigan work

How does the Michigan research shape up in terms of the six criticisms levelled earlier in this chapter at the Ohio researchers?

1　*Discrepant findings.* The early research tended to confirm the superiority of employee-centred and general supervision. Little contradictory evidence was found though some disconcerting aspects of the findings were pinpointed. The later Michigan research suffers from the problem of presenting its findings as both composite indices and as separate dimensions of leadership. It may be that findings relating to the composite indices obscure discrepant findings for the individual scales. This possibility is certainly implied by some of the very low correlations discerned in the Bowers (1975) study. The picture is confounded by the fact that the strength of many of the relationships cited above declines with time. It is not clear from the theoretical work emanating from the researchers what significance one should attach to this pattern. One would always anticipate declining effects over time of an antecedent variable, but in the absence of a yard-stick for specifying 'proper' time-lags the question of whether evidence is confirmatory or not is problematic.

2 *Absence of situational analysis*. In the early Michigan work and the initial phases of the four-factor research, there was relatively little attention paid to variables which might impinge on the various empirical relationships. Bowers's (1975) analysis has gone some way towards this problem, though the overall pattern of results is not at all easy to interpret. In this context, a study of US destroyer ships by Butler and Jones (1979) is worthy of mention. These researchers distinguished between more hazardous areas on the ship (engineering divisions) and those which were less hazardous (deck divisions). Their research found that the four dimensions of Supervisory Leadership had no impact on the number of accidents in the former environment. By contrast, in the less hazardous deck divisions, greater Supervisory Goal Emphasis, Work Facilitation, and Interaction Facilitation were all associated with fewer accidents. The impact of leadership upon frequency of accidents seemed to vary, in other words, according to the dangerousness of the work context. Further, research based on civil service and military employees by Jones, James and Bruni (1975) found that the effects of the four Managerial Leadership dimensions on the amount of confidence and trust in their leader was moderated by respondents' job involvement scores. Correlations between the Managerial Leadership dimensions and confidence and trust were significantly lower (though still positive) among respondents who were involved in their jobs.

In summary, there seems to be a greater awareness of the need to include situational factors in the work of the later Michigan researchers. This develoment parallels the systematic inclusion of such factors in the various approaches outlined in Chapter 5 and the growing interest in them displayed by researchers employing the Ohio instruments.

3 *The problem of causality*. The early Michigan writers were clearly aware of the problem of inferring cause-effect relationships from their studies, and their reports make frequent reference to the need for caution (e.g. Kahn, 1956, p. 43). The Bowers and Seashore (1966) and Bowers (1975) studies manifest the same problems, while the Taylor and Bowers (1972) and Franklin (1975) studies include longitudinal research designs. However, as stated above, there is a very real problem of what the appropriate lag should be under such circumstances.

The Morse and Reimer (1956) study appears to provide a strong test of some of the early Michigan ideas in the sense that it is an experimental study. However, as indicated above, its results in connection with productivity were equivocal. Two other problems remain. First, the precise relationship between the two experimental treatments and the early Michigan general/close and production/employee-centred contrasts is not absolutely clear. Second, in terms of the issue of causality, the study is not entirely virtuous in spite of the use of an experimental design, because the members of the two treatment programmes were aware of the differences between them. They often had strong feelings about the programmes that they were not in (Zimmerman, 1978), implying that the two conditions were not entirely independent. Clearly, then, a large proportion of the

Michigan work manifests problems of causality, in spite of the fact that causal inferences are often made by commentators on the work.

4 *Problem of the group*. Both early and later Michigan researchers have tended to use group averaging methods when analysing subordinates' accounts of leader behaviour. Such procedures have been questioned by proponents of individual-based accounts. According to the advocates of the VDL approach, much of the Michigan research may have ignored intra-group variations in how leaders are perceived as behaving.

5 *Informal leadership*. Both early and later Michigan traditions derive the bulk of their information about leadership on reports and impressions of the practices of designated supervisors. However, the railroad study was deemed to shed some light on informal leadership, though one may validly question whether 'speaking up' for the group (see above) is genuinely indicative of leadership. Nonetheless, such items of information do shed some light on informal processes. The emphasis on Peer Leadership in the later work also acknowledges informal leadership in that the group functions performed by formal leaders 'may be provided by anyone in a work group for anyone else in that work group' (Bowers and Seashore, 1966, p. 249). However, the provision of such benefits may occur on an equal exchange basis, so that whether this is indicative of informal *leadership* is a moot point. Indeed, the later Michigan researchers are cautious not to equate Peer with informal leadership. Consequently, it is necessary to conclude that informal leadership processes are generally underplayed in the Michigan research.

6 *Non-observation of leadership behaviour*. With the exception of the Morse and Reimer (1956) study, 'measures' of leadership practices have been gleaned from subordinates', and occasionally supervisors', own reports. Consequently, the research is open to all of the problems indicated in the comparable section dealing with the Ohio research. In particular, the problem of implicit leadership theories may apply to the Michigan research too. An investigation which is relevant to this possibility is a study of Israeli students (Eden and Leviatan, 1975) which asked subjects to rate an imaginary manufacturing plant in terms of the leadership items in the *Survey of Organizations* questionnaire (Taylor and Bowers, 1972). The resulting analysis points to a conceptual structure being used which is almost identical to the four-factor approach. In other words, when asked about an imaginary plant, rather than their own work experiences, people employ implicit leadership theories which guide their perception of the leadership processes in the firm. People seem to carry around in their heads a view of leadership which they deploy in respect of answering questionnaires relating to both imaginary and real leaders. A similar study on American undergraduates by Weiss and Adler (1981) confirmed these results. In addition, these researchers found that the tendency to describe an imaginary supervisor in terms of the conceptual structure of the four-factor approach was unaffected by variations in the cognitive

complexity[4] of subjects. Such findings raise very disturbing questions about the meaningfulness of questionnaires which are devised to provide descriptions of the behaviour of leaders. That these findings are similar to those discerned in the context of the Ohio dimensions (Rush *et al.*, 1977) is not surprising in view of the conceptual symmetry between the two approaches.

Leadership style studies and the development of normative approaches

It is clear from the preceding discussions that the Ohio and Michigan approaches have had a considerable impact upon leadership researchers. But the research which has emerged out of these two traditions has also had an impact upon the development of ideas about what leaders *should* do in order to enhance their effectiveness. These kinds of orientation have been dubbed 'Normative Leadership Approaches' by Barrow (1977). Two examples of a normative approach, both of which appear to have been heavily influenced by the Ohio and Michigan studies, will now be examined. Both of them are important because of their commitment to applying their schemes in organizational settings.

The Managerial Grid

The Managerial Grid was conceived by Blake and Mouton who in a series of publications (e.g. 1964) have developed an approach to organizational development which is one of the best known in the literature. The infrastructure to their approach is a contrast between two approaches to the managerial role: 'concern for production' and 'concern for people'. Blake and Mouton take the view that both concerns are essential ingredients of effective management. Each concern is conceptualized as a nine-point scale, thus yielding eighty-one possible combinations of managerial behaviour. In fact, in most of their writings, Blake and Mouton focus solely upon five combinations, as the simplified diagram (Figure 3.5) suggests, which are:

(1) 1,1 is called 'Impoverished management' and is characterized by low scores on both dimensions, a context in which conflict is likely to be rife.
(2) 1,9 is 'Country club management', with a high score on Concern for People only. While camaraderie may be at a peak, people are not pushed to produce.
(3) 9,1 is 'Task Management' which sees people as merely suppliers of labour. Management, as the high score on Concern for Production implies, sees its job primarily in terms of controlling and directing subordinates and planning their work.
(4) 5,5 is a middle-of-the-road position in which there is some emphasis

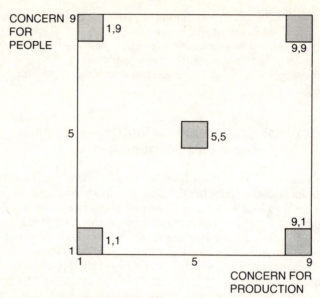

Figure 3.5　*The Managerial Grid schema*

on both dimensions.

(5) 9,9 is called 'Team Management' and constitutes the recommended managerial stance in that both task and people imperatives are being met. It is a participative system, since people responsible for the production are also supposed to be involved in work planning and execution. Real Team Management conditions exist when 'individual goals are in line with those of the organization' (Blake and Mouton, 1964, p. 180).

According to Blake and Mouton managers often oscillate between 9,1 and 1,9 styles: the former in response to a need to enhance output, the latter when interpersonal relationships suffer. They advocate that the inculcation of 9,9 values in an organization should be undertaken in stages, starting with off-site training in Grid principles and then on-site training. Managerial Grid Training is a vital first step in developing the two constituent concerns, as well as an awareness of the desirability and means of generating openness of communication and participation among managers.

Does the Managerial Grid approach work? The evidence is mixed. Blake and Mouton are clearly impressed with the evidence emanating from research on 800 managers and supervisors in a large petrochemical firm (Blake, Mouton, Barnes and Greiner, 1964), which experienced considerable cost savings and enhanced productivity and profits after the introduction of the Grid programme. Greater cooperativeness among plant personnel was also discerned. The study suffers from severe methodological weaknesses which arise fundamentally because of the absence of control groups. One is left with the possibility that the observed effects could have occurred anyway, or that some other form of managerial training would have had the same (or even a greater) effect. Further, as Campbell, Dunnette, Lawler and Weick (1970, p. 291) have observed, output at the plant did not increase. The productivity gain was achieved by a large decrease in the work force. Since then, it is suggested:

> most Grid programs are either not evaluated at all, or are evaluated by low-rigour methods. What few rigorous studies there are have generated mixed and often contradictory conclusions. (Filley, House and Kerr, 1976, pp. 505-6)

A study of the effect of Grid Training on a division of a glass work in the USA by Beer and Kleisath (1975) suggests that it leads to enhanced employee satisfaction, a drop in turnover, better communication and a number of other intended effects. However, the absence of any kind of control group renders such a study extremely difficult to interpret.

In a more recent paper, Blake and Mouton (1982) point to more rigorous research on two subsidiaries of a company which had many similar or identical characteristics. One subsidiary experienced the Grid programme, while the other did not. A ten-year comparison suggests a gain in profitability over the matched control of 400 per cent, although the significance of this finding is questionable in view of Beer and Kleisath's (1975, p. 345) assertion that such criteria are not necessarily appropriate for evaluating Grid training. Another experimental study suggests that 9,9 sales personnel are much more likely than those without this orientation to make a sale. It is important to realize that it is still necessary to have information on the effectiveness on other management and organizational change programmes before definitive conclusions about the Grid as such can be deduced. Nor is it easy to interpret research which shows that managers with a 9,9 orientation are more likely to rise up the career ladder (Blake and Mouton, 1982, p. 283; Hall and Donnell, 1979), especially since its presence in a manager may not be due to Grid training. Further, Blake and Mouton (1982) cite a study in which managerial personnel were asked to choose between managerial situations based on a 9,9 orientation or those based on Hersey and Blanchard's (1977, see Chapter 5) Situational Leadership approach. Respondents were asked to rank the relative effectiveness of the 9,9 and Situational Leadership approaches in dealing with particular managerial situations. In fact, 9,9 alternatives were typically preferred, but to deduce that these findings lead to 'an acceptance of the 9,9 orientation as the most valid basis for exercising effective leadership' (Blake and Mouton, 1982, p. 282) is foolhardy, since the Hersey-Blanchard approach is only one of a number of possibilities that could have been selected for comparison.

There is a clear resemblance between the two Grid dimensions and the Ohio State preoccupation with Consideration and Initiating Structure, such that there is often an implicit view among many writers that the former arose out of the latter. When writing about the Grid, for example,

Sashkin and Garland (1979, p. 76) refer to Consideration and Initiating Structure rather than the two 'concerns'. In their examination of the effects of Grid training on leadership attitudes, Beer and Kleisath (1975) employed the LOQ and its associated conceptual schema to denote the concern for production and people. It is easy to see why this association should occur, for there is a clear symmetry between the bi-polar pairs. Further, Blake and Mouton's early work makes many references to Ohio research.[5] More recently, Blake and Mouton (1982) have expressed the distinctiveness of their perspective from approaches such as that of the Ohio researchers which talk about people and task orientations as separate dimensions which imply the possibility of leader profiles. The profiles typically comprise varying combinations or degrees of, say, Consideration and Initiating Structure. By contrast, the Grid dimensions are interdependent. Employing an analogue from chemistry when comparing the concern for people revealed in 1,9 and 9,9 orientations, they suggest:

> Both 9s signify the same magnitude of concern [i.e. for people] but qualitative differences in thought, feeling and behaviour are shown in the compound resulting from the interaction between these two interdependent variables. (Blake and Mouton, 1982, p. 279)

This suggests that the '9' in 1, 9 is not identical in constitution to the '9' in 9,9. While this statement may help to clarify the distinctiveness of the Grid approach from that of superficially similar approaches, the presence of equivocal findings is not conducive to an overly sanguine view about the overall validity of the schema. The pattern of inconclusive results is highly reminiscent of much Ohio-based leadership research, while the persistent emphasis upon a 'one best way' of managing will continue to hamper progress in discerning the viability of the Managerial Grid. Given the doubts about the validity of even the Ohio 'Hi-Hi' leader style (see above), which is very reminiscent of a 9,9 orientation (notwithstanding Blake and Mouton's clarification), it is not surprising there is some unease among leadership researchers over the Grid programme.

Likert's System 4

While the Blake and Mouton Managerial Grid seems to have been influenced by the Ohio researchers, the idea of System 4 developed by Likert (1961; 1967) is a systematic development of the ideas and research generated by the Michigan leadership studies (Likert, 1979, p. 153). The basic tenet upon which Likert builds his approach is the 'principle of supportive relationships':

> The leadership and other processes in the organization must be such as to ensure a maximum probability that in all interactions and in all relationships within the organization, each member, in the light of his background, values, desires, and expectations, will view the experiences

as supportive and one which builds and maintains his sense of personal worth and importance. (Likert, 1961, p. 103)

In addition, Likert advocates that supervisors should seek to cultivate group problem-solving by consensus and, consonant with this preference, a structure within the organization of overlapping groups, such that each work group is linked to the wider organization. High performance goals and technical competence on the part of supervisors and managers are also necessary. It is easy to see in these ideas the early Michigan preoccupations with employee-centred and general supervision, as well as the importance of group relationships.

On the basis of this conceptual infrastructure, Likert distinguishes four kinds of management system:

(a) System 1 – an 'exploitive authoritative' system.
(b) System 2 – 'benevolent authoritative' management.
(c) System 3 – 'consultative' management.
(d) System 4 – 'participative group management'.

As one moves from System 1 to System 4 management, the principles advocated by Likert are more in evidence and participation by organiz-ational members increases. Consequently:

System 4 harnesses human motivation in ways that yield positive cooperation rather than fearful antagonism on the part of the people in the organization; by contrast, Systems 1 and 2 tend to develop less favourable attitudes, more hostile attitudes, or more submissive attitudes. (Likert, in conversation with Dowling, 1973, p. 34)

According to Likert, provided a manager plans well, has high performance goals, and is technically competent the causal relationships summarized in Figure 3.6 can be expected. The closer a management system is to System 4 (Box 1), the better will be the intervening 'morale' variables in Box 2, and the organization will experience greater performance in terms of the outcomes specified in Box 3.

These are not idealized speculations on Likert's part, even though they smack of constituting a management panacea. Likert deploys a massive array of data in seeking to demolish traditional management systems and erecting System 4 in their place. Leadership occupies an important place in the scheme since it is reflected in the supervisory and managerial practices which underpin the principles upon which System 4 (as well as the three others) is based. Many of the studies reported in Likert's work provide only inferential support as they reflect only relationships among some of the variables which comprise the System 1 to 4 approach, e.g. studies revealing the superiority of participative management for job satisfaction, performance, group cohesion, and the like. What we really need to know is whether System 4 as a package is superior to the other management systems. Before examining some of the relevant evidence, however, a word

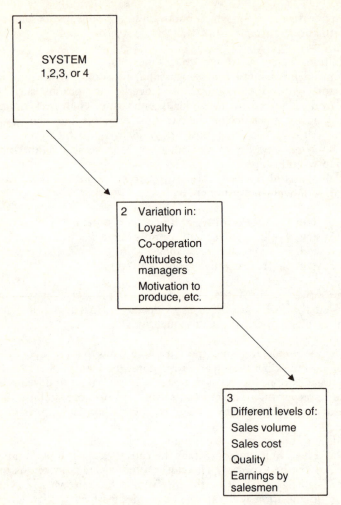

Figure 3.6 *Causal flow in Likert's approach*

of caution is necessary. While Likert's System 4 approach is often treated as a scheme which is indicative of a leadership style approach (e.g. Yukl, 1981; Albanese and van Fleet, 1983), there is more to the assessment of organizations in System 1 to 4 terms than leadership alone. For example, when an organization is to be infused with a System 4 programme, Likert and his colleagues advocate that it is necessary to discern where it is on the System 1 to 4 continuum. In fact, most firms tend to approximate to System 2 management systems (Dowling, 1973, p. 44). But this assessment does not simply involve looking at leadership styles in the firm. Communication flows, decision-making and control processes and procedures, patterns of interaction influence, and the like, are all elements to be analysed and possibly changed. While leadership style may affect some of these variables, its impact on them is often unstated and in any event it is at least analytically separate from them. The reader should be cautious in believing that the evidence to be examined provides test cases for Likert's approach to the study of leadership.

A classic study of the introduction of System 4 is that provided by the Weldon Manufacturing Co., a garment manufacturer, which in 1962 was taken over by the Harwood Manufacturing Co., which itself had been the focus of a classic study of participation (Coch and French, 1948 – See Chapter 4). At the time of the take-over Weldon was a disaster in performance and human relations terms – poorly managed, bad record of union disputes, high labour turnover, outdated machinery (Marrow, Bowers and Seashore, 1967). The Institute of Social Research at Michigan was called in to introduce System 4 into the firm which in 1962 was virtually at the System 1 end of the continuum. This operation was carried out by means of a combination of management training in human relations and participation principles, reducing the very high degree of centralized decision-making and authority, and changing the attitudes of managers and supervisors regarding their subordinates.

One difficulty with treating Weldon as a test case is that other changes were introduced which are unrelated to System 4. Changes in work-flow and distribution, the acquisition of new machinery, new methods of record keeping and other changes were simultaneously introduced. So too were a new incentive pay scheme and a new approach to selection and training. Further, a peaceful settlement with the Amalgamated Clothing Workers Unit was achieved at a relatively early stage. The fact that non-System 4 features were introduced simultaneously, coupled with the absence of a 'control' makes the results difficult to interpret. Nonetheless, by 1964 Weldon was a System 3 firm and was exhibiting a marked surge in a variety of indicators of productive efficiency, such as return on capital invested, as well as lower operator turnover and absenteeism (Marrow *et al.*, 1967, p. 147). A 30 per cent increase in productivity was reported, but only a small percentage of this increase seems to have been due to System 4 elements (Marrow *et al.*, 1967, pp. 181-2). Much more crucial to the surge in productivity were the new incentive scheme and 'the weeding out of low earners'.

While the authors of the main report maintain that the System 4 approach was really much more crucial than such calculations imply (Marrow *et al.*, 1967, pp. 182-4), there is little doubt that the findings are disconcerting in that they shed some doubt on the real impact of System 4 on the increases in production efficiency and the lower turnover and absenteeism rates. Also, the changes in employee attitudes, motivation, and satisfaction were much less pronounced than might have been expected (Marrow *et al.*, 1967, ch. 14). Quite apart from the fact that this pattern of results for these morale variables is contrary to expectations, it poses problems for Likert's overall model. Since they are Box 2 variables (see Figure 3.5) one would have expected increases in them to be the cause of increases in the performance variables. But the latter increased independently of demonstrably superior ratings on the Box 2 variables, lending strength to the interpretation that the non-System 4 changes had a more sizeable impact than anticipated.

A second test case is a comparison of two General Motors plants, Doraville and Lakewood, undertaken by the Michigan team which was started in 1969 (Dowling, 1975). In spite of similar working conditions, size, and character, the two plants differed markedly in performance: Doraville being described by Dowling as a highly successful plant; Lakewood as a 'disaster area'. The latter plant was found to be a System 2 operation by the Michigan researchers who set about moving it in a System 4 direction:

> Training sessions were held for staff members and then for the rest of the supervisory force. Mutual understanding, trust, and teamwork were stressed. Special emphasis also was given to improving the effectiveness of all supervisors in such key areas as communication, goal setting and team building. (Dowling, 1975, p. 26)

In addition, very considerable effort was expended on enhancing the information that each employee had on the firm, products, costs, facilities, and so on.

Between December 1969 and August 1970, a very short space of time indeed, the firm's organizational climate improved, leadership behaviour moved in a System 4 direction, group processes (following the four-factor approach – see above) were enhanced, and a range of satisfaction measures showed improvement. This apparently favourable response to System 4 techniques was not matched by the performance measures employed. Indeed, direct and indirect labour efficiency both declined. Indirect labour efficiency continued to decline to the end of 1970, while direct labour efficiency improved. However, both indicators had improved considerably by the end of 1972, and there was also evidence of improved quality and fewer grievances over the 1969-72 period. Results such as these strongly suggest that there is a considerable lag in the impact that System 4 can have on performance.

Again, caution in the interpretation of these apparently impressive results is necessary. There is no control group so that we do not know what would have happened without System 4. In all probability, circumstances would have continued to be dreadful and may even have deteriorated. What we cannot be certain about is that System 4 was the best way of dealing with the Lakewood problems, rather than a Grid approach or any other programme for organizational change. This is particularly the case with instances like Lakewood and Weldon where the programme is introduced into firms which are poor performers and abysmally managed. In such circumstances, virtually any reasonably well considered change programme should make things better. Indeed, the very fact that a firm appears to be prepared to do something constructive about its predicament may have a beneficial effect on morale. The possibility of an unintended 'Hawthorne effect' at Lakewood cannot be discounted either.

This is not to say that System 4, any more than Grid organizational development, is of no use. In each case, the evidence is both ambiguous and open to a variety of interpretations. Again, we should not be surprised at the fact that the results of these studies do not always conform to expectations, because in spite of an occasional sensitivity to the importance of situational factors which may impinge on their viability (e.g. Likert, 1961, p. 89), writers like Likert still operate with roughly the same 'one best way' approach that the early researchers on leadership style found so difficult to substantiate.

Summary

The disillusionment with the trait approach, in tandem with the other factors mentioned at the start of this chapter, was highly instrumental in the surge of interest in the study of leader behaviour in organizations. Arguably, the Ohio State programme is the most famous and influential of the approaches that this change of direction spawned. For thirty years, researchers have found the contrast of Consideration and Initiating Structure to be a highly resonant and fruitful contribution. The programme's commitment to the precise operationalization of leader behaviour dimensions was in substantial synchrony with developments in social science methodology. However, the Ohio approach has been plagued with inconsistent findings and methodological difficulties, this latter malady afflicting the Michigan approaches too. This chapter has sought to explicate the major theoretical (such as they are) and empirical thrusts of the Ohio and Michigan approaches and to elaborate six criticisms which can be levelled at them. The six criticisms do not constitute an exhaustive list but they do raise fundamental problems about the practice of research into leadership of the kind developed by these two traditions. They will be referred to again in relation to some of the other approaches which will be examined in later chapters. The Ohio and Michigan approaches do not fare too well in terms of the six criticisms. However, as later chapters will reveal, their impact has been enormous in that the people-versus-task dimension which both approaches exhibited, along with the Michigan focus on the participative approach to leadership (in the form of 'general' supervision), have been enduring concerns for researchers. The two normative approaches – Grid and System 4 – were introduced and assessed by virtue of their apparent connection with many of the ideas associated with the early research on leadership style. However, a number of methodological and substantive problems were apparent in the evidence associated with both of the normative approaches.

4

LEADERSHIP STYLE II: PARTICIPATION, REWARDS, MOTIVATION AND CONTROL

The discussion of the Ohio and Michigan research sought to bring out both the unique and similar characteristics of the two schools. A convergent element of the two schools is one to which other writers often draw attention (e.g. Schein, 1980; Bass, 1981), namely a recurring contrast between task-centred/directive/instrumental/initiating leadership and employee-centred/supportive/considerate/human relations leadership. The former emphasizes the group task which must be achieved and the means for its attainment; the second cluster denotes an orientation to the affective, social and emotional needs of the group and its members. The task-centred emphasis is manifested in the Ohio dimensions called Initiating Structure and Production Emphasis, the early Michigan idea of production orientation, and the four factor notions of Goal Emphasis and Work Facilitation. Likewise, the leader's supportive behaviour is denoted by Consideration and Sensitivity in the Ohio research, employee-centredness in the early Michigan investigations, and Support and Interaction Facilitation by Bowers and Seashore (1966, see Table 1). The contrast is present in the work of many other writers, one of the more prominent of whom is Bales (e.g. Bales and Slater, 1955) who, in his experimental work, wrote about the differential propensity of leaders to fulfil the task and 'socio-emotional' needs of the group.[1] The review of the evidence in Chapter 3 can leave one with little doubt that the evidence for the supposed benefits of both task-centred and person-centred leadership are mixed. There are tendencies for task-centred leadership to be associated with greater subordinate performance and for a person-centred style to be associated with greater subordinate satisfaction. But these *are* tendencies, and there is too much conflicting evidence to be confident in drawing definitive conclusions.

At least three possible reasons exist for this state of affairs. One possibility is that we are asking too much of the task-centred/person-centred contrast in expecting it to have universal predictive utility. Secondly, it may be that the methodological difficulties inherent in much of the work on leadership (e.g. the problem of causality and the non-observation of leadership practices) has contributed to the inconclusiveness of much leadership research. This is a recurring problem to which the reader's attention will continue to be drawn. Thirdly, it may be that the labels are too broad and do not take sufficient account of the strategies employed by leaders in dealing with their subordinates. Alternatively it may be that the wrong aspects of leader behaviour are being addressed; for example, that Consideration and Initiating Structure are not really so important. It is to this third pair of related possibilities that the writers associated with the frameworks presented in this chapter have implicitly addressed themselves. Four areas of leadership behaviour will be examined: the enormous and burgeoning literature on *participative leadership*, an area which was addressed in some of the material examined in the last chapter, and the behaviour of leaders in terms of their *reward*, *motivational* and *control* strategies.

Participation

How much influence a leader should permit his subordinates over matters relating to their jobs is an important decision that all leaders face. This is the fundamental issue which underpins the widespread interest in how 'participative' a leader should be, that is, how far he should allow subordinates to determine how the work, for which he is responsible, should be done; how closely he should supervise them; and how far he should take their views into account.

The possible importance of being participative was evident in some of the research reviewed in the last chapter. The Iowa childhood studies of Lewin, Lippitt and White seemed to show that when participative climates were created, there was greater satisfaction in the groups, less aggression, and there was some evidence that they were more productive. The Relay Assembly Test Room study was often taken as evidence of the superiority of participative supervision, as the experimental conditions were taken to imply that the workers had greater control over how the work should be done. The Morse and Reimer study directly manipulated the amount of influence that clerical workers had at their disposal, a factor which affected turnover and satisfaction beneficially. The early Michigan contrast between close and general styles of supervision was also essentially a reflection of degrees of participativeness. The general style essentially indicates allowing subordinates greater freedom and latitude at the work place. Finally, both of the normative approaches examined in the last chapter, Blake and Mouton's 9,9 management and Likert's System 4, are essentially statements of the superiority of participative systems.

Given such a heritage, participative leadership clearly warrants examination side by side with the 'task' and 'people-centred' contrasts of the Ohio and Michigan researchers. Yukl (1971) has argued for the examination of participativeness among leaders, as a dimension of leader behaviour distinct from Consideration and Initiating Structure. The Ohio scales often obscure participativeness when there is an exclusive reliance on these two notions. The SBDQ, for example, includes statements like the following as indicators of Consideration:

- He changes the duties of people under him without first talking it over with them (reverse).
- He insists that everything should be done his way.

The Initiating Structure items include:

- He waits for his foremen to push new ideas before he does (reverse).
- He lets others do their work the way they think best (reverse).

Items like these appear nominally to be about the amount of participation a supervisor allows his subordinates, so that the Ohio scales which stress only these two dimensions tend to obscure this aspect of leadership. This difficulty adds weight to Yukl's advocacy of the treatment of participation as a separate dimension of leadership behaviour.

An example of an approach to the study of leadership behaviour which focuses exclusively on participative leadership is the influential framework adopted by Tannenbaum and Schmidt (1958). The title of their work was 'How to choose a leadership pattern'. In fact, the framework is about how to choose a *participative* leadership pattern, as the article is effectively about what degree of participation ought to be allowed to subordinates and under what circumstances. They conceptualize the range of leadership behaviours as a continuum with 'boss-centred leadership' and 'subordinate-centred leadership' as the two poles. On the basis of these notions, they distinguish between seven types of leadership behaviour which are as follows:

1　Manager makes the decision and announces it. From a consideration of the possible alternatives to achieving a goal, a manager chooses one and simply tells his subordinates to implement his choice.
2　Manager 'sells' his decision. This is the same as 1 except that the manager attempts to persuade his subordinates that he has made the appropriate choice.
3　Manager presents his ideas and invites questions. The manager informs subordinates of his chosen programme of action and invites a response to them from his subordinates, so that they can understand his aims better.
4　Manager presents a tentative decision subject to change. While the manager initiates a solution to a particular problem, it is not presented as an absolute one, and so may be changed provided that the manager agrees about his subordinates' reservations.
5　Manager presents the problem, gets suggestions, and then makes his decision. In this instance, the subordinates get an opportunity to be influential at the outset of a decision-making sequence, but the manager reserves the right to be the arbiter of the solution which

will be implemented.

6 Manager defines the limits and requests the group to make a decision. The manager indicates the problem to be solved and then passes the discussion and choice of a solution to the group, of which he is a part.

7 The manager permits the group to make decisions within prescribed limits. Within 'prescribed limits' the manager allows the group to be responsible for the identification, as well as the solution, of problems. The manager becomes 'merely' a member of the group.

Movement from 1 to 7 implies a trend away from the manager's use of authority to greater freedom for subordinates. As Tannenbaum and Schmidt recognize, the seventh pattern is rarely found. Most notions of participative leadership are really referring to the sixth pattern, though some approaches are probably referring to the fifth pattern.

Participative leadership, then, involves a shift away from authoritarian, highly directive forms of leadership towards a broader range of individuals being allowed and encouraged to play a part in decision-making. The idea that greater participation must be encouraged in contemporary organizations is widespread in the literature. Mulder (1971, p. 31) calls it 'the most vital organizational problem of our time', while Preston and Post (1974) refer to participative management as the 'third managerial revolution'. Social scientists have often been at the forefront of the advocacy of participative management, largely because they espouse what McGregor (1960) has referred to as Theory Y values and presuppositions, while spurning Theory X ones. McGregor employed this dichotomy as a shorthand for the divergent behavioural assumptions of two different approaches to management's task. Under Theory X, management is responsible for organizing and directing resources and people in the interests of organizational goals. People must be directed, persuaded, rewarded, even cajoled such that they submit to the needs of the organization. This approach presupposes that people are viewed as lazy, dislike responsibility, are insensitive to broader goals, recalcitrant and none too bright. McGregor argued that these assumptions and beliefs are incorrect, and that the opposite invariably pertains. As such, management must review its role in relation to people and must encourage people to fulfil themselves at work. In this light:

> The essential task of management is to arrange organizational conditions and methods of operation so that people can achieve their own goals *best* by directing *their own* efforts toward organizational objectives. (McGregor, 1960, p. 315)

Further, Theory Y values are often depicted as highly consonant with modern day values of self-determination and self-realization. In any event, the idea of allowing greater participation at work seems to be a central ingredient of such ideas.

The general drift towards Theory Y reasoning has been charted by a number of writers (e.g. Miles, 1965; Perrow, 1972) and need not be explored here. It is, however, important to discuss the reasons for believing that participative management is advantageous. Anthony (1978, pp. 27-9) cites eight possible advantages:

1   Greater readiness to accept change. People will be fearful and possibly mistrustful of change if they are not involved in decisions relating to it. At a time when organizations and their members are being encouraged to be more responsive to change (Bryman, 1976), this is a not inconsiderable benefit.

2   More peaceful manager-subordinate relations. Participation allows people to voice, rather than bottle up, worries and grievances.

3   Increased employee commitment to the organization. Participation enhances people's sense of being valued members of the organization and so induces a more favourable attitude towards it.

4   Greater trust in management. Participation enables people to understand the issues and problems which confront management, so that they comprehend managerial behaviour and objectives better.

5   Greater ease in the management of subordinates. If advantages 2, 3 and 4 obtain, then people will be easier to manage.

6   Improved quality of management decisions. If a broader spectrum of people let their views be known, as the idea of participation implies, then management decisions should be of better quality.

7   Improved upward communication. Participation ensures feedback from subordinates.

8   Improved teamwork. Participation enables managers to build coordinated work groups.

Other benefits of participation are often mentioned in the literature: for example, under participative management people identify more with a decision and often see themselves as having an investment in it; participation leads to a better understanding of the organization; it enhances people's self-development; and so on. Potential disadvantages are often mentioned in the literature on participation: it may bring conflicts into the open to such a degree that the organization falters; it may lead to time-consuming decisions and possibly ones which are based too much on compromise, as the old adage 'Too many cooks spoil the broth' recognizes; managers may be riddled with anxiety if they are faced with being responsible for large numbers of decisions with which they have little agreement; and so on.

The evidence relating to participative leadership

Much of the interest in participative leadership derives from the apparently encouraging evidence from research about the introduction of participative *systems* or *programmes* in organizations. The Morse and Reimer study is one such example, and a number of other field experiments exist. A difficulty with such studies, which is often insufficiently recognized in the literature, has to do with the implications of the findings for the benefits of the amount of participativeness exhibited by particular leaders. Participative programmes are often introduced into organizations such that there is a fairly substantial change in its internal structure and a range of concomitant or even independent changes. In the last chapter, it was suggested that the range of changes involved in the Harwood study makes it very difficult to interpret how far System 4, or even the leadership element within System 4, contributed to the various observed outcomes. The correlational studies are different in that they typically treat participativeness as a behavioural attribute of individual leaders, so that it is assessed as a variable like Consideration or Initiating Structure. But participative leaders are often discerned by such techniques in a range of organizations – those with and those without broader participative systems. In the field experiments in which participative programmes are introduced, leaders are typically trained in the precepts and techniques required. One presumes that all leaders become participative, though the effects of possible deviant styles (i.e. non-participative, authoritarian) in such milieux warrants greater study. While the differences between field experiments and correlational studies dealing with participative leadership are fully recognized in the literature (e.g. Wall and Lischeron, 1977), these contextual issues are given somewhat less attention.

One of the difficulties inherent in reviewing the literature on participation is simply that researchers differ in what they mean by it. In consequence, it is necessary to adopt a loose definition of what is in any case an imprecise concept. The studies which will be examined all relate to the intentional involvement of subordinates in decisions relating to work. The research can be grouped into three main headings (Lowin, 1968): experimental studies in non-organizational settings, field experimental studies in organizations, and correlational studies in organizations.

1 *Experimental studies of participation in non-organizational settings*
This group includes research conducted in both laboratories and settings which are in the field but not based in formal organizations. The Iowa studies (e.g. White and Lippitt, 1960) are an example of the latter. From the point of view of the study of leadership in organizations, while such research is suggestive, even if relatively consistent findings in favour of participative leadership had been discerned, the question of their relevance to 'applied' contexts would still need to be verified. Consequently, research within this genre will be reviewed much more briefly.

Lowin's (1968) review of this group of studies includes not only the Lippitt and White research but also the Day and Hamblin (1964) study of general and close supervision referred to in the last chapter. While he found that studies like those of Lippitt and White and Day and Hamblin suggested that participative leadership was beneficial (e.g. in terms of group attitudes or productivity), he also recognized that 'there are at least as many problematic ones' (Lowin, 1968, p. 87). In part, these discrepant findings were attributable to situational factors which mediated the participation-response relationship, a point which will be returned to below. Some of the negative findings could not be explained away by the intrusion of such contaminating variables.

A review of the relevant laboratory studies of participative leadership by Filley, House and Kerr (1976, p. 223) confirmed an absence of consistent findings. All eleven studies examined the effect of participative leadership on productivity, of which seven confirmed a positive relationship. However, Filley *et al.* point out that in three of these seven studies the participative leadership-productivity relationship was moderated by other variables. Only four out of eleven seem to reveal entirely general positive relationships between participative leadership and productivity. Only three of the eleven studies examined the impact of participative leadership on satisfaction; the relationships were found to be positive in all cases.

A more recent review of eighteen laboratory studies of the effects of participative decision-making confirms that it seems to be no more effective than directive methods in terms of productivity (Locke and Schweiger, 1979). The evidence in respect of satisfaction was, on balance, more supportive of the benefits of participative decision-making, although two of the studies reviewed imply the superiority of directive methods.

The experimental studies of the effects of participative leadership are somewhat equivocal. The results for productivity are particularly problematic, suggesting that at best a range of contextual factors needs to be taken into account. The absence of any relationship in a number of instances is particularly disconcerting, though it may be that unexplored situational variables were operating in these studies. Ironically, the Lippitt and White research which is one of the best known studies in this group is much more problematic in respect of the issue of productivity than is often recognized. This is because the impact of the different leadership climates on productivity was not part of the focus of investigation, so that no direct measure of either efficiency or productivity was devised. That the participative leadership climate had a beneficial impact upon productivity is largely inferred from their data (e.g. greater 'work-mindedness') rather than a definitive finding. The recent work of Latham and Saari exemplifies the problem of inconclusive evidence. In one study (Latham and Saari, 1979a) college students were allocated to experimental conditions of assigned and participatively set goals, and were given a brainstorming task. The researchers could find no significant differences in respect of measures of performance, goal performance, goal attainment, or goal acceptance. These findings were confirmed in a related study by Latham, Steele and Saari (1982) which adopted a similar research design. A participative goal setting condition was compared with three conditions in which goals were assigned but in different ways. There were no differences between the two main types of condition in respect of either task-related goal acceptance or performance. Indeed, the group with the highest performance was an assigned goal group which had been allocated a particularly difficult goal, which matched the more difficult of the goals set in the participative condition. To complicate matters even further, another laboratory study by Latham and Saari (1979b) found that the opportunity to set goals led to better performance than when goals were assigned. Although the balance of the research associated with these authors points to participation having no impact on performance, the evidence is still equivocal.

However, there seems to be a fairly consistent tendency for greater participation to be associated with job satisfaction and other indicators of satisfaction. The tendency for findings relating to satisfaction to be more consistent than for performance seems to be a recurring problem in studies of leadership.

2 Experimental studies of participative leadership in organizational settings

There are two 'classic' studies within this group. One is the Morse and Reimer (1956) study of clerical workers reported in the last chapter; the second is that of Coch and French (1948). This study was conducted at a garment manufacturer, Harwood Corporation, the company which eventually took over Weldon which was itself the focus of research by Marrow *et al.* (1967 – see last chapter).

While the particular Harwood factory, which was the target of the research, displayed good industrial relations, the work force (predominantly female) fiercely resisted necessary changes to procedures for doing their work. In order to find out how resistance might be overcome, Coch and French set up four experimental conditions designed to examine the effects of participation. Firstly, a 'no participation' group of eighteen workers who were merely informed of intended changes, along with an explanation of them. Secondly, a 'participation through representation' group (thirteen workers). With this treatment the group selected a number of operators to be trained in the new methods. Subsequently, the new job methods and associated piece rates were presented to all of the workers. The special operators trained their peers in the new methods. Finally, there were two 'total participation' groups of eight and seven members each. In this condition, all members of both groups participated in the design of jobs. The four groups were similar in terms of productivity prior to the introduction of the experimental changes (i.e. the new work methods). The 'no participation' group's level of productivity fell sharply after the experimental change from around 60 units per hour to just under 50. This level of productivity was largely maintained for the following thirty days. In addition, Coch and French report strong expressions of aggression against management representatives, as well as output restriction. By the end of the first forty days, 17 per cent had asked to leave. The productivity of the 'representation' group dropped sharply too, but after fourteen days it was returning to its pre-experimental levels and was slowly climbing. The atmosphere was much more cooperative in this group and nobody left within the first forty days. The two 'total participation' groups exhibited slight falls in productivity in the immediate period after the experimental changes, but thereafter the level of productivity was invariably higher than the two other groups (around 71 to 72 units per hour) and showing a tendency to improve. There were no indications of aggression. Eventually, the 'no participation' group was broken up and dispersed throughout the factory. Two and a half months later, the thirteen remaining original members were re-assembled and transferred to a new job, using the 'total participation' approach. The same group which was producing at the level of 50 units per hour in the post-experimental period of the initial experiment was producing at around 70 units in this second experiment. Coch and French attribute this contrast in performance (and the associated lack of aggression in the second experiment) to the different mode of participation.

On the face of it, the Coch and French study is very supportive of worker participation. There are some reservations which can be levelled against the study, however. Both Lowin (1968) and Zimmerman (1978) have observed that the company was somewhat atypical, not least because of the commitment of the company's president, A.J. Marrow, who was later so involved in the Weldon research (Marrow *et al.*, 1967 – see last chapter), to both the participative system idea and to psychological research. Further, French had been associated with the company since 1937. Zimmerman also observes that due to a high level of turnover among new recruits, for some time the company had been giving them special training to counteract this tendency. He also points to the fact that there was a 'climate' of participation at the plant due to a policy of using referenda among all employees to resolve problems. Further, as Lowin observes, the presence of a control group (the 'no participation' group) does not remove the possibility of a 'Hawthorne effect'; a point which applies to many field experiments in this area. This is particularly a problem in studies like that of Coch and French and Morse and Reimer, where the experimental groups are mutually aware of each other, possibly engendering feelings of jealousy, or of being advantaged or disadvantaged, as the case may be. Finally, the implications of the use of very different group sizes for the three experimental treatments seems to have been accorded scant attention in the literature, an issue which raises questions of the equivalence of the groups.[2]

Further research with which French was associated has not always been as supportive of participative decision-making as the Harwood study. In their research on the introduction of a new manufacturing process in a Norwegian factory, French, Israel and As (1960) set up four control groups which did not participate in decisions relating to the changes. There were five experimental groups, two of which were permitted a particularly wide-ranging selection of areas in which they were allowed participation, including training and the assignment of work. The five experimental groups certainly experienced more participation than the controls (as revealed in post-experimental questionnaires). However, there was virtually no difference in productivity between the two sets of groups, and even little evidence that participation made a great deal of difference to satisfaction issues. A further study at Harwood (French, Ross, Kirby, Nelson and Smyth, 1958) in which there was no control group found that the introduction of participation had some effect on productivity, though the evidence was not overwhelming. Turnover rates decreased but had been declining prior to the study, so that the impact of participation is questionable. Grievance rates actually increased in concert with participation, though this may have been partly due to new work methods.

Consequently, even by taking the work associated with one researcher, it is possible to discern some fairly contrasting findings in respect of field experiments on participation. Reviewers of these studies are not always in agreement over whether the research supports a participative approach or not. The reviews by Lowin (1968) and Wall and Lischeron (1977), for example, tend to regard the research as relatively unfavourable to participation, whereas Filley, House and Kerr (1976, p. 223) conclude from an appraisal of the field experiments that 'participative leadership generally has a positive effect upon both satisfaction and productivity'. The more comprehensive review of seventeen studies by Locke and Schweiger (1979) is at variance with this latter conclusion. Their review of field experiments (which took place in both organizational and non-organizational settings) concluded that the evidence for the superiority of participative decision-making on performance was inconclusive. However, the evidence regarding satisfaction was more favourable to participation though over 40 per cent of the field experiments 'showed no general superiority' (Locke and Schweiger, 1979, p. 316). A comprehensive and more recent assessment by Yukl (1981, p. 215) concluded 'that participation is successful in some situations but not others, and is more likely to improve satisfaction than performance'. Yukl's review included seventeen studies (originally eighteen, but one study was a simulation). Of the sixteen studies which examined productivity, participation had a positive impact in six cases, a negative impact in three, and there was no difference from non-participation conditions in seven studies. Participation generally had a positive impact on satisfaction issues. The measurement time spans of the studies varied from one month (the Coch and French research) to eighteen months. Whether variations in the life of these studies is a contributory feature to the equivocal findings is impossible to ascertain, but Likert (1977) has consistently argued for longer term research in respect of evaluations of his System 4 approach, itself a participative approach.

Yukl's (1981) review of the field experimental literature dealing with the relationship between participation and satisfaction tends to be somewhat more supportive than that of Locke and Schweiger (1979), though both point to the balance of the evidence being positive. In part, this disparity derives from apparent differences in interpretation of the findings by the two reviews.[3] Another reason is that the studies which were reviewed are not identical. One piece of research which was reviewed by Locke and Schweiger, but not by Yukl, is a British field experiment on participation carried out by Wall and Lischeron (1977, ch. 7), which failed to confirm that satisfaction was enhanced by increased participation. The research was based on 150 male workers in the Outdoor Services section of a local authority. This group held regular meetings with managers and were to participate more in what the authors call 'medium level' decisions (e.g. training, promotion of workers, purchase of materials and equipment) and 'distant level' decisions (e.g. budget allocation, policy making, hiring and firing of managers). Another group of Outdoor Services workers served as control. The participation scheme seems to have resulted in greater perceived influence, especially in respect of 'medium-level' decisions. However, there were no differences in a range of satisfaction measures (job, pay, the organization, etc.) between the experimental and control groups.

Since Yukl's (1981) review, some further major studies within the field experiment framework have appeared. Firstly, a piece of research by Dossett, Latham and Mitchell (1979) on sixty female clerical personnel who were randomly assigned to participative and non-participative conditions is of interest. The clerks were requested to carry out a test. 'Participation' in this study denoted whether goals (number of items answered) were participatively set. The non-participative treatment was referred to as an 'assigned' goals condition. The researchers found performance to be unaffected by the presence or absence of participation. Indeed, goal attainment was greater in the assigned condition. A follow-up study based on employees from the same sample in a different context (a 'performance appraisal' setting) found that assigned goals led to better performance than did participatively set ones, although this difference was found to disappear after four months. A field experiment by Latham and Marshall (1982) on supervisors in a US governmental agency confirms some of these findings. Subjects were assigned to three goal-setting conditions: participatively set, self-set, and assigned goals. Measures of goal attainment and productivity were not significantly different between the three conditions. This study confirmed other experimental work (both laboratory and field) associated with Latham which suggests that the emphasis on participation directs too much attention to the 'how' of goal-setting, when it is apparent that ensuring that specific goals are set is much more important to productivity.

Finally, in a study of nursing and clerical personnel in a hospital outpatient facility by Jackson (1983), subjects were assigned to an 'increased participation' in decision-making condition and to a control condition. The outcome measures were assessed after both three and six months. Participation was found to have a clear negative relationship to both role conflict and role ambiguity, especially after six months. These variables have often been recognized as having deleterious consequences for individuals (e.g. stress, turnover). Also, as expected, people in the experimental condition were more likely to perceive themselves as having greater influence which was itself related to both overall job satisfaction and whether they intended to leave the hospital. Thus, insofar as greater participation leads to greater perceived influence, it has a strong indirect relationship with such 'outcome' variables. While this last point raises the issue of moderating variables in participation-outcome relationships (which will be addressed in detail below), it is also worth making in this context. Greater perceived influence does not flow automatically from participation for all subjects in such experiments. Indeed, in Jackson's experiment the relationship between the amount of participation, as manipulated in the experiment, and perceived influence is not large. While studies of participation programmes often examine the impact on subjects' perceived influence (e.g. Morse and Reimer, 1956), the effect of this latter variable on the anticipated outcomes is often not fully addressed. It may even be that some of the conflicting evidence arises out of a failure to take into account whether the experimental manipulations really do have an impact upon the perceptions of subjects and what the implications of variations in perceptions might be.

It would seem, then, that the experimental research relating to the effects of participation in formal organizational settings is inconclusive. There is more evidence to suggest that it enhances satisfaction than performance, but there are many studies which imply that excessive confidence in the beneficial effects of participation is unwarranted.

3 Correlational studies of participation

The first two groups of studies of participation involve the introduction of programmes of participation. On either a small or a large scale, groups of individuals are allowed greater say in their work, or the running of their departments, and so on. As has already been suggested, this type of study is not as obviously related to participative leadership, which relates to what individual leaders do. Within any firm there will be putative leaders who vary, often a good deal, on any scale of participativeness. Participative leaders may be quite few in number and often dispersed throughout the firm. Most of the correlational studies are concerned with the consequences (and often the causes) of variations in the degree of participative leadership for subordinates. This is quite different from an experimental study in which a participation programme is introduced and leaders are trained in its underlying principles. The context of participative leadership is different, as in one it operates at a system level and in the other it relates to the behaviour of individual leaders (though there may be a number of broad constraints as will be discussed below). The fact that the introduction of participative systems is often accompanied by other organizational or technical changes, particularly in the field studies, only serves to raise further difficulties in connection with precisely what the experimental studies imply about participative leadership.

Nonetheless, many writers draw direct comparisons between the experimental and correlational studies, a procedure which has been followed in this book but with the foregoing reservations very much in mind. The correlational studies typically treat participative leadership as an independent variable and then seek to discern, usually in a static sense, its consequences. Another kind of study assesses the amount of power or influence groups of workers say they have and relates variation in this attribute to outcomes, such as satisfaction or performance. The reference point is not what the subjects of this second kind of investigation say their superiors do but the amount of influence the former claim to possess. The early Michigan research on general and close supervision would be included in such types of investigation. So too is an investigation of twenty research laboratory directors by Baumgartel (1956), which was carried out under the auspices of the Institute at Michigan. Baumgartel was able to classify eighteen of the directors in terms of the Lippitt and White scheme, of participatory, directive, and *laissez-faire* leadership. In the participatory pattern which occurred in seven laboratories, the research director is described as having moderate influence on his subordinates (research scientists) who feel that they have much influence over him. This leadership pattern was characterized by frequent director-subordinate contact. In addition, 'subordinates feel that joint discussion and joint decision with the director is the most typical pattern of decision-making' (Baumgartel, 1956, p. 26). Scientists operating in this pattern tended to be better motivated, to have a stronger sense of progress toward scientific goals and be favourably inclined toward their leader. However, these effects tended to be strongest when comparing the participatory and directive leader. Differences were much less strong, unlike in the Lippitt and White study, in respect of comparisons between participatory and *laissez-faire* leaders. In particular, there was very little difference between these two styles of leadership in terms of the amount of task motivation towards the goals of science that was engendered. Further, these leadership differences had no impact at all on a broader range of subordinate attitude and satisfaction issues.

Lowin's (1968) review of the correlational research included the early Michigan research, but omitted Baumgartel's work. His review suggested that the results taken as a whole were inconclusive, a conclusion which would not have been altered had the Baumgartel study been included. A systematic review by Filley, House and Kerr (1976) cites eleven correlational studies of participative leadership. All of the nine studies which examined its effects on satisfaction found a positive relationship. Only one of the nine studies which examined the relationship between participative leadership and productivity failed to provide a positive correlation. However, as Filley *et al.* observe, four of the eleven studies only discerned positive relationships when moderating variables were introduced. Similarly, a review by Wall and Lischeron (1977) points to a more consistent set of empirical relationships in the correlational evidence than in the experimental studies. Locke and Schweiger's (1979) assessment of twenty-five studies was less encouraging for the proponents of participative leadership. In their view the balance of the evidence suggests that participative decision-making approaches are not superior to non-participative approaches when productivity is the criterion. However, participative approaches do seem to make an impact on satisfaction, although over 40 per cent of the evidence reviewed could not confirm a positive effect.

An example of one of the studies often reviewed can briefly be mentioned. A study by Argyle, Gardner and Cioffi (1958) of British foremen found that a 'democratic' style led to lower absenteeism but did not affect turnover. Such supervision only had a general impact upon productivity when combined with 'non-punitive' practices. Insofar as a democratic style is indicative of participative leadership (many writers follow this convention), such findings are quite promising. However,

Argyle *et al.* also examined the effects of 'general' supervision, which is conceptually and empirically similar to participative leadership. In line with the findings of the early Michigan research, general rather than close supervision was related to greater productivity, but unrelated to both absenteeism and turnover.

A study by Sadler (1970) sheds some interesting additional light on participative leadership. Sadler compressed the Tannenbaum and Schmidt (1958) continuum into four styles: the leader 'tells', 'sells', 'consults' and 'joins'. With this last style, the manager delegates the right to make a decision to the group, but defines the problems and the appropriate limits to decision-making. A film was produced to present these four styles to four separate groups of people, including R & D staff, salesmen, systems analysts, and members of computer service bureaux in a marketing company. Most people indicated that they preferred to work for a boss exhibiting the 'consults' style, though a marked sex difference was evident in that 61 per cent of men preferred it, against 35 per cent of women. However, only 26 per cent and 14 per cent of men and women respectively felt that their own manager employed this style. Among those who did perceive their own superior in terms of the 'consults' style, satisfaction with the job and company was greatest, as was confidence in management.

Some of Bass's recent work sheds some light on the effects of participative leadership (e.g. Bass and Valenzi, 1974; Bass, Valenzi, Farrow and Solomon, 1975). This group of investigators has developed a research instrument which enables five styles to be distinguished on the basis of subordinates' reports of their leaders:

(i) directive–desired ends attained by telling subordinates what to do and how it should be done;
(ii) negotiative – the deployment of bargaining to achieve ends;
(iii) consultative – discussion with subordinates before making a decision;
(iv) participative – subordinates take part in decision-making processes;
(v) delegative – subordinates are left free to make their own decisions.

The last three styles are indicative of participative leadership, albeit in differing degrees. Indeed, the three styles are closely inter-related (.66 to .84) suggesting that there is a tendency for participative leaders also to delegate and to allow consultation. All three styles were found in a study of subordinates in a wide range of organizations to be related to work group effectiveness and satisfaction with supervision and with one's job.

Further evidence on the effects of participative leadership derives from research into its effects on managerial advancement. Hall and Donnell's (1979) study of 12,000 managers found that high 'achievers' in career terms were much more likely to employ participative practices in relation to their subordinates. They were also much *less* likely than average and low achievers to endorse values associated with McGregor's Theory X, a highly authoritarian system. This issue was also explored by Heller and

Wilpert (1981) in an investigation of managers in seven countries and points to a style which emphasizes participative decision-making being a fairly important contributor to managerial career success, especially among more senior subjects. Such findings need to be treated with some caution, as suggested in the previous chapter, particularly in view of the fact that managerial advancement is a rather individualistic criterion of effectiveness.

Further evidence about participation derives from a study of forty-eight middle-level, cost-centre managers in a large company by Brownell (1983). This study will be returned to below, but the pertinent feature for the current discussion is Brownell's investigation of the effects of 'budgetary participation'. This notion refers to the managers' ability to influence budgets. Brownell found this variable to be largely unrelated to both job satisfaction and self-assessed performance.

Similar equivocal evidence derives from Wall and Lischeron's (1977) research on British nurses. The investigators distinguished between 'local' influence (referring to influence in respect of jobs and duties), 'medium' influence (over duty rotas, routine, holidays and the like), and 'distant' influence (over selection and appointment of nurses, choice and purchase of expensive equipment, budgets). Wall and Lischeron found that, while many of the correlations between perceived influence and satisfaction were positive, they were small and not statistically significant. A comparable study by these researchers of skilled and unskilled factory workers revealed a mixed picture. Those who see themselves as having a good deal of local influence tend to be more satisfied with the organization, supervision, and co-workers in particular, but many of the correlations are again small and non-significant. For the perception of medium and distant influence, few of the correlations are large. Indeed, among unskilled workers, the more distant influence workers thought they had, the *less* satisfied they were with the organization, the job, supervision, and overall. Finally, in their study of ninety-four local authority manual workers, Wall and Lischeron (1977) found much stronger evidence for a positive relationship between perceived influence and a range of satisfaction issues. It is worth pointing out that only the research on local authority workers was reviewed by Locke and Schweiger (1979). Had the two other samples – nurses and factory workers – been included in their review, the balance of the participation–satisfaction literature might well have shifted against a clear positive relationship between these two variables.

Finally, research carried out with the employment of the Michigan Organizational Assessment Questionnaire (MOAQ) has provided recent evidence on participative leadership which also post-dates the literature reviews cited in this section. The MOAQ is a general research instrument designed to glean data on the perceptions of people working in organizations (Cammann, Fichman, Jenkins and Klesh, 1983). One of its components is a module on Supervision, a constituent dimension of which is 'Participation', a two-item scale which measures the extent to which subordinates perceive their supervisors as involving them in decisions. Data on over 400 employees from a wide range of work contexts indicate that the more participation a supervisor allows, the greater are levels of subordinate job satisfaction, job involvement, job effort, job challenge, and both intrinsic and extrinsic reward satisfaction (Cammann *et al.*, 1983, p. 109). Such findings appear to provide strong, unequivocal support for participation, but some caution is advisable before jumping to such a conclusion. The Supervision module contains another dimension, 'Decision Centralization', which refers to: 'the extent to which the supervisor makes important decisions without involving subordinates' (Cammann *et al.*, 1983, p. 105). This component of supervision is usually, and quite properly, taken to be the obverse of participation (e.g. Yukl, 1971). Indeed, the correlation between the two-item Decision Central-ization scale and Participation was found to be −.56, although it is slightly surprising that the magnitude of the coefficient was not greater. Nonetheless, one might expect that this dimension would be negatively correlated with the six outcome measures with which Participation was positively and strongly correlated. This was the case, but in each instance the size of the correlation was considerably smaller than that for Participation. Indeed, the correlations between Decision Centralization and both job involvement and job effort failed to achieve statistically significant levels. It is somewhat disconcerting when two highly kindred notions like Participation and Decision Centralization produce somewhat discrepant findings in the context of the same research instrument administered to the same group of respondents at the same time.

While Wall and Lischeron (1977) are probably correct that correla-tional research has more readily pinpointed the apparent advantages of participative styles of leadership, there is a good deal of contradictory evidence among studies employing this design too, particularly in respect of performance outcomes. Overall, the evidence drawn from the three main research designs which have been employed to examine participation-outcome relationships does not encourage too much confid-ence in the advantages of participative leadership.

The problem of discrepancies

While there is a fair amount of evidence to suggest that participation contributes to satisfaction, as well as performance (to a lesser extent), and other supposedly 'good' outcomes (e.g. low turnover and absenteeism), there is too much unsupporting evidence to be too confident. What factors might account for these discrepancies? Two key possibilities can be cited. Firstly, the studies reviewed cover a variety of different types of participation, so that a failure to take into account the diversity of forms of participation and their relative effects has contributed to a field in which comparisons between different investigations are not always entirely sensible. Secondly, it has long been recognized that participative leadership-outcome relationships are likely to be situationally contingent. The failure to take such contextual factors into account may on occasions have led to the various discrepancies. Each of these issues will be dealt with in turn.

Firstly, then, there is a range of generic types of participation. A fundamental point is that participation and participative leadership vary in the *degree of influence* that is involved. In the Tannenbaum and Schmidt (1958) continuum, the last three types of leadership pattern could all be called participative. The Bass and Valenzi (1974) trinity of consulting, being participative, and delegating could be seen in similar terms. Next, participation is likely to vary in terms of whether it is *direct or indirect*, that is, whether it is undertaken directly by the individual or mediated by representatives. Most experimental studies deal with the former, but correlation studies which ask people about how much influence they have may obscure this distinction. Participation may be *formal* or *informal*. Many of the experimental studies deal with formal participation only, but it may be that many of the correlation studies are reflecting mixtures of both formal and informal participation. They may be confounding participation which is official and that which is at the discretion of individual leaders. The two are related, but leaders may permit participation over and above officially sanctioned amounts. Further, studies may obscure *hierarchical differences*, that is, whether it is leadership in relation to immediate or relatively distant layers that is in question. Data on senior managers reported by Heller and Yukl (1969) suggest that less participative methods are deployed in relation to immediate subordinates: influence-sharing styles in relation to subordinates two levels down in the hierarchy. The importance of hierarchical issues are also evident in Wall and Lischeron's (1977) research which implies a need to take into account the areas in which participation might take place. Some areas are immediate ('local' in their terminology) ones, largely to do with the organization of subordinates' work. Other areas are much more distant (e.g. personnel issues, matters of policy), decisions about which are usually made at quite senior levels. It is worth observing that it is precisely this latter kind of participation that is not usually at the behest of the individual leader. While field experiments are occasionally able to investigate quite pervasive systems of participation (e.g. the Wall and Lischeron, 1977, local authority field experiment), this topic is unlikely to be an element in studies of the effects of different degrees of participativeness in leaders. Research of this latter kind is typically concerned with participation in more immediate work-related issues.

A further set of distinctions can be made, following Sashkin (1976), in terms of *forms of participation*. Sashkin suggests that participation can take place in four areas: in goal setting, in decision-making, in solving problems, and in the development and implementation of change in the organization. The studies reviewed above reflect concerns in all of these forms of participation, yet the differential implications of these four forms are not fully addressed. Direct comparisons are often made between studies, as has been done above, yet the possibility that the results discerned are in part a function of the form of participation is rarely addressed systematically. Yet another, albeit simpler, classification of participative leadership has been provided by House and Baetz (1979) who distinguish between *participative decision-making* and *participative super-*

vision. The former denotes the attempts by leaders to ensure that their subordinates are able to influence the final decision relating to a problem at hand. Participative supervision refers to patterns of daily interaction between leader and subordinate, in which the latter is encouraged to make suggestions about the work that has to be done and its execution. It would appear from these deliberations that there are at least six dimensions on which participation can vary, which is rarely taken into account in comparing studies of participative leadership. It is no wonder that inconsistent findings exist, particularly when these differences are added to the divergent methods for investigating participative leadership and its effects.

A second reason for the inconsistent findings is that many of the studies have failed to take into account the situational factors which impinge upon participative leadership-outcome relationships. A good deal is known about such variables nowadays and an attempt will be made to summarize the more important facets of this now voluminous literature. This set of issues will be returned to in the next chapter in which the major 'Contingency' theories of leadership will be examined. Two of the approaches to be examined – the path-goal (see especially House and Mitchell, 1974) and the Vroom and Yetton (1973) approaches – place the contingent nature of participative leadership at the forefront of their concerns. Both approaches seek to develop this interest within a theoretical framework, which in large part differs from the research to be addressed below. By and large, it is possible to group the research in which situational factors were found to be of importance under a number of sub-headings. In each case, the findings point to participative leadership having an anticipated effect (e.g. on job satisfaction) in some instances but not others, or even having a negative impact upon such posited effects.

1 Task characteristics

The reviews of the relevant literature by Filley *et al.* (1976), House and Baetz (1979), Singer (1974), and Yukl (1981) all point to the importance of this mediating variable. It seems that when task requirements are repetitive and routine to subordinates, participative leadership is less likely to have an impact on satisfaction and performance (e.g. Schuler, 1976). If tasks are unambiguous and routine the areas to which participation can be applied are more limited; when tasks are more complex, a variety of views is beneficial and subordinates are more likely to respond positively to being involved. For example, in their research on British foremen Argyle *et al.* (1958) found that the relationship between democratic and general style of supervision and productivity was stronger in those departments in which work was not machine-paced (i.e. less routine, more complex). Unfortunately the two types of department – machine-paced and those not – also differed in method of wage payment, which makes it less easy to discern the direct effect of the nature of the work being done. Nonetheless, there is a marked consistency in studies suggesting that the routine nature of the task is an important mediating variable. This suggests that participative leadership is more likely to display its supposed effects in

manual jobs which require a considerable skill input and as one ascends
the white-collar hierarchy. Above routine clerical jobs in this hierarchy
work becomes increasingly less 'programmed' (March and Simon, 1958)
and so more amenable to participative schemes. If the proponents of job
enlargement and job enrichment schemes have an impact on routine work
by making it more varied, they will widen the range of tasks with potential
for participative leadership. However, it should not be assumed that this
issue is clear-cut. A study of managers by Bass and Valenzi (1974) found
that among organizations classified as 'varied' (i.e. non-routine) the
relationship between participative leadership and job satisfaction was
negative; in 'routine' organizations it was positive. While this is not quite
the same level of analysis as that implied by research emphasizing task
characteristics, the results are rather starkly opposite to that which the
research on task requirements would lead one to expect.

2   *Personality characteristics of subordinates*
A number of characteristics have been addressed, but one of the best
known studies is an investigation by Vroom (1959). In this study,
supervisors in a large delivery company were asked to indicate the amount
of influence they had and their job satisfaction. In addition, personality
scales of both authoritarianism (indicative of rigidity, dogmatism and a
preference for autocracy) and 'need for independence' were completed.
Among authoritarian supervisors with a low need for independence score,
participation had no impact on satisfaction. Among non-authoritarian
supervisors with a high need for independence scores, there was a clear,
positive relationship between the two variables. A similar pattern was
evident when the dependent variable was a measure of performance.
However, a study of managers by Tosi (1970) failed to support these
findings, in that levels of authoritarianism and need for independence
among subordinates failed to mediate an overall relationship between
participation and satisfaction. Tosi found a fairly strong positive
relationship between participation and job satisfaction irrespective of the
levels of authoritarianism and need for independence reported by
subordinates. However, there was no relationship at all when performance
was the outcome measure, and the two personality characteristics again
failed to moderate this finding. A laboratory experiment conducted by
Wexley, Singh and Yukl (1973) also failed to support the importance of
authoritarianism and need for independence. Subjects were exposed to
three treatments which entailed different levels of participation in an
'appraisal interview', in which the interviewee's strengths and weaknesses
are discussed. In the least participative treatment, subjects are told of their
strengths and weaknesses and are told by the interviewer how he feels they
should be improved. The participative condition entailed an opportunity
for the interviewee to present his own thoughts regarding possible
solutions to problems. The results point to greater participation having a
marked positive effect on both subordinate satisfaction and motivation to
improve performance. Neither subordinate authoritarianism nor need for
independence affected this finding. Clearly, the nature of the moderating

effects of subordinate authoritarianism and need for independence are much less clear-cut than early research indicated.

Research on employees occupying a range of hierarchical positions in a US manufacturing company by Schuler (1976) sheds further light on this issue. This research suggests that participation is conducive to job satisfaction among subordinates who exhibit little authoritarianism irrespective of the level of task repetitiveness; it is conducive to satisfaction among authoritarian subordinates only when tasks exhibit little repetitiveness. It would seem that subordinate authoritarianism only moderates participation-satisfaction relationships when there is a high level of task repetitiveness. Finally, an investigation by Runyon (1973) of employees in a large US chemical company, found that subordinates' scores on the Internal-External Locus of Control scale (see Chapter 2) was an important variable. The relationship between the amount of participation and job satisfaction was particularly strong among 'internals'. A laboratory experiment by Ruble (1976) also suggests that internals are more productive when they can participate in the planning of a task; externals exhibit better performance when planning is imposed. Such relationships seem to arise largely because 'internals' tend to prefer to be able to participate in decisions relating to their work, suggesting that the desire to participate is likely to be an important mediating variable.

3 The desire to participate

The likely importance of the desire to participate has been argued by a number of writers such as Mulder (1971). Logically, one might expect that among individuals with little desire to participate, the responses to the opportunity to be involved in work-related decisions will not be great. How widespread is the desire for participation? There have been many studies of the desire for participation among manual workers. A review of some of the evidence by Wall and Lischeron (1977, pp. 12-13) points to around 50 to 61 per cent of manual samples desiring participation. In their own research on nurses these writers found the desire to be stronger over 'local' and 'medium' level decisions. The desire for preferred participation varied by job level, with Auxiliary Nurses showing a strong tendency not to seek involvement. Comparable results were discerned for their sample of factory workers and local authority manual workers. Research among shop floor workers in three British firms by Ramsay (1976) confirms a desire for participation particularly in respect of the sample's own work and working conditions (84 per cent of the sample), but only 37 per cent wanting more say in company level decisions. Clearly there is a greater desire for participation in matters which impinge on one's work either very or fairly directly. Sadler's (1970) aforementioned research suggests a general preference for participation among managerial workers. Clearly, the desire for participation is a variable in that it is not universally preferred, and we can justifiably anticipate that it mediates participation-outcome relationships. People with a pronounced desire for participation are more likely to respond positively to it.

4   The position of the leader

Research by Pelz (1951), while not directly concerned with the impact of participative leadership, suggests that the amount of power that the leader has by virtue of his position affects subordinates' responses to leadership style. Subordinates respond better to the leader in terms of the extent to which the latter can facilitate the attainment of their own goals by having influence in the organization at large. We would anticipate that the relationship between participative leadership and outcomes will be affected by the leader's status and influence within his own organization. Under conditions of little influence, participative leadership would have little impact on subordinates. Similarly, Yukl (1981, p. 215) has suggested that the amount of support that leaders have from higher management levels for their participative practices will influence subordinate responses. A further aspect of the leader's position is his or her 'expert power', which refers to the amount of knowledge and expertise possessed by the leader. Mulder (1971) suggests that if expert power is too great, the introduction of participative programmes will founder, since participation provides leaders with high levels of expert power the opportunity to assert their position. Furthermore, the greater the expertise of subordinates the more able they are to take advantage of the opportunities of participation. Consequently, it has been shown by Mulder and Wilke (1970) in laboratory experiments that the leader's knowledge relative to that of subordinates moderates the effects of participation. Cammalleri *et al.* (1973) have demonstrated with a 'Lost on the Moon' laboratory situation that autocratic leaders who are well informed stimulate their groups to be more accurate than do democratic leaders. When misinformed the performance of autocratic leaders was worse than that for similarly misinformed democratic leaders.

5   The interaction of participative leadership with other leadership styles

In view of the diversity of leadership styles (see Chapter 3 and below), it is surprising how little research has been conducted on combinations of style and that it is not a more prominent topic in discussions of participative leadership. Some evidence certainly exists on these issues. For example, Argyle *et al.* (1958, cited above) found that democratic supervision among foremen primarily had an effect on productivity when accompanied by a non-punitive style. In addition, Yukl (1971) has pointed to the possibility that participation would be more effective if accompanied by high Consideration. The study of cost centre managers by Brownell (1983) provides an example of the effects of participation in relation to other styles. Brownell examined the effects of managers' budget participation and the Consideration and Initiating Structure of their superiors. This research shows that participation has a deleterious effect on both performance and job satisfaction if accompanied by high levels of Initiating Structure, and little Consideration. As Brownell (1983, p. 328) observes: 'participation will be ineffective if accompanied by a supervisory leadership style dominated by structuring behaviour'. It was also found that the effects of budget participation on performance were much more pronounced when accompanied by higher levels of Consideration. Yukl's hunch was not confirmed, however, in that Consideration was positively associated with job satisfaction irrespective of the amount of participation experienced by managers. Such findings point to the possibility that the effects of participation are mediated by other leadership variables.

Overview of participation

It has been suggested that the variety of findings noted earlier in the chapter can be partly attributed to two factors. Firstly, a wide range of types of participation has been explored, so that it may be that dissimilar forms of participation are being compared. In other words, discrepant findings may be due to divergent participative forms and practices having been examined by researchers. Secondly, there is the possibility that a variety of situational factors impinge upon the participation-outcome relationships. Three points need to be asserted about the review of situational factors. Firstly, it is incomplete. It was decided to concentrate upon those which seem particularly important in the literature. Bass and Valenzi's (1974) research, for example, pinpoints a number of organization-level factors which have an impact on the effects of participative leadership (e.g. the extent of disorganization) which have not been covered. Secondly, even the role of some of the situational factors appears to be contentious. The effect of authoritarianism and task routineness on participation-outcome relationships is not at all certain. Thirdly, there are almost certainly combined effects of the situational variables. Personality characteristics of subordinates and their desire for participation may well have a combined effect over and above their unique impacts. Schuler's (1976) research points to the possibility of combined effects being an important area of study. Similarly, House and Baetz (1979, p. 367) have suggested that personality factors only affect participation-outcome relationships when a task is not 'ego-involving' to subordinates. If tasks are 'ego-involving' then people will be generally predisposed to enjoy the effects of participation.

Even if it were possible to present the findings relating to participative leadership such that the evidence appeared more conclusive, one would still be faced with the problem of causality. The Lowin and Craig (1968) experiments referred to in the last chapter strongly suggest that poor subordinate performance leads to 'closer' (i.e. less participative) supervision. Barrow's (1976) experiment not only confirmed this finding, but also ascertained that as subordinate performance deteriorated, 'leader' behaviour became more autocratic.

Furthermore, participation is just one of a number of means of motivating employees which has been considered over the years, so that it is relevant to compare its relative effectiveness with other approaches. While such comparisons are often implicit in experimental studies, Locke *et al.* (1980) have performed a useful service in reviewing the literature relating to the impact of participation in decision-making on employee performance in the context of three other methods of motivating people. The three other approaches are: goal setting – the assignment of specific and/or challenging goals as against easy or 'do your best' goals; job enrichment – instilling greater variety, challenge and responsibility; and money – the employment of pay incentive schemes. Their analysis of the literature points to money being the most effective motivational technique, followed by goal setting, then job enrichment, and lastly participation. The median performance gains achieved for each cluster of studies were 30 per cent, 16 per cent, 17 per cent and 0.5 per cent respectively. Both money and goal setting engendered performance gains in all of the studies reviewed: 92 per cent of job enrichment studies showed a gain, and finally only 50 per cent of participation studies revealed a gain in performance. The robust evidence for money as a motivator is interesting in the light of a field experiment conducted in a small US manufacturing firm by Jenkins and Lawler (1981). In this study, employees were given the opportunity to participate in the design of a pay plan, as a consequence of which pay improved by an average of 12.9 per cent. While it is not easy to disentangle the effects of participation from other possible influences, the authors concluded that a number of positive reactions (e.g. satisfaction with pay and job, less turnover, better management-employee relations) were attributable to it. It may be that participation in pay-related matters is beneficial by dint of the importance of pay *per se* as a motivational factor.

One of the more interesting conclusions emanating from this study is the investigators' suggestion that the pay plan was more effective at least in part because 'understanding and commitment were high' (Jenkins and Lawler, 1981, p. 125) as a result of the participation. This suggestion is interesting in the context of Locke's hunch that, although the evidence about the effects of participation on satisfaction and performance is not strong (Locke and Schweiger, 1979; Locke *et al.*, 1980), participation may be useful 'as a means of obtaining ideas which lead to better quality decisions' (Locke, 1981, p. 427). One of the most successful studies of the effects of participation, he observes (Locke *et al.* 1981, pp. 379-80), was a field experiment with hospital laundry workers by Bragg and Andrews (1973), in which there was a 42 per cent surge in productivity as well as improvements in employee attitudes and absenteeism. While there are a number of methodological problems with the study (e.g. experimental and comparison groups were neither randomly assigned nor matched), an important aspect of it was that workers were highly involved in discussions about work procedures, conditions, hours, and the like. It may be that the level of decision quality emerging from the participation process was superior to that which would have been obtained by an alternative method. Yet although the level of decision quality is acknowledged to be a possible benefit of participation, it has tended to be neglected in empirical research, with the exception of work deriving from the Vroom-Yetton model considered in the next chapter. A preoccupation with productivity has tended to blind researchers to this issue.

However, the relevance of participative leadership for notions of work performance is problematic. It has already been suggested that a good deal of the early interest in this issue sprang from early human relations research which was stimulated by the Hawthorne Studies. There can be little doubt that the energies of early writers within this tradition were directed to the improvement of morale in plants in order to raise productivity in the manner of the Relay Assembly Test Room study. However, since the late 1950s, a number of writers (e.g. Miles, 1965; Strauss, 1969) have observed that the tradition shifted towards a greater concern for the self-actualization of the individual worker. The latter is seen as a valuable organizational resource whose full potential must be unleashed and not stultified and constrained. By allowing people of all levels to participate in decision-making, organizations enable them to make a full and worthwhile contribution which enables them to develop their nascent abilities. Within this framework – generally attributed in varying degrees to Argyris, Likert, McGregor and Bennis – the development of the individual is an end in itself and not a means to an end, viz. higher productivity. Ironically, then, there is some doubt as to whether 'performance' is a suitable yardstick against which to judge the benefits of participative leadership.

The area of participation is a confused and confusing one. This is the case not only because of the disparate findings, but also because the implications of many of the studies for what leaders as such do is unclear. As has been observed above, much of our understanding about participation derives from studies of the implementation of participation programmes. Even if such evidence had been unequivocal, the implications for the study of leadership would still have been ambiguous in that the relevance of the evidence for leader behaviour would not be obvious. A study by Nightingale (1981) of twenty Canadian industrial organizations has a bearing on this point. The author matched ten formally participative organizations with ten hierarchical ones and examined leadership styles in each. While the author found that participative 'supervisory practices tend to be found in formally participative organizations' (Nightingale, 1981, p. 1127), 42 per cent of pairings of style and structure were incongruent. In other words, in 42 per cent of instances of supervisory practice, participative leaders were to be found in non-participative organizations *or* non-participative leaders were to be found in participative organizations.[4] The majority of incongruent pairings were of the former type. Findings such as these underscore the author's misgivings about the implications of field experiments concerned with the effects of the introduction of participation *programmes* for the study of participative *leadership*.[5] Further, research which relies on respondents' responses to questions about how much participation they have is rendered questionable by Nightingale's findings, since it is not possible to discern whether the effects are due to a participative structure or participative leadership or a combination of both. The distinction between these levels of analysis is an important one in the context of the study of leadership as such. Nightingale's study is also interesting because his findings suggest that participative styles of supervision had a more pronounced effect than participative structures on subordinates' reported levels of alienation, attitude toward change, organizational commitment, and attitudes toward management. Again, such findings point to the necessity of disentangling these two elements in the study of participation. In any event, the case for participative leadership is a good deal less than established and even the importance of particular situational factors is not completely clear.

Rewards

Given the prevailing focus within leadership research upon the leader and a group of subordinates, it is not surprising that the rewards that the former offers to the latter should attract attention. Could it be that the reward strategies employed by leaders have an impact upon the kinds of outcome variables which preoccupied the Ohio and Michigan researchers, for whom this aspect of leader behaviour was not a focal concern? While the role of pay and other rewards as determinants of people's satisfaction and performance at the workplace has been explored by many researchers, the nature of the non-material rewards leaders provide for their subordinates is also an important topic which did not receive systematic attention until the work of Sims and Szilagyi surfaced in the mid-1970s.

The hub of their approach is a distinction between positive and negative leader reward behaviour, which denotes whether subordinates view the rewards they receive (whether positive or negative) as contingent upon their work performance. This distinction is gleaned from the Leader Reward Behaviour Instrument (LRBI) which comprises sixteen items reflecting positive reward behaviour and six punitive reward behaviour questions. Each item is a statement about the supervisor to which the subordinate is meant to indicate the degree of his agreement on a seven-point continuum. Examples of positive LRBI statements are:

— Your supervisor would personally pay you a compliment if you did outstanding work.
— Your supervisor would help you get a transfer if you asked for one.
— Your supervisor would encourage you to do better if your performance was acceptable but well below what you are capable of.

Examples of punitive LRBI statements are:

— Your supervisor would get on to you if your work was not as good as the work of others in your department.
— Your supervisor would recommend that you get no pay increase if your work was below standard.
— Your supervisor would recommend that you not be promoted to a higher job level if your performance was only average.

Researching on supervisory personnel and their subordinates in a university medical centre, Sims and Szilagyi (1975) sought to discern whether these two behavioural strategies were associated with a range of satisfaction measures (work, pay, co-workers, etc.) and performance (as indicated by supervisors' assessments of each subordinate). The analysis was conducted for each of four occupational skill levels – administrative, professional, technical, and service personnel. The results revealed a strong tendency for positive LRB to be associated with a range of satisfactions for all occupational groups, and to be related to performance except for the administrative group. By contrast punitive LBR was associated with lower satisfaction among technical and service groups, but *greater* satisfaction among the administrative group. This latter, possibly surprising finding, was explained by virtue of the fact that role ambiguity was greatest among this group, and that punitive LRB was clarifying the subordinates' role positions. Overall, however, positive LRB was more strongly related than punitive LRB with role ambiguity. Subordinates with supervisors who exhibited higher levels of positive LRB were also more likely to believe that their rewards were contingent upon their job performance.

It would seem that positive LRB is associated with greater satisfaction, less role ambiguity, to some extent better performance, and a belief in the contingent nature of rewards on their performance. The effects of punitive LRB are more variable, with a tendency to be associated with lower subordinate performance for three of the four occupational groups (only two statistically significant). As always with cross-sectional, correlational research designs the direction of causation is problematic. Is LRB a cause or consequence of the various satisfactions and performance? This is particularly problematic for the LRB approach as the measurement items deal with statements about how the supervisor responds to subordinate performance.

Consequently, studies since the early medical centre research have used longitudinal research designs. Keller and Szilagyi (1978) report a study of managerial, engineering and supervisory employees in a large US manufacturing organization in which the LRBI and a number of outcome measures were distributed twice, one year apart. Szilagyi (1980) examined these variables among clerical workers in a retail organization, with a three-month time lag. Sims (1977) administered the LRBI to MBA evening students drawn from a variety of organizations and work contexts. Each respondent had his or her performance evaluated by their supervisors. The instruments were re-administered six months later. This study seems to have employed a shorter LRBI, but also suggests an additional type of Leader Reward Behaviour. This category was labelled 'Advancement reward behaviour', and comprises three items which form part of the positive LRB sub-scale in the other studies. It denotes 'the degree to which the leader administers promotion recommendations contingent upon high performance' (Sims, 1977, p. 125).

There are some differences in findings between these studies which, to some extent, are a function of the degree of time lag between the two administrations of the research instruments (Sims and Szilagyi, 1979). With shorter time lags, correlations tended to be larger. Nonetheless, some general findings are:

1 Positive LRB enhances performance and satisfaction with work and other issues. Also, positive LRB enhances a belief among subordinates that their efforts will lead to better performance.
2 Punitive LRB causes dissatisfaction with work and related issues, though the early Sims and Szilagyi (1975) study is slightly at odds with this finding.
3 Poor subordinate performance (and to a lesser extent, absenteeism) induces more punitive reward behaviour by leaders.
4 Punitive LRB has a deleterious effect upon performance, especially when accompanied by a low emphasis upon advancement reward behaviour (Sims, 1977).

The reader should note that findings 3 and 4 imply reciprocal causation, that is, subordinate performance is both a cause of punitive LRB and a consequence of it, though the Szilagyi (1980) study strongly suggests that it is more important (in statistical terms) as a cause than as a consequence of such leader behaviour. It would seem that not only does punitive LRB have a deleterious effect on performance, but it is also more likely to be in evidence when performance is poor. This finding strongly implies a vicious circle in which punitive LRB is employed to deal with underperforming subordinates, resulting in dissatisfaction, possibly absenteeism, and poorer performance, which results in more punitive behaviour. The performance LRB findings have been confirmed in a laboratory experiment by Sims and Manz (1984) carried out on university MBA students. Positive and punitive LRB were indicated by the observation and recording of the 'leaders'' verbal behaviour, rather than the questionnaire approach of other research in this tradition. In particular it was found that punitive LRB was a response to poor performance, confirming the longitudinal investigations summarized above. One area in which this study is somewhat incongruent with the earlier research is the positive LRB-performance relationship. Sims (1977) found that positive LRB induced better performance, but that better performance resulted in *less* positive LRB. The Sims and Manz (1984) experiment found that: 'When performance was high, leader positive reward behaviour was also high' (p. 229). Clearly, some resolution of this apparent discrepancy is needed.

The implications of an emphasis upon leader reward behaviour has been taken a step further in a study by Podsakoff, Todor, Grover and Huber (1984). These authors emphasize the importance of distinguishing contingent from non-contingent LRB. Contingent LRB indicates that the leader responds with praise (reward behaviour) or reprimand (punishment behaviour) to good or bad subordinate performance respectively. The idea of non-contingent rewards points to reward or punishment behaviour that is administered irrespective of the subordinate's performance. This conceptual scheme suggests four kinds of LRB, in that both positive and punitive behaviour (to use the terms associated with Sims and Szilagyi) can be either contingent or non-contingent. The authors sought to relate these four types of LRB to performance (a measure based on each subordinate's evaluation by his or her supervisor) and job satisfaction. The measurement of the four types of LRB was based on each respondent's scaled responses to questionnaire items. The data were drawn from samples of US local government workers, hospital pharmacists, and state government employees. This research constitutes a significant improvement over the Sims and Szilagyi research which did not adequately distinguish between contingent and non-contingent LRB. This is an important distinction in that one might expect that subordinates will respond differently to punitive behaviour which is a response to their poor performance from that which is administered independently of how well they perform. Contingent reward behaviour (i.e. positive) was found to be related positively to both performance and a number of measures of satisfaction (with job, supervisor, co-workers, etc.). Non-contingent punishment behaviour led to poorer subordinate performance and generally lower levels of satisfaction (only with supervisors, co-workers, and pay, not work). Contingent punitive behaviour was unrelated to all measures of satisfaction as well as performance; so too was non-contingent reward behaviour, except that it seems to lead to lower levels of work satisfaction. A further interesting feature of this research is that it examined a much wider range of potential moderating variables which might impinge on the LRB-outcome relationships than in the research associated with Sims and Szilagyi. Included in the list of potential moderators were role conflict and ambiguity, task-related measures like variety, autonomy, and routineness, aspects of the organizational context, workers' commitment, and locus of control. These moderating variables had virtually no impact on the two-variable findings, suggesting that they have considerable generalizability to a wide domain of contexts.

This research also points to two important qualifications to the earlier LRB research. Firstly, it suggests that it is not positive reward behaviour *per se* which is of benefit to individuals and their organizations, but that which is contingent. Secondly, it also implies that it is non-contingent punitive behaviour that is most likely to have a deleterious impact. Non-contingent positive reward behaviour and contingent punitive behaviour are somewhat neutral in their effects. The main difficulty with this study is that it is static, so that while the findings provide important extensions of earlier research emphasizing LRB, the direction of causal effects cannot be readily imputed. The research is nonetheless important in suggesting that we should not too readily assume that all leader behaviour-outcome relationships are contingent.

From the research on LRB we can suggest that positive (especially contingent) rewards are much more effective than punitive ones. They seem to induce greater satisfaction and better performance, whereas punitive rewards have a deleterious impact on both. Even when faced with poor performance, the leader should resist the temptation to act punitively. Some confirmation of these ideas, presented in an intuitive rather than rigorous form, is evident in the parable of 'The One Minute Manager' (Blanchard and Johnson, 1982). The parable is not a fiction as it is based upon the authors' management and medical experiences respectively. It tells of the utility of 'the one minute praising' whereby the manager, when confronted with a new subordinate, strives to praise him or her at the earliest opportunity even if the pretext is relatively trivial. Blanchard and Johnson recommend that the person should be told what was right or good in what they did; then informed about how good the manager feels about the person's performance 'and how it helps the organization and the other people who work there' (p. 44); encourage similar performance; and so on. In addition, there is the 'one minute reprimand' which is really a positive response to a disappointing performance. The manager lets the subordinate know in clear terms as quickly as possible what is wrong and how he or she feels about it. But the manager also reassures the subordinate, reaffirms how much that person is valued and how much is thought of them in spite of the poor performance. Further, when the reprimand ends, it is not carried over into other situations. Both the one minute praising and the one minute reprimand are highly congruent with the idea of positive LRB. On the face of it, the one-minute reprimand is a form of contingent punishment behaviour. In fact, the brevity of the reprimand, coupled with the reassurance that the subordinate receives, seem to make it a sub-type of positive reward behaviour. It would seem that Blanchard and Johnson's work points to a need to assess the form that rewards and punishments take in organizations so that adequate classifications may ensue. It suggests that an emphasis on making the individual feel good, even when having to be reprimanded for a disappointing performance, is a better platform for the management of subordinate performance than a punitive strategy.

In terms of the first three of the six areas of criticism levelled at the Ohio studies – discrepant findings, absence of situational analysis, and the problem of causality – the emphasis on LRB appears very promising. It fares less well in terms of the other three. While research does not always indicate whether group average or individual level measures of LRB were used, some studies seem to adopt the former strategy which is open to some criticism. The Podsakoff *et al.* (1984) study seems to have used individual-level analyses. Secondly, there is no examination of informal leadership and the possible administration of informal rewards. Finally, LRB is not observed (except possibly in a loose sense by Blanchard and Johnson) but gauged from questionnaire responses. Consequently the forms that rewards and punishments assume are not adequately ascertained. Nonetheless, the consistency of the findings within this emerging research tradition is highly encouraging.

Motivation

The idea of motivation seems to be at the very core of the idea of leadership. In an article by Oldham (1976) it is the starting point for another categorization of leadership behaviour. Oldham uses the term 'motivational strategies' to refer to the techniques supervisors employ to provide the conditions for the motivation of subordinates. 'Conditions', according to Oldham, may mean a number of things: such as, enabling subordinates to fulfil personal needs or goals or providing the groundwork for accomplishing work. The idea of a motivational strategy is more than a depiction of what supervisors do; it denotes a conscious plan of action to mould the appropriate organizational conditions which will enhance motivation.

Oldham's analysis is based upon a distinction between six motivational strategies:

1 Personally rewarding strategy – indicates that the supervisor rewards his subordinates for good work by congratulating them, or by positive gestures (e.g. smiling, pat on back).
2 Personally punishing strategy – indicates a punitive response to poor work by shouting at, ignoring, or being unpleasant to the subordinate.
3 Setting goals strategy – the establishment of specific performance goals. This strategy provides direction to subordinates.
4 Designing feedback systems – involves ensuring that subordinates are fully appraised of the adequacy of their performance.
5 Placing personnel strategy – indicates that supervisors attempt to assign people to jobs which 'stretch' them. This strategy involves ensuring that subordinates are given a good deal of challenge at work.
6 Designing job systems – means that the supervisor arranges the tasks of his subordinates such that they are made more challenging.

Initially, three further strategies were conceptualized, but were dropped when Oldham's research evidence suggested that they were largely determined by the supervisors' organizations and so were not areas over which they had any control. The first two strategies bear a strong conceptual resemblance to the Sims and Szilagyi Leader Reward Behaviour notions.

The research was conducted in ten stores in the USA which were part of a nationwide chain. Data were collected on forty-five middle managers in the stores. Each of the six strategies was measured by only one questionnaire item. However, a composite index of each strategy was built up on the basis of reports in terms of each questionnaire item by subordinate ratings, supervisors' self-reports, and the store managers' ratings. Hence, while only one item per strategy was employed, each item, appropriately amended, was submitted to each of the three different respondents. Oldham assessed these depictions of motivational strategy in relation to two dependent variables: motivational effectiveness (how good each middle manager was at motivating subordinates to work hard and well) and subordinate effectiveness (the productivity of each middle manager's subordinates). Ratings of these two dimensions were made by both store managers and assistant managers, and Oldham's analysis distinguishes between the two sets of ratings.

With the exception of the Personally Punishing strategy, all of the motivational strategies were positively correlated with motivational effectiveness, irrespective of whether store manager or assistant manager reports were used. Personally Punishing was negatively related to motivational effectiveness, though only significantly in respect of assistant manager ratings. The pattern of results in connection with subordinate effectiveness was less systematically correlated to the six strategies. There was a fairly clear-cut tendency for Personally Rewarding and Designing Feedback systems to be positively correlated with this variable. In addition, Designing Job Systems was positively correlated with store manager ratings of subordinate effectiveness.

An additional feature of Oldham's study is that he also produced measures of Consideration and Initiating Structure. Separate indices of these two dimensions were built up from middle managers' self-reports through the Ohio LOQ, and subordinates' reports by means of the LBDQ. While Initiating Structure showed significant relationships to store manager ratings of motivational and subordinate effectiveness, the overall pattern was that 'the motivational strategies are better predictors of middle manager effectiveness' (Oldham, 1976, p. 83).

Oldham's research is clearly suggestive of an important aspect of leadership, namely the extent to which the leader can manipulate the organizational environment of his subordinates such that they are motivated to better work performance. There are a number of weaknesses to the study. While the measurement of the six strategies in terms of three sets of reports is praiseworthy, the use of only one indicator for each respondent is a disadvantage. Indices or scales are typically used in the literature in case a particular item may either be an unstable measure or may not encapsulate the full range of meaning of the concept it is supposed to be measuring. The study is also deficient in respect of five of the six criticisms raised in relation to the Ohio research. The exception is that of discrepant findings in that the Oldham scheme does not seem to have generated a research tradition and so we have little subsequent evidence with which to compare it. In this connection, it is noteworthy that the results for the Personally Rewarding and Personally Punishing strategies are broadly congruent with those discerned in the work stimulated by Sims and Szilagyi reviewed in the previous section. However, there is no situational analysis, though Oldham (1976, p. 84) recognizes its potential in relation to his research. The causal direction of variables has to be assumed, but is not established, so that motivational effectiveness could be a cause of the motivational strategies. For example, could it be that the Designing Job Systems strategy is used in relation to groups of subordinates who are already highly motivated? Further, Oldham employed averaged group measures of all of the leadership variables (including the Ohio ones) he examined. There is no examination of informal leadership. Finally, leader behaviour is gleaned from question-naire responses rather than observed.

Control

A fourth formulation of leader behaviour has been provided by Jones (1983) around the theme of control. While this theme is a prominent one in organization theory (e.g. Etzioni, 1961; Woodward, 1970; Perrow, 1972), as Jones observes, it has not been a prominent feature in leadership research. To some extent this is surprising in view of the possible congruence between the pervasive idea of leadership as a social influence process and the procedures adopted by leaders to control their subordinates' behaviour. On the basis of a review of the literature, as well as consultation with colleagues, Jones developed a list of twenty-two control methods. These were presented in varying combinations, to sixty-three senior undergraduates in business studies who were asked to 'evaluate the similarity of pairs of twenty-two methods supervisors might adopt to alter the effectiveness of the work group for which they are responsible' (Jones, 1983, p. 162). An analysis was conducted to extract any underlying dimensions to the twenty-two methods. Four such dimensions were derived from the analysis. One dimension is expressed as obtrusive control versus unobtrusive control, involving methods like close supervision, directive supervision, punitive rewards at the former end and providing people with information and taking an interest in subordinates at the latter end. The second dimension was labelled situational against personal control. The former emphasizes changing the physical structure of the workplace and altering work relationships; while personal control is indicated by setting an example or establishing clear output goals and standards. Thirdly, Jones distinguishes between professional and paternalistic control. Professional control entails 'controlling the information available to . . . perform work tasks' (Jones, 1983, p. 167). By contrast, paternalistic control denotes the use of 'personal and material rewards and punishments' to control subordinate behaviour. Finally, Jones's analysis suggests a fourth dimension of process versus output control, indicating a choice between controlling how work is done and setting goals and standards.

Jones's research provides an interesting taxonomy of the control choices open to leaders. It departs, in methodological terms, substantially from other research on leadership behaviour and so it seems difficult to evaluate it by the six criteria which we have previously employed. Two main problems can be discerned with this research. Firstly, many of the control methods are not 'clean' in relation to the dimensions; in other words, they are constitutive of more than one dimension. In particular, as Jones recognizes, the professional-paternalistic dimension involves a considerable number of items present in other dimensions. Such overlapping causes problems of interpretation which are common to these kinds of statistical procedure and it is a moot point whether another writer would interpret the categorization in quite the same way. Secondly, the generalizability of the research is open to question in view of the fact that the research was conducted neither on real supervisors or leaders nor in a work context. In this light Jones's (1983, p. 170) assertion that the study is important for showing 'that when selecting an appropriate means to select a desired goal, supervisors have a number of strategies they may follow' seems to stretch the evidence slightly.

The idea of leadership style

An examination of the literature on leadership styles reveals that very often categories of leader behaviour are referred to almost as though they are attributes of the people described. The image, often unintended, is that of leadership style being fixed and inert. Clearly, this is not the case and there is ample evidence to suggest that leaders adjust their behaviour to a diversity of contexts, situations, and subordinates.

There is a good deal of evidence to suggest that leaders do not use just one style, or even a fixed combination of styles as in the Ohio 'Hi-Hi' duet (see Chapter 3). Bass and Valenzi (1974) asked subordinates which of the five styles they examined were exhibited by their superiors: direction, manipulation, consultation, participation, and delegation. Only 2 per cent of the sample indicated that their bosses used a single style; 1 per cent that a dual (i.e. two styles in combination) approach was employed; and over 90 per cent indicated that three or more strategies were used. Similarly, Hill's (1973) study of middle and first level British supervisors found that only 14 per cent used the same one of four styles across four hypothetical situations. Finally, a study of German and British managers by Heller and Wilpert (1977) examined the range of styles employed by respondents. Five decision-making styles were distinguished forming a continuum of participative leadership similar to that of Tannenbaum and Schmidt (1958) and Sadler (1970): the manager makes his own decision without detailed explanation; own decision with detailed explanation; prior consultation with subordinate; joint decision-making with subordinate; delegation of decision to subordinate. These five styles were examined across twelve decision areas to see which styles were used in relation to which decisions. Data were collected on senior managers' reports of their behaviour and on their subordinates' behaviour. The decision styles of the latter group, who were also fairly senior managers, were based on reports by their own subordinates. For both groups only around 1 per cent of managers appear to use one style alone. Taking both groups of managers together, over half the sample used four or five styles (72 per cent and 58 per cent of British and German managers respectively).

Further evidence that leaders do not adopt single, inflexible styles emerges from the Vertical Dyad Linkage (VDL) approach briefly mentioned in the last chapter. The study by Danserau, Graen and Haga (1975) provides an empirical example of these ideas. The research investigated the immediate post-reorganization period of a housing division in a large public US university. Sixty managers at the top of this division were examined. Because the research took place after a period of reorganization, the vast majority of leader-subordinate relationships which were examined were new 'vertical dyads'. The authors draw a useful distinction, derived from the work of Jacobs (1971), between leadership and supervision which denote respectively influence in respect of subordinates without authority and influence which is based only upon authority. In the latter context, the leader has recourse to his own position and that of his subordinate to enforce compliance. In the view of these authors:

> In general, the greater the latitude initially given to the member to negotiate job-related matters, the higher is the probability that the superior is attempting leadership and the lower is the probability that he is using supervision with his member. (Danserau *et al.*, 1975, p. 50)

Interviews were conducted with the sixty managers and their superiors, though some of the focal managers were interviewed as managers too. The interviews were conducted in four 'waves'. At a relatively early period it was apparent that roughly half of the managers formed an 'in-group' with high negotiating latitude; the other half an 'out-group' with little latitude. In terms of the researchers' conceptual framework, the two groups were the recipients of leadership and supervision respectively. According to the VDL theorists, subordinates are selected as in-group members by virtue of their greater competence and skill, their greater trustworthiness, and their more pronounced motivation to assume responsibility. Danserau *et al.* found that the in-group members received more leadership attention, felt that they had little difficulty in dealing with their superior, and perceived him as more responsive to their job needs. The in-group was more active in connection with communicating and administering group activities and was revealed as behaving in closer correspondence to each member's and superior's preferences for the group. In-group members also expressed higher levels of intrinsic work satisfaction, better interpersonal relations with their supervisor and were more positive about the supervisor's technical competence and the value of their job performance rewards.

A field experiment involving 106 form-processing employees of a large US public service organization by Graen, Novak and Sommerkamp (1982) sought to investigate some of the ramifications of these ideas. For one of the experimental treatments managers were given training in the ideas of Leader-Member Exchange, such that each of them was encouraged to think about, be sensitive to, analyse and act upon the nature of the relationships they had with each subordinate. Such training elicited strong gains in productivity and subordinate job satisfaction, as well as a number of other positive side effects. Research by Vecchio and Gobdel (1984) in a bank setting confirms that 'in-group' status is associated with better subordinate performance and satisfaction with supervision, lower turnover, but not with greater job satisfaction. Parenthetically, these investigators, as well as Graen and Cashman (1975), have registered some doubts over whether leader-subordinate relationships can be meaningfully rendered down into an 'in-group' as against 'out-group' contrast. More recent empirical work suggests that there may often be a middle group which experiences both high and low latitude relationships (presumably on different occasions). In their own research, Vecchio and Gobdel operated with this tripartite notion, as has more recent research by the model's proponents (e.g. Liden and Graen, 1980). Such problems aside, the implications of these ideas for leadership research are many, but for the present discussion it is important to note that leaders behave in different ways to their subordinates. Further, important consequences seem to flow from the differentiation of leader-member dyads.

There appears to be little to justify treating leadership styles as fixed, rigid phenomena. Leaders vary their styles considerably, but in relation to what? What kinds of factors affect or influence the leader's style and how is it affected? The following is a brief list of factors which have been found to be relevant.

1   The specific task at hand

It is evident that leaders are flexible in their leadership styles in that they adopt different patterns for particular tasks. The research by Heller and Wilpert (1977) found that managers behaved in a more or less participative manner (in terms of the authors' five decision styles) across the twelve decision areas. They were more participative in connection with decision areas like: choosing between applicants who will work for the manager's subordinate, promotion of a person working for the manager's subordinate, and firing one of the subordinate's employees. They were much less participative in relation to areas such as increasing the salary of a direct subordinate, purchase of equipment over a certain sum of money, and budgetary issues.

2   The general nature of the task

The nature of the work carried out by subordinates seems to have an impact on leader behaviour. A laboratory experiment conducted on male undergraduates was conducted by Hill and Hughes (1974). Subjects were assigned to three task conditions and variations of leader behaviour were examined in terms of four categories (based on the work of Bales): positive socio-emotional, directive, non-directive, and negative socio-emotional. The researchers found clear differences in the extent of reliance on each of these categories across the three tasks, suggesting that the type of task affects leader behaviour. In particular their research suggests that more uncertain tasks require more directive acts. Further evidence can be derived from studies cited in this and the previous chapters. Barrow's experimental research (1976) suggests that leaders are more task-oriented (roughly synonymous with Initiating Structure) when faced with complex tasks. Similarly, the cross-sectional research on managers by Bass *et al.* (1975) found task complexity to be of importance, but not in the same way that Barrow's research indicates. Bass *et al.* found that task complexity was important in predicting in a positive direction the amount of both negotiating and delegating behaviour exhibited by managers. It was not a factor in the amount of direction they displayed, as Barrow's research would lead one to anticipate. Further, a variable called 'clearer task objectives' was found to lead to more directive activity, the opposite of what the research by Hill and Hughes would lead one to expect. There was strong evidence that less routine tasks were associated with more consultative, participative and delegating activity. This latter finding is broadly consistent with the idea that the benefits of participation are more likely to be discerned where tasks are more uncertain and there is more to participate about.

In contrast to the findings of Bass *et al.*, but in line with those of Barrow, a study of personnel in three different types of organization found task routineness to be strongly and positively related to Initiating Structure (Ford, 1981). However, Sheridan and Vredenburgh's (1978) study of head nurses in the USA found task routineness to be unrelated to both Initiating Structure and Consideration. Although the nature of the task appears to have an impact on leader behaviour, the evidence relating to the complexion of its effects is somewhat equivocal. It may be that the divergences in some of the findings are in part due to methodological differences between the studies. Further evidence in connection with task-related sources of variation in leader behaviour is evident in a study within the Michigan four-factor tradition by Taylor (1974). This investigation of a large sample of individuals drawn from seven firms sought to discern the effect of the degree of technological sophistication encountered by work groups on some of the measures of leader behaviour associated with this approach. Taylor found that technological sophistication was associated with greater supervisory work facilitation and support, but only in those firms which had determinedly adopted a participative form of management. Among those firms which had adopted participative management as a last resort, after other methods had failed, the effect of technological sophistication on these two leader behaviour dimensions was not only less marked but in a negative direction. Such findings point to the likelihood of the prediction of leader behaviour being contingent upon the situation.

3 Performance and performance-related attributes of subordinates
This aspect of the causation of leader behaviour has already been indirectly tackled in this and the previous chapter. When examining experimental and panel studies of the relationship between leader behaviour and performance, it has been pointed out that the evidence suggests that the latter often causes the former. The evidence that has been previously examined suggests that poor subordinate performance leads to more directive/structuring behaviour (Barrow, 1976; Greene, 1975; Lowin and Craig, 1968), less Considerate/supportive behaviour (Barrow, 1976; Greene, 1975; Lowin and Craig, 1968), more punitive leader reward behaviour (Sims and Manz, 1984), and less positive leader reward behaviour (Sims and Manz, 1984). It will be recalled that Barrow's research is particularly interesting in the context of the present discussion in that he was able to document that as subordinate performance changes so too does leader behaviour. Other research confirms the role of subordinate performance as a cause of leader behaviour. Barrow's study suggests that leaders respond to poor subordinate performance with more autocratic behaviour. Lowin and Craig's (1968) study also indicates that

poor performance engenders closer supervision, an approach that is usually indicative of a less participative style.

Subordinate competence is also related to how leaders behave. In the Heller and Wilpert (1977) research on British and German senior managers, the impact of the perceived managerial skills of subordinates (e.g. technical competence, entrepreneurial skills) affected how leaders behaved. The more a manager judged the skill requirements of his job to be greater than that of his immediate subordinate, the less likely he was to use a participative decision style.

4   *The leader's power*

The role of the amount of power enjoyed by a leader as a possible determinant of managerial style is evident in research on Israeli managers (Chitayat and Venezia, 1984). Their investigation of the determinants of managerial styles, as categorized according to the Bass *et al.* (1975) framework, found that in business organizations the more power enjoyed by executives the more likely they were to be directive. In non-business contexts the relationship between power and directiveness was negative. The leader's power to employ performance-contingent rewards and punishments also seems to be an important determinant of his or her reward behaviour. For example, a study by Greene and Podsakoff (1981) found that when leaders lose control over performance-contingent rewards, their use of punishment behaviour seems to grow. Additional evidence regarding the leader's power as a determinant of his or her leadership style emerges from Heller and Wilpert's (1981) survey research on managers in a number of different countries. It was found that when managers lack 'role authority' they are more likely to use centralized (i.e. non-participative) decision-making styles. It would seem that the amount of power that a leader has is an important constraint on, and determinant of, the style adopted.

Many other factors impinge upon leader behaviour – this list merely provides some of the more prominent areas in the literature (see Yukl, 1981, ch. 7). In Chapter 6 a further group of variables will be considered, namely those which derive from characteristics of the organizations in which leaders find themselves. For the time being, it should be apparent that leaders rarely have fixed styles and that they respond to the contexts with which they are faced. Such evidence raises a question about the meaning of the numerous cross-sectional/correlational studies of leadership style in the Ohio, Michigan and other traditions. Not only does a particular leader behave in different ways to subordinates, as Danserau *et al.* (1975) observe; they also react to each subordinate in different ways at different times. While Schriesheim's (1979) research was cited in the last chapter as implying that the former point does not necessarily make too much difference, it is nonetheless clear that many studies of leadership merely provide a snapshot in which very broad statements of leadership are pictured. Leaders described as high on Initiating Structure and low on Consideration in the Ohio studies may become low on both, high on both, or reverse their relative emphases within fairly short spaces of time after the studies were conducted! They may also exhibit different emphases to different subordinates. It is small wonder that so many investigators have found that their research only partially confirmed that of other investigators. As statements about *tendencies* in relation to how leaders behave the hundreds of studies of leadership style are valuable. The problem that we are witnessing is, of course, one that has been encountered before. Virtually no study of leadership *observes* in detail what leadership involves in the real world – how it affects subordinates and how the context in which the leader finds himself affects what he does. In this light it is small wonder that writers like Adair (1983) and Mintzberg (1982) have suggested that the practical implications of research on leadership style are not at all clear-cut.

Overview

The research covered in this chapter seems to reveal a slightly greater specificity in the depiction of leadership style. There seems to be a gradual move away from the general themes of Consideration/Initiating Structure and Production/Employee-centred to the ideas of rewarding, motivating, and controlling in which very specific behavioural phenomena are being addressed. Indeed, it may be more accurate to refer to the Ohio and early Michigan research as studies of leadership *style*, with later research (e.g. rewarding, motivating) being more to do with leader *behaviour*, to denote a contrast between fairly general and specific formulations. This tendency has progressed further with the publication of Yukl and Nemeroff's (1979) paper in which fourteen leader behaviour categories were generated from a number of studies and a review of the literature. The most recent formulation (Yukl, 1981) lists nineteen categories. This development is consistent with the work of writers like Oldham (1976) and Jones (1983), in arguing that more specific categories are more helpful in 'determining what makes a leader effective in a particular situation' (Yukl, 1981, p. 120). The nineteen categories are: performance emphasis, consideration, inspiration, praise-recognition, structuring reward contingencies, decision participation, autonomy-delegation, role clarification, goal setting, training-coaching, information dissemination, problem-solving, planning, coordinating, work facilitation, representation, interaction facilitation, conflict management, and criticism-discipline.

This is a very comprehensive list indeed whose ultimate utility, as Yukl recognizes, may well depend upon the adequacy of its measurement. On the face of it, it seems quite difficult to imagine what combinations of overall leader behaviour across nineteen categories are conducive to greater effectiveness in particular situational contexts. This development is somewhat redolent of the quest for more and more traits deemed to be relevant to leadership which was encountered in Chapter 2. The problem with the quest in that context was that, quite aside from the inconsistent findings, it was difficult to envisage which traits, or combinations of them, were particularly crucial to leadership ability. The conceptual parsimony of the early style researchers with their stark dichotomies now appears a haven! Developments such as Yukl's, comprehensive and specific though they are, may well engender the same kinds of practical difficulty for researchers and practitioners that the proliferation of traits did for an earlier generation of investigators. Yukl has developed research instruments to tap the nineteen styles in a military context. Noting that his schema implies much more specific denotations of leader behaviour than within traditions like the Ohio school, he concludes:

> Performance emphasis, role clarification, goal setting, training-coaching, planning, problem solving, coordinating, and work facilitation are all part of a general task-oriented category of leadership behaviour, and the differential results for these behaviours would have been masked if only the broader measure had been used. (Yukl and van Fleet, 1982, p. 107)

A parallel and fairly similar trend can be discerned in the development of the Supervision module of the Michigan Organizational Assessment Questionnaire in which the relative parsimony of the four-factor approach has given way to a scheme which specifies twelve dimensions: production orientation, control of work, work-facilitation-goal setting, work facilitation-problem solving, work facilitation-subordinate relations, bias (towards subordinates in respect of race or sex), consideration, participation, decision centralization, supervisory competence, use of contingent reward allocation, and interpersonal competence (Cammann *et al.*, 1983, pp. 103-11). Classification schemes of leader behaviour such as this, as well as that of Yukl, constitute a shift towards both greater specificity of leader behaviour and greater inclusiveness. As such, there is a very evident simultaneous shift away from classifications of leadership style as general orientations to the leadership role towards the minutiae of leadership behaviour.

Researchers who have emphasized the importance of the leader's orientation to the task have tended to focus either on the leader's 'structuring' behaviour – making clear to subordinates the nature of the task and the means for its attainment – or the prominence accorded by the leader to task attainment. Another facet of task orientation is what Cooper (1966) has (possibly misleadingly) dubbed 'task relevance' which denotes 'having considerable job skill together with an abundant concern for performing his duties well' (p. 57). In a study of British industrial supervisors he found that operatives tended to prefer superiors who exhibited both task-relevant and considerate behaviour. They were much less favourably disposed to '*laissez-faire*' supervisors and those who displayed high levels of Initiating Structure. Cooper also found that the subordinates of supervisors who stressed task relevance made significantly fewer work-related errors and exhibited lower levels of absenteeism than their peers whose supervisors exhibited lower levels in respect of this variable. Such evidence strongly suggests that leaders serve as models for their subordinates, and that those leaders who are highly competent and motivated will be preferred (see also Weiss, 1977). The extent to which leaders serve as models for their subordinates has been rather underplayed in the literature on leadership although Yukl's (1981) reference to the 'inspiration' element in leader behaviour goes some way in this direction. Yukl's data on military leader effectiveness (Yukl and van Fleet, 1982) suggests that it is an important component in this context. Further, Adair's (1983) training programme emphasizes the importance of setting an example as a vital element in effective leadership. The key issue is to ensure that leaders provide 'good' models, though what constitutes a good model may be more problematic than writers like Adair seem to indicate. Nonetheless, the capacity of leaders to inspire others by presenting themselves as appropriate models has been somewhat neglected in the literature, even though it seems to strike at the very heart of the common notion of leadership as entailing a propensity to motivate.

Unfortunately, the proliferation of new classifications and measures often renders the inter-relationships among the various categories of leadership style impossible to discern, as researchers often employ their own schemes to the exclusion of others. This is not always the case, however. In Table 4.1 the observed correlations between a number of approaches which have been explicated in this and the previous chapter and the basic Ohio dimensions of Consideration and Initiating Structure have been brought together. The correlations between both Consideration and Initiating Structure and the categories developed by the LRB, motivational strategies, and four-factor approaches are presented. In addition, correlations with participation are presented, but for this aspect of the presentation some licence has been taken. The correlations with participation are drawn from three studies. Firstly, a study by Yukl (1971) of sixty-seven supervisors' 'decision-centralization', estimated in terms of the five decision areas used subsequently by Heller and Wilpert (1977 – see above). Since this is a measure of the amount of centralization of decision-making, the sign is reversed in the table (i.e. plus instead of minus). Secondly, data from Brownell's (1983) study of managers are based on his index of *budget* participation. Finally, data are drawn from a number of studies by Stogdill, Goode and Day who presented a (then) new set of Ohio sub-scales, one of which is 'Tolerance of Member Freedom'. This sub-scale measures how much scope for initiative, decision and action the leader allows.

Following Yukl's (1971) suggestion, this sub-scale has been treated as a surrogate for participation. The nature of the Ohio research instrument is given where known. According to Table 4.1 Considerate leaders score high in terms of all of the four-factor dimensions, exhibit more positive LRB, exhibit more personally rewarding and less personally punishing behaviour, are more inclined to design feedback systems, and are more participative. Structuring leaders also score high on all of the four-factor dimensions, exhibit more of *both* positive and punitive LRB, and emphasize setting goals, designing feedback systems, and placing personnel. As Yukl (1971) has argued, Initiating Structure is unrelated to participation. Clearly, there is a good deal of conceptual and measurement

Table 4.1 *Correlations between Consideration, Initiating Structure, and other dimensions of leader behaviour*

	Consideration	Initiating Structure	
Four-factor approach[1]			
Supervisory support	.74**	.41**	(Form X11)
Supervisory goal emphasis	.64**	.76**	(Form X11)
Supervisory work facilitation	.56**	.64**	(Form X11)
Supervisory interaction facilitation	.66**	.61**	(Form X11)
Leader reward behaviour[2]			
Positive LRB	.66**	.51**	(Form X11)
Positive LRB	.81**	−.07	(SBDQ)
Punitive LRB	−.01	.33**	(Form X11)
Punitive LRB	−.01	.49	(SBDQ)
Motivational strategies[3]			
Personally rewarding	.15	.20	(LOQ)
Personally rewarding	.50**	−.07	(SBDQ)
Personally punishing	−.10	.21	(LOQ)
Personally punishing	−.49**	−.31*	(SBDQ)
Setting goals	.18	.36*	(LOQ)
Setting goals	−.18	.44**	(SBDQ)
Designing feedback systems	.12	.46	(LOQ)
Designing feedback systems	.37*	.09	(SBDQ)
Placing personnel	.19	.23	(LOQ)
Placing personnel	−.09	.43**	(SBDQ)
Designing job systems	.22	.26	(LOQ)
Designing job systems	.20	.19	(SBDQ)
Participative leadership			
Decision-participation (Decision-centralization with sign reversed)[4]	.24*	N.S.[10]	(Not known)
Budget participation[5]	.12	−.12	(Form X11)
Tolerance of member freedom			
(a) Community leaders[6]	.40**	.05	(Form X11)
(b) Ministers of religion[6]	.49**	−.05	(Form X11)
(c) US Senators[7]	.50**	.22	(Form X11)
(d) Corporation presidents[8]	.41**	−.20	(Form X11)
(e) Presidents of labour unions[9]	.42**	.04	(Form X11)

1 Yunker and Hunt (1976)
2 Szilagyi and Keller (1976)
3 Oldham (1976)
4 Reported in Yukl (1971)
5 Brownell (1983)
6 Stogdill, Goode and Day (1962)
7 Stogdill, Goode and Day (1963a)
8 Stogdill, Goode and Day (1963b)
9 Stogdill, Goode and Day (1964)
10 Reported in Yukl (1971) as non-significant but no details given

N.B. All significance levels are based on two-tailed significance tests, and have been estimated or re-estimated by the author in these terms.
* p<.05   ** p<.01

overlap between the descriptions of leader behaviour, though this varies according to the Ohio instrument employed. The very fact that the Consideration and Initiating Structure categories occasionally overlap (but in other instances do not) with other dimensions suggests that greater attention ought to be directed to the impact of combinations of styles on the various outcomes in which leadership researchers have been interested. It is also necessary to sort out how much of the overlap is due to methodological artefacts, such as the inclusion of items indicative of participative leadership in Ohio measures of Consideration, to which the reader's attention has already been drawn. Issues such as these point to the very real measurement difficulties which have beset leadership researchers over the years.

In more recent years, the role of situational contingencies has become much more prominent. In large part, this emphasis has become more pronounced due to the growing recognition of the equivocality of so many findings associated with the study of leader behaviour. In the next chapter, a number of theories in which situational factors are integral elements are discussed.

5

CONTINGENCY APPROACHES TO THE STUDY OF LEADERSHIP

The approaches discussed in this chapter take as their central focus the possibility that the effectiveness of particular leadership styles is situationally contingent. This means that a particular style or pattern of behaviour will be effective in some circumstances (e.g. when a task is intrinsically satisfying, or when the personalities of subordinates predispose them to a particular style) but not others. The basic structure of 'contingency approaches' is expressed in Figure 5.1 Contingency approaches explicitly draw attention to the notion that there are no universally appropriate styles of leadership; particular styles have an impact on various outcomes in some situations but not others.

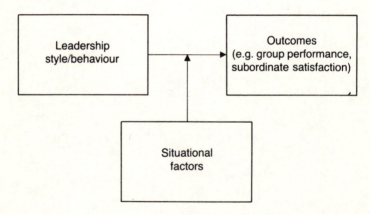

Figure 5.1 *The basic structure of contingency approaches of leadership*

This idea has been encountered in the context of the last two chapters, so that it is pertinent to enquire what distinguishes the perspectives addressed in this chapter from previous references to this conception. In fact, there is no hard and fast distinction between early research in which situational factors were evident and the later approaches discussed here. To a significant extent, it was the apparent lack of evidence for universally superior leadership styles coupled with scattered indications of their situational specificity which acted as an impetus for the contingency approaches. The early findings and these newer theories are distinguishable in at least two ways. Firstly, in the contingency approaches discussed in this chapter, the situationally specific nature of effective leadership is an explicit and prominent focus, whereas in the earlier research situational factors were generally somewhat residual variables. To put it another way, situational factors were not usually central planks of a researcher's investigation. Secondly, in the early research, situational variables were introduced into the analysis in a rather unsystematic and *ad hoc* manner, whereas the newer contingency approaches attempt to provide a theoretical justification in the context of a general model for the inclusion of such variables in their purview. The idea that a particular situational factor moderates a leadership style-outcome relationship is given a theoretical justification in terms of a general model, although as will become evident, the theoretical elaboration of specific findings is frequently *ex post facto*.

Four examples of the contingency approach are explored in this chapter. In the author's view, they constitute the four most important perspectives in terms of either having generated strong research programmes (the Fiedler and path-goal approaches) or for having achieved prominence in the field of organizational behaviour for their theoretical or practical implications (the Vroom-Yetton and Hersey-Blanchard approaches).

Fiedler's Contingency Model of leadership effectiveness

In the work of Fred E. Fiedler (see especially 1967, 1971, 1972, 1978a, 1978b, 1978c) can be found the earliest systematic attempt to develop a contingency approach to the study of leadership style. The research conducted by Fiedler and his various co-workers has been carried out in a wide range of settings in industry, the military, sport, and elsewhere. Unfortunately, as will be evident from the discussion below, the model is bedevilled by controversy, with reviewers of the immense research literature that it has generated appearing incapable of even a modicum of agreement over its validity.

The *leitmotif* of Fiedler's approach is a scale which is administered to people in leadership positions. The respondent is asked to think of a co-worker who is the person with whom he or she has least liked working, known as the 'least preferred co-worker' (LPC). The object of the exercise is for the respondent to rate his or her LPC in terms of eight-point, bipolar adjectives. Examples are:

Pleasant	8	7	6	5	4	3	2	1	Unpleasant
Friendly	8	7	6	5	4	3	2	1	Unfriendly
Rejecting	1	2	3	4	5	6	7	8	Accepting
Distant	1	2	3	4	5	6	7	8	Close

The number of pairs of adjectives is somewhat variable and can be as few as sixteen and as many as twenty-five. Nowadays, the scale tends to comprise eighteen pairs with the following pairs being additional to those cited above: tense-relaxed; cold-warm; supportive-hostile; boring-interesting; quarrelsome-harmonious; gloomy-cheerful; open-guarded; back-biting-loyal; untrustworthy-trustworthy; considerate-inconsiderate; nasty-nice; agreeable-disagreeable; insincere-sincere; kind-unkind. It is evident that the respondent's LPC can be described in a positive or favourable fashion (e.g. pleasant/friendly/accepting/close/etc.) or in a negative or unfavourable manner (e.g. unpleasant/unfriendly/rejecting/distant/etc.). The scale enables a researcher to distinguish between leaders who provide favourable depictions of their LPCs (often called 'high LPC' leaders) and those whose descriptions are unfavourable ('low LPC' leaders). In much of the early research there was a tendency among many writers to refer somewhat crudely to high and low LPC leaders as a simple dichotomy. In his most recent work, Fiedler (e.g. Fiedler and Chemers, 1984) operates with three categories: high LPC leaders (with LPC scores of 73 and above on the 18 item scale), middle LPC leaders (LPC score of 65-72), and low LPC leaders (64 and below). However, a great deal of the written material relating to the LPC scale endorses, at least implicitly, a dichotomous image of high and low LPC leaders.

On the basis of his own and other researchers' evidence, Fiedler has consistently maintained that high LPC leaders extract superior perform-ance from their subordinates in some circumstances; but in other contexts, low LPC leaders will do better. In other words, Fiedler maintains that the type of leader required in order for group performance to be enhanced is situationally contingent. In considering the particular circumstances which may affect the relationship between LPC and performance, Fiedler focuses upon the extent to which the situation is favourable to the leader. This notion is usually referred to as the 'situational favourableness' dimension, but in more recent years it is often referred to as the degree of 'situational control'. The argument is that the degree to which the situation is favourable (or unfavourable) to the leader mediates the LPC-performance relationship. Situational favourableness is taken to comprise three factors which together denote how far the context in which the leader operates facilitates his or her ability to influence the group. These three components of the situation are:

1   Leader-member relations (often called 'Group atmosphere').
This aspect of the situation refers to the quality of personal and affective relations between the leader and group members. If relations are good, such that the leader is liked and accepted, then it is likely to be easier for

him or her to lead as group members are likely to feel better disposed towards complying with his preferences.

2   Task structure.

Fiedler believes that the leader's position is facilitated by tasks which are clear and unambiguous rather than those which are unstructured. The leader who faces a structured task knows exactly what has to be done and so can issue directions and monitor group performance much more easily. Furthermore, the leader's subordinates are likely to have a better understanding of what has to be done in order to accomplish a task.

3   Position power.

This aspect of the situation refers to the extent to which a leader has the ability to administer rewards and punishments to group members and to enforce compliance. If the leader is in a weak position within an organization, then his ability to lead effectively may be adversely affected by a recognition among his subordinates that he does not have the means to reward or punish good or bad performance respectively. The ordering of these three components is not accidental, in that it forms a hierarchy of importance in respect of the favourableness of the situation with leader-member relations being the most important, and position power the least important, aspects. By rendering each component into a dichotomy, Fiedler produces eight possible combinations (usually called 'octants') which vary from highly favourable to highly unfavourable situations (see Figure 5.2). This scheme yields eight possible descriptions of the extent to which the situation is favourable to the leader.[1]

Table 5.1 *Summary of findings relating to Fiedler's Contingency Model*

Octant	1	2	3	4	5	6	7	8	Row No.
Median correlations in original studies[1]	−.52	−.58	−.33	.47	.42		.05	−.43	1
Range of correlations in subsequent studies[2]	−.43	.60	.10	.00	.03	−.45	−.27	−.51	2a
	−.77	−.55	−.80	.71	.28	.67	.62	.60	2b
Median correlations in subsequent studies[2]	−.59	−.10	−.29	.40	.19	.13	.17	−.35	3
Range of correlations in adequate tests[3]	−.43	.50	.60	−.36	.03	−.52	−.30	−.59	4a
	−.77	−.55	−.80	.46	.28	.39	.62	.60	4b
Median correlations in adequate tests[3]	−.64	−.10	−.26	.10	.19	.13	.17	−.33	5
West Point study[4]	−.43	−.32	.10	.35	.28	.13	.08	−.33	6

1 from Fiedler (1967)
2 from Fiedler (1978c)
3 from Hosking (1981)
4 from Chemers and Skrzypek (1972)

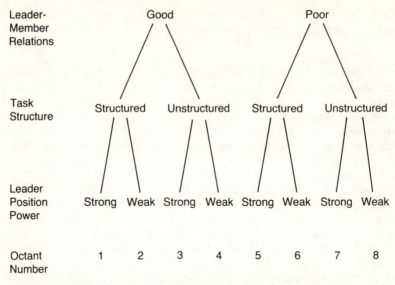

Figure 5.2   *Fiedler's notion of situational favourableness (control)*

The key to Fiedler's model is that when the correlations from various studies between LPC scores and performance are arrayed along the eight octants, a patterning of the correlations appears to become evident. If only the median correlations for each octant are considered, then as rows 1 and 3 in Table 5.1 reveal, in highly favourable (Octants 1, 2 and 3) and highly unfavourable situations (Octant 8) there tend to be negative correlations between LPC and group performance. In situations of intermediate favourableness (Octants 4, 5, 6, and possibly 7) the LPC-performance correlations are positive. Figure 5.3, which is drawn from a summary of the early studies (Fiedler, 1967), displays this curvilinear tendency.

Such findings strongly imply that when situations are very favourable or very unfavourable to the leader, low scoring LPC leaders will extract better group performance. In the intermediate contexts, however, high LPC leaders will do best in this respect.[2] The controversy regarding this model has continued unabated since its introduction in the 1960s. In order to cut a path through this abundant and often highly complex discussion, two areas will be focused upon in this discussion: the interpretation of the LPC scale and the validity of the model as a whole.

What does the LPC scale mean?

Textbooks on research methods in fields like social psychology and sociology convey an image of the research process in which the investigator narrows down his or her interests within a particular domain of study and seeks to 'operationalize' the focal concepts of interest in order to examine relationships among them. There are few areas of investigation

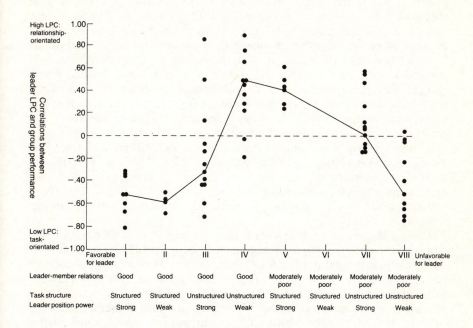

Figure 5.3   *Correlations between LPC scores and group effectiveness plotted for each octant*

Note: Each dot represents one study which has been aligned with its appropriate octant. Its position in respect of the vertical axis reflects the magnitude of the LPC-group performance correlation. The line links the median correlations across the octants.
Source: F.E. Fiedler, *A Theory of Leadership Effectiveness* (McGraw-Hill, 1967), p. 146. Reproduced with permission.

within the social sciences which provide a better example of the tenuous correspondence that this view of the research process has with reality than the LPC scale, which is, in the words of Schriesheim and Kerr (1977, p. 23), 'a measure in search of a meaning'. The most frequently cited interpretation is that high LPC leaders are relationship-oriented, in that they seek out satisfying relationships. Low LPC leaders tend to emphasize successful task performance. As such, whilst the high LPC leader tends to be 'permissive, human relations-oriented, and considerate of the feelings of his men', the low LPC leader 'tends to be managing, task-controlling, and less concerned with the human relations aspects of his job' (Fiedler, 1965, p. 116). This juxtaposition of leaders in terms of an emphasis on personal relationships versus task orientation seems to place it squarely within the ideas associated with other leadership researchers such as the Ohio and Michigan approaches. Indeed, Fiedler seems to have recognized a congruence between this interpretation of the LPC scores and the Ohio Consideration-Initiating Structure pairing (Fiedler, 1967, p. 45). This is somewhat surprising in that Fiedler's notions of relationship and task orientation are of an either-or nature, whereas the Ohio researchers conceptualized such notions as separate dimensions of leadership behaviour.

One of the major problems with this interpretation is that researchers have often failed to show a correspondence between LPC scores and their supposed behavioural implications (Rice, 1978a). For example, a study of foremen by Stinson and Tracy (1974) found low correlations between respondents' LPC scores and descriptions of their behaviour by subordinates in terms of Consideration and Initiating Structure as measured by the LBDQ. One might have anticipated a large positive correlation between LPC and Consideration; but the correlation was $-.026$. A more recent laboratory experiment by Singh (1983) has also had difficulty in supporting this interpretation of the LPC scale.

Two further interpretations have been offered. One is to suggest that high LPC persons are more cognitively complex than low LPC persons (Foa, Mitchell and Fiedler, 1971). In part, evidence for this contention derives from the achieved correlations between LPC scores and scales of cognitive complexity. It would imply that high LPC leaders are more likely to differentiate among objects in their environment and to be less inclined to perceive phenomena in stereotypical ways. However, while this interpretation of the LPC scale has received support (e.g. Rice and Chemers, 1975), others have failed to confirm it (e.g. Larson and Rowland, 1974). In other words, this interpretation seems to have fared fairly poorly in a manner not unlike its predecessor. Indeed, it seems to have given way to the 'motivational hierarchy' interpretation as early as 1972 (Fiedler, 1972). This interpretation posits a hierarchy of motives in which high LPC leaders are seen as exhibiting a relationship orientation as a primary goal, but have a task orientation as secondary goals which surface when the primary goals are satisfied. The goal hierarchy of the low LPC person is the opposite of this profile, in that the task is the chief area of concern, whilst relationships are secondary goals. This interpretation would go a long way towards explaining why, for example, low LPC persons are not always as task oriented as the early interpretation of the scales implied. It could occur because the low LPC leader would be expected to emphasize personal relationships when the situation is very favourable. In less favourable circumstances, the primary goal of an emphasis on the task is evident. This interpretation has also been found empirically wanting (e.g. Rice and Chemers, 1975).[3]

Schriesheim and Kerr's (1977) suggestion that LPC is a measure in search of a meaning would seem to have considerable substance. Even Fiedler has expressed his exasperation:

> For nearly 20 years we have been attempting to correlate it with every conceivable personality trait and every conceivable behaviour observation score. By and large these analyses have been uniformly fruitless. (Fiedler and Chemers, 1974, p. 74)

In part, much of the controversy about the meaning of the LPC scale derives from Fiedler's insistence that it provides a measure of leadership *style*. As Rice (1978a) has observed, this view implies a rather idiosyncratic notion of leadership style. In the bulk of leadership research, 'style' and 'behaviour' are used virtually interchangeably (although it was suggested at the end of the last chapter that there may be a case for treating them as distinct from one another). Yet in Fiedler's conceptualization 'leadership style refers to the underlying needs and motives of the leader, not the overt behaviour patterns displayed by the leader' (Rice, 1978a, p. 1231). For example, in referring to the LPC scale as a measure of 'a very important personality variable' (Fiedler and Chemers, 1974, p. 74), Fiedler's underlying conceptualization of leadership style seems to clash with the interpretation with which researchers have typically operated. Consequently, Fiedler's somewhat unusual understanding of the concept may have made many researchers uneasy about the implications of his model for leadership research in general.

The validity of the Contingency Model

Quite aside from what the LPC scale means, writers on leadership have clashed a great deal over whether the Fiedler model is correct. It is easy to see why from Table 5.1, for an examination of rows 2a and 2b reveal often wide disparities in the magnitude and direction of the correlations for each octant, which an emphasis upon median correlations (row 3) tends to obscure. This summary of the findings, which was gathered from Fiedler's (1978c) own review, is supported by a slightly later one by Hosking (1981) which examined only those studies which constituted 'adequate tests' of the model.[4] In effect, Hosking's review entailed rejecting examinations of the model which departed significantly from its technical requirements or its underlying presuppositions. A comparison of rows 2a and 2b with 4a and 4b confirms a wide range of findings. Only octants 1 and 5 seem to result in relatively consistent findings. Fiedler appears relatively unconcerned about the range of findings that the model seems to engender in respect of each octant, largely because the vast majority of the correlations are in the direction predicted by the model. Others have been dissatisfied with this suggestion pointing out that the majority of correlations do not achieve statistical significance (e.g. Ashour, 1973).

One of the chief problems with assessing the validity of the model, then, is that there is disagreement over whether or not tests of it are supportive. Unfavourable reviews of the evidence by a number of writers (e.g. Ashour, 1973; Schriesheim and Kerr, 1977) bring forth protests from Fiedler (1973; 1977 respectively) to the effect that his reading of the evidence points to the validity of the model. One of the studies most frequently cited by Fiedler as providing strong support for the model is an experimental study carried out at the US Military Academy at West Point (Chemers and Skrzypek, 1972). None of the studies which make up the basis for the summary provided in Table 5.1 examined all eight octants within a single research design. The West Point study sought to redress this possible problem. The eight octants were experimentally created. Leaders were assigned to four-man cadet groups in terms of how well they were liked, thereby creating favourable and unfavourable leader-member relations contexts. Task structure was manipulated by assigning one of two tasks which differed in this respect. Position power differences were created by telling some groups that the leader's evaluation of their performance could contribute to their future military careers by virtue of the grades they received; the other groups were told that the evaluation would have no effect. The correlations obtained for each octant are arrayed in row 6 of Table 5.1. When compared with either rows .1 or 3, it can be seen that the pattern of correlations is highly congruent with the pattern of median correlations obtained in a range of studies reviewed by Fiedler. However, Hosking (1981) suggests caution in following Fiedler's enthusiasm, since the magnitude of these correlations is rarely great, suggesting that the amount of variation being 'explained' by the LPC scale is fairly small. Further, none of the correlations seems to achieve statistical significance.

Other issues which have a bearing on the model's validity may be mentioned. The assumption of the model that leadership affects group performance may be questioned. Research on students reported by Farris (1975) found that as group performance improved, 'leaders' ' LPC scores increased, while poorer performance led to a tendency for LPC scores to decline. Indeed, the degree of stability of LPC scores has been a general area of controversy. Correlations between initial and subsequent adminis- trations of the scale to samples varies enormously from .01 to .92 with a median of .67 (Rice, 1978b), but writers differ substantially in respect of whether they take the LPC scale to be unstable (Rice, 1978b; Schriesheim, Bannister and Money, 1979; Rice, 1979). In any event, the possibility of the pattern of causality being the reverse of that assumed by the model is disconcerting. Secondly, the tendency for most researchers to administer the LPC score to designated or putative leaders obviates the possibility of examining informal leadership processes. An exception to this statement is an experimental study using undergraduates as subjects, in which leaders were allowed to emerge in small task-centred groups (Schneier, 1978). The evidence suggests that the study had Octant 2 characteristics. It was found that the correlation between the LPC score of the emergent informal leaders and group performance was $-.55$, which is not only consistent with the model but also the largest negative correlation achieved for Octant 2. It would seem that the distinction between appointed and emergent leadership is of considerable interest to the Fiedler model.

Thirdly, there has been a tendency for writers on the Contingency Model to stress the differences between high and low LPC leaders. However, as Shiflett (1973) has observed many people to whom the scale is administered will fall within a middle range, thereby engendering problems of interpreting their leadership styles. This problem was addressed by Kennedy (1982) in an analysis of data collected on thirteen independent samples from a number of contexts, though predominantly military. Kennedy was able to conduct his analysis across all eight octants. He found that middle LPC leaders produced better performance scores than either high or low LPC leaders in five of the octants (2, 4, 5, 6 and 7). In fact, the performance of middle LPC leaders was consistently high in terms of all eight octants. Kennedy regards this finding as not just an important qualification to the model, but also providing support for it. However, since these findings suggest that the situation had little impact on whether the middle LPC leader is effective or not, the general import of the model is not confirmed. Nonetheless, as pointed out above, in his more recent work, Fiedler (Fiedler and Chemers, 1984) has introduced the notion of the middle LPC leader more systematically, but even here there is a tendency to polarize the discussion in terms of high and low LPC scores.

Fourthly, the adequacy of the conceptualization of 'the situation' may be questioned in view of the limited range of attributes which it is usually taken to comprise. Fiedler seems aware of this problem (Fiedler, 1978c, p. 66) and mentions that moderating variables like situational stress and leader experience and training are increasingly being considered. Of particular interest to the student of organizations is the inclusion by Csoka (1975) of the mechanistic/organic distinction associated with Burns and Stalker (1961). This pairing denotes whether an organization is highly structured and stable (mechanistic) or unstructured, fluid, and imbued with ambiguity (organic). A study of Army dining hall stewards suggests that low LPC leaders generate better performance in a mechanistic context, whereas high LPC leaders do better in an organic situation.

By now, the reader should have a sense of the very considerable controversy which surrounds the Contingency Model. Many researchers within the field of leadership would find it difficult to agree with the bold assertion that it is 'one of the . . . best validated theories' (Fiedler and Chemers, 1984, p. 6). The fact that there are leadership researchers who would agree with this statement merely testifies to the controversies which surround it. Indeed, many commentators like Ashour (1973) would take issue with the statement simply in terms of whether it is a 'theory'. In the light of so much discord over the model, it is possibly surprising to the reader that in more recent years Fiedler has been shifting his attention increasingly towards the application of its constituent ideas. It is to this area that we shall now turn.

The Leader Match concept

Fiedler's views about the practical implications of his ideas first gained a public airing in a classic article graphically entitled 'Engineer the job to fit the manager' (Fiedler, 1965). He suggests that the traditional approaches to seeking to develop effective leadership in organizations – selection and training – are not necessarily the best. A reliance on selection is a problem because it may be very difficult to find people with appropriate combinations of technical qualifications and leadership style. Training, by contrast, is 'difficult, costly, and time-consuming' (Fiedler, 1965, p. 721). In proposing an alternative, Fiedler draws on the Contingency Model and suggests that a particular leadership style (as measured by the LPC) will be more effective in some situational contexts (as indicated by the three dimensions of situational favourableness) but not others. Accordingly he proposes:

> It is certainly easier to place people in a situation compatible with their natural leadership style than to force them to adapt to the demands of the job. (Fiedler, 1965, p. 121)

In other words, the focus of diagnosis and change is not the leader's style but the situation.

Out of this broad orientation Fiedler developed the Leader Match approach to leadership training. The chief emphasis of this approach is a self-teaching manual (Fiedler and Chemers, 1984) which contains explanations of the central ideas, instruments which the leader completes to ascertain his LPC score and situational context, and self-administered tests of the trainee's understanding of the programme. The aim of the approach is for the leader to learn how to diagnose the favourableness of his situation and, in the light of his LPC score, to change it so as to match his leadership style. Alternatively, he may seek to engineer himself into jobs within his firm which better fit his leadership style. Leaders are described as relationship-motivated, task-motivated, and socio-independent in accordance with whether they achieve high, low or medium LPC scores respectively. The underlying understanding of leadership style is the 'motivational hierarchy' approach briefly summarized above. The emphasis within the manual seems to be on the high and low LPC leaders, with those scoring in the middle of the range tending to be seen as a residual category.

Fiedler and his co-workers have conducted a number of validation tests of the Leader Match programme, most of which are briefly summarized in the first chapter of the new manual. These studies, which have been conducted in a diversity of settings, all suggest that leaders with Leader Match training perform better than those with either no training or who have undergone an alternative programme. However, it is difficult to avoid being uneasy about a training programme whose theoretical and empirical basis many commentators believe to be at the very least contentious. As Hosking and Schriesheim (1978, p. 500) have succinctly put it: 'If the Contingency Theory is invalid, so is leader match.' A further difficulty to which both they and Kabanoff (1981) have drawn attention is that the dimensions of situational favourableness may themselves contribute to group performance. For example, in a re-analysis of the Chemers and Skrzypek (1972) West Point study, Shiflett (1973, p. 434) found that leader-member relations had a very strong independent effect on performance. It was by far the most important contributing factor to variation in performance, much more so than any of the leadership style plus situational context combinations which the model suggests should be more important. It may be that the positive findings of validation studies which compare Leader Match trained groups with control groups can in part be explained by such effects.

The Leader Match idea is likely to remain controversial as long as the Contingency Model from which it is derived suffers from conflicting views about *its* validity. The main contribution of the Contingency Model has been to provide an approach to the study of leadership in which situational factors are not merely residual phenomena but central ingredients of an account of leadership effectiveness. While the Fiedler approach has attracted a good deal of controversy, the essence of the model has been enormously influential. The suggestion that a leader's effectiveness is contingent upon the situation has found much more favour than the specific model with which Fiedler has been associated. The contingency approaches to the study of leadership which will be discussed below can be seen as alternative formulations to Fiedler's Contingency Model.

House's path-goal theory of leadership

While Fiedler's approach to the study of leadership has often been denigrated for lacking a theoretical framework (e.g. Ashour, 1973), the same cannot be said of House's influential path-goal approach which in large part is an application of the ideas of the 'expectancy theory' of work motivation to the domain of leadership. While a number of varieties of this theory exist, the fundamental tenets have been retained in most of the formulations. In essence, expectancy theorists propose that people choose levels of effort at which they are prepared to work. The choice of a high level of effort is contingent upon their assessment of whether it leads to good performance and the value (called 'valence' in the language of expectancy theory) of good performance to them. While the theory has been subjected to considerable criticism and the research which emanates from it is fraught with methodological difficulties (Mitchell, 1979), it has been adapted by Robert J. House to the context of the leader's ability to motivate his subordinates.

The early formulation supplied by House (1973) was rapidly revised (House and Dessler, 1974; House and Mitchell, 1974) and it is upon the more recent versions that the following explication draws. According to this formulation:

> the motivational functions of the leader consist of increasing personal payoffs to subordinates for work goal attainment, and making the path to these payoffs easier to travel by clarifying it, reducing roadblocks and pitfalls, and increasing the opportunities for personal satisfaction en route. (House and Dessler, 1974, p. 31)

In other words, the leader is an important source of motivation insofar as his behaviour can enhance the desirability of good performance in the eyes of his subordinates and facilitates goal attainment for them. If the subordinate believes that a high level of effort and hence good performance lead to desirable outcomes, he or she will work harder. Desirable outcomes might involve greater pay or prestige. If the perceived outcomes are undesirable, the subordinate will not be motivated to work hard. Undesirable outcomes might include loss of prestige, or greater personal risk. The most recent formulations of the approach (House and Mitchell, 1974; Filley, House and Kerr, 1976) examine four kinds of leader behaviour which may have an impact upon the motivational processes which the theory emphasizes:

1   Instrumental Leadership (sometimes called 'Directive'). This form of leader behaviour entails a systematic clarification of what is expected of subordinates, how work should be accomplished, each person's role and the like.
2   Supportive Leadership. Such behaviour entails a concern on the leader's part for his subordinates' well-being and status. The supportive leader tends to be friendly and approachable.
3   Participative Leadership. This notion, which will be familiar from the last chapter, denotes a consultative approach in which the leader seeks to involve subordinates in decision-making.
4   Achievement-oriented Leadership. Such leaders set high performance goals and exhibit confidence in their subordinates' ability to attain lofty standards.

According to the path-goal theory, the extent to which each of these categories of leader behaviour will have a beneficial impact upon subordinate performance and job satisfaction is contingent upon two broad classes of situational factors. The first of these is the personal characteristics of subordinates. According to House and Mitchell (1974), subordinates' characteristics are likely to affect their perception of whether the leader's behaviour is 'an immediate source of satisfaction or as instrumental to future satisfaction' (p. 85). Attributes such as their level of authoritarianism or whether they are 'externals' or 'internals' in terms of the Locus of Control scale or their perceptions of their task-related abilities are proposed as potential moderators of the effects of particular types of leader behaviour. The second broad class of situational factors is 'environmental' and comprises: the nature of the subordinates' tasks, the formal authority system of the organization, and the primary work group. It may be, for example, that the subordinates' task is highly structured. It is clear to them what needs to be done, as well as how and when. Instrumental leadership may lead to excessive control of subordinate behaviour, and so occasion resentment and dissatisfaction. When the task is unstructured, subordinates may experience confusion and role ambiguity, so that their ability to recognize how their effort will lead to better performance is jeopardized. When such conditions exist, it is necessary to clarify the task and the procedures for task accomplishment, implying that instrumental leadership is likely to be preferable.

The bulk of the research emanating from the path-goal tradition has tended to focus upon the instrumental and supportive leader behaviour types. Initially, the Ohio scales of Initiating Structure and Consideration were used as surrogate measures for these ideas, but more recent researchers have tended to develop their own instruments or derivatives of the Ohio scales. A number of outcome measures have been examined, including job satisfaction, subordinate performance, and the like, in spite of the fact that ultimately the path-goal approach seems to relate primarily to issues concerned with task achievement and performance. There has been a tendency for the role of the personal characteristics of subordinates as a potential mediating variable in respect of leader behaviour-outcome relationships to be under-researched. Among the environmental group of situational factors, the degree of task structure, the subordinate's hierarchical level or perceived role ambiguity have been prominent foci of attention. The early studies which the theory spawned tended to use static correlational research designs, but more recently researchers have been employing longitudinal designs in their investigations. In spite of the relatively short life of this tradition, it has attracted a good deal of empirical attention to which it is now proposed to turn. The procedure adopted by other writers (e.g. House and Mitchell, 1974; Filley, House and Kerr, 1976; Yukl, 1981) of summarizing the research evidence under each of the four categories of leader behaviour will be followed.

1 Instrumental Leadership (IL)

Since IL is supposed to involve the imposition by the leader of a high level of structure on the task at hand, when the latter is highly structured this form of leadership may be unnecessary. This proposition would suggest that the level of task structure will moderate the effects of IL. One might also anticipate that the subordinate's level in the hierarchy will moderate its effects in a similar fashion, as higher level jobs tend to be less routine and more ambiguous. One of the first tests of these ideas was a study by House and Dessler (1974) of employees at a range of hierarchical levels in each of two companies. The researchers examined the impact of a derivative of the Ohio Initiating Structure measure (as a surrogate for IL) on perceived role clarity, intrinsic and extrinsic satisfaction, and on subordinates' expectations of the extent to which their effort has an impact on their task performance and of the likelihood of good performance being rewarded. These two expectations are referred to in the research literature as Expectancy I and II respectively. It was found that IL is negatively correlated with subordinate satisfaction when tasks are highly structured; when there is little structure, the relationship becomes positive. There was also some evidence to suggest that when task structure is fairly high the impact of IL on the two notions of expectancy is negative, but when it is low the relationship is positive. The relationship of IL with role clarity failed to follow any clear pattern when degrees of task structure were investigated as potential moderators. This is surprising because the theory suggests that when task structure is low, IL compensates for the ensuing role ambiguity that is inherent in such circumstances by clarifying what the subordinate is supposed to be doing. This in turn clarifies the expectancies held by subordinates who are better able to perceive how their effort can relate to their performance and the implications of their performance for likely rewards. As a result, they are likely to be more satisfied and their performance will be enhanced. Quite apart from the difficulties inherent in inferring a sequence of events such as this from a static study, the apparently indeterminate effects of IL on role clarity (the obverse of role ambiguity) under varying degrees of task structure poses a difficulty for the theory. Nonetheless, the House and Dessler study was one of a number of investigations which, according to House and Mitchell (1974), provide support for the path-goal theory's hypothesis about the effects of IL on satisfaction.

A number of studies have failed to provide support for these ideas, however, as House and Mitchell (1974) recognized in their review. An early example is an investigation of paramedical and support personnel in a US university medical centre by Szilagyi and Sims (1974). The impact of IL (as measured by Initiating Structure) on subordinate satisfaction was investigated. The results were somewhat mixed in that perceived role ambiguity only exhibited a strong moderating relationship on one of the four occupational clusters examined. Even more disconcerting was the finding that the path-goal theory predictions for the effects of IL on performance were not confirmed. Szilagyi and Sims found that role ambiguity had virtually no effect on the relationship between IL and subordinate performance. A study by Stinson and Johnson (1975) drawing on data on military officers, civil service personnel, and project engineers found that both the amount of task structure and task repetitiveness moderated the effects of Initiating Structure on subordinate satisfaction, but in a manner opposite to that which path-goal theory would lead one to anticipate. In other words, there was a strong positive correlation between Initiating Structure and measures of satisfaction among those subordinates with *higher* levels of task structure and task repetitiveness. Among those with low scores on these two task attributes, the correlations between

Initiating Structure and satisfaction were either negative or weakly positive. A pattern of mixed findings of this kind was apparent in a review by Schriesheim and von Glinow (1977) of studies which examined the suggestion that lower levels of task structure engender a strong positive relationship between IL and both job satisfaction and role clarity. The balance of the findings was slightly in favour of the path-goal hypotheses about IL.

One reason for the mixed pattern of support may be that there are problems with the measurement of IL. Schriesheim and von Glinow suggest that studies which use the Ohio SBDQ measure of Initiating Structure and its derivatives tend to produce results which fail to confirm path-goal theory predictions. Those which are based on the LBDQ-X11 or its derivatives (like House and Dessler's measure) tend to confirm the notion that task structure or role clarity moderate the effects of IL on satisfaction. Another attempt to come to terms with the pattern of mixed results is House and Mitchell's (1974) suggestion that the personal characteristics of subordinates may moderate the effects of IL. They point to an unpublished study which indicates that the level of authoritarianism exhibited by subordinates is an important moderating variable. Among workers in a manufacturing firm doing routine, repetitive work IL was preferred by authoritarian, closed-minded individuals, but non-instrumental leadership was preferred by those who exhibited little authoritarianism. However, this study also found that when faced with non-routine, ambiguous tasks, IL was preferred irrespective of levels of authoritarianism. A finding such as this may go some way towards explaining the discrepant findings.

More recent research reveals a similar pattern of mixed findings. Dessler and Valenzi's (1977) research in a manufacturing company found that among those workers doing routine, structured tasks Initiating Structure and intrinsic satisfaction were strongly correlated in a positive direction. Among those doing less routine work, the effect of Initiating Structure was negligible. These findings are in direct contrast to the path-goal-theory notion that people doing unstructured tasks will welcome IL, whereas those involved in routine work will react against it. Research by Schriesheim and Schriesheim (1980) on managerial and clerical workers in a US public utility found that levels of task structure did not moderate the effects of IL on a variety of job satisfaction measures. By contrast, a study of bank and manufacturing employees by Schriesheim and De Nisi (1981) found that the amount of task variety (a similar notion to lack of task structure) moderated the effects of IL on subordinate satisfaction with supervision in a manner congruent with path-goal theory.

Clearly, then, the evidence is mixed, although there is a fair degree of support for the tenets of path-goal theory. While the effects of IL on satisfaction measures have been emphasized in this section, it should be borne in mind that when performance has been the dependent variable results have been less favourable to path-goal theory (Mitchell, 1979). Where possible, the studies reported in this section will be used in discussing the three other categories of leader behaviour.

2   Supportive Leadership (SL)

According to path-goal theory 'supportive leadership will have its most positive effect on subordinate satisfaction for subordinates who work on stressful, frustrating or dissatisfying tasks' (House and Mitchell, 1974, p. 91). When work exhibits such characteristics, SL goes some way towards anaesthetizing its effects by making it more bearable. When tasks are not stressful, frustrating or dissatisfying it is assumed that SL will not make a great deal of difference to subordinate satisfaction or the amount of effort someone is prepared to expend. When tasks are stressful, by contrast, SL may enhance the subordinates' confidence and underline the important contribution they make so that they may more readily perceive the relationship between their effort and goal attainment. House and Dessler (1974) proposed that the level of task structure would moderate the effects of SL. They argued that unstructured tasks are more complex and varied, and hence more intrinsically satisfying, thereby rendering SL redundant. When tasks are highly structured SL will be positively related to satisfaction and the 'expectancies' because 'supportive leadership is assumed to reduce frustration resulting from highly structured dissatisfying tasks' (House and Dessler, 1974, p. 41). This suggestion received some support in their research in that SL seems to have a stronger positive impact on intrinsic satisfaction when task structure is high. The same was only true in respect of the relationship with extrinsic satisfaction for one of their two samples. The evidence was only partially supportive of the view that task structure would moderate the effects of SL on the 'expectancy' notions. In the Szilagyi and Sims (1974) university hospital study, the administrative sub-group exhibited a high level of role ambiguity, but was also found to reveal strong relationships between SL and satisfaction. According to path-goal theory, the impact of SL should have been negligible since their level of task structure was low. In the Stinson and Johnson (1975) study, leader Consideration seems to have had a more pronounced impact on satisfaction measures when task structure and repetitiveness were high, thereby providing some confirmation of path-goal hypotheses.

In their review of the relevant research, House and Mitchell (1974) felt that the predictions of path-goal theory regarding the effects of SL had received a great deal of confirmation. By the time of Schriesheim and von Glinow's (1977) later review there seemed to be more evidence which was not supportive, though Mitchell (1979) is probably correct in his view that the balance of evidence is less mixed than for IL. The more recent research by Schriesheim and Schriesheim (1980) found that SL had a very strong impact on a range of satisfaction measures (work, pay, supervision, etc.) and job clarity, but that task structure levels did not moderate the relationships to any substantial degree. This finding suggests that, contrary to what path-goal theory would lead one to expect, SL is strongly related to a number of dependent variables, but that the relationships are in large part not situationally contingent.

The overall balance of the evidence is fairly supportive of the predictions derived from path-goal theory regarding this dimension of leader behaviour. Nonetheless, the number of studies which have failed to provide confirmation is slightly disconcerting.

3   Participative Leadership (PL)

This notion was addressed in some detail in the last chapter, but it is necessary to return to it in this context, because path-goal theory provides a particular formulation of the reasons for the potential impact of PL on an individual's productivity. Mitchell (1973) provides four possible reasons for believing that PL enhances subordinate motivation. Firstly, in a participative climate people are likely to be better informed, so that they will have a more complete understanding of the relationships between the amount of effort they expend and goal-attainment. They will also better understand which task-related patterns of behaviour are rewarded and which are not. Participation, then, clarifies the relationships between paths and goals. Secondly, Mitchell suggests that subordinates are more likely to be able to select goals they value under PL. For example, they may select goals whose attainment directly reflects the amount of effort they are prepared to expend. Thirdly, subordinates operating in a participative environment are likely to select goals to which they are more personally attached, so that the motivation to perform well may be generated by the subordinate's 'ego-involvement' in the task. Finally, Mitchell points out that participation enhances the individual's control over his work and suggests that people are more likely to work harder under such circumstances, since people will recognize that the consequences of their effort depend more upon themselves than upon others or external factors.

The evidence which has been accumulated on the impact of situational factors on the PL-outcome relationship within the path-goal tradition has pointed to the need to take into account environmental and subordinate characteristics simultaneously. An exploratory investigation of the role of task structure as a moderator in the House and Dessler (1974) study failed to find a clear pattern of relationships in both samples. Further, in their review of the relevant literature, House and Mitchell (1974) recognized that subordinates' personal characteristics, such as authoritarianism, do not always moderate the effects of PL as the Tosi (1970) study mentioned in the last chapter indicates. An investigation of employees at a range of hierarchical levels in a manufacturing firm by Schuler (1976) points to the need to take into account both environmental and personal characteristics. It seems that people are more interested in work which is unstructured because of the variety and challenge it involves. When tasks are unstructured the impact of PL on job satisfaction is unaffected by subordinates' personal characteristics. However, when the task was highly structured, PL led to job satisfaction only for subordinates who exhibited high scores on a scale of authoritarianism. Thus, it seems that among people with a strong drive for independence and self-direction, PL leads to job satisfaction. Clearly, people's preferences about self-control in their activities have an impact on the relationship between PL and job satisfaction only when tasks are routine. When the task is unstructured and ego-involving, PL enhances job satisfaction irrespective of their personal characteristics.

While interesting, these ideas rest uneasily with evidence that people are often confused by unstructured, unclear situations (Bryman, 1976) and often seem to prefer the directiveness of instrumental leadership where such circumstances exist (see above). Sometimes, unstructured tasks seem to be presented by path-goal theorists as a 'problem' for subordinates which IL may help to alleviate; on other occasions, they are presented as ego involving and obviate the need for PL. It may be that Schuler's operationalization of task characteristics as 'task repetitiveness' refers to a very specific aspect of the task but insofar as it measures 'the variety of task activities and the frequency of occurrence of similar task demands' (Schuler, 1976, p. 322) it is highly congruent with the idea of task structure. This confusion needs to be reconciled before the elaboration of path-goal theory can proceed very far. Nonetheless, the path-goal formulation of the potential effects of PL is an interesting one which departs from the atheoretical content of much of the evidence presented in the previous chapter.

4   Achievement-Oriented Leadership

According to the path-goal theory 'achievement-oriented leadership will cause subordinates to strive for higher standards of performance and to have more confidence in the ability to meet challenging goals' (House and Mitchell, 1974, p. 91). As such, leadership of this kind enhances the subordinate's expectation that difficult goals can be achieved through greater effort. Very little research has been conducted in relation to this aspect of leadership but an unpublished investigation suggests that when subordinates are performing ambiguous, non-repetitive tasks, achievement-oriented leaders are more likely to enhance their confidence that their effort would yield effective performance (reported in House and Mitchell, 1974, p. 91). When tasks were only moderately ambiguous achievement-oriented leadership had little effect on subordinate expectations.

General problems with path-goal theory

The path-goal approach shares many of the same problems that were identified in relation to approaches to the study of leadership style, like the Ohio tradition. To some extent, this is not surprising in view of the heavy reliance on Ohio measures that pervades a good deal of the research within the path-goal tradition. The problem of discrepant findings, the frequent employment of group average methods of describing leaders, the near absence of the investigation of informal leadership, and the non-observation of leader behaviour are all evident in the studies emanating from the theory. The criticism levelled at the Ohio studies that there is insufficient attention devoted to situational factors is not appropriate, since this kind of analysis is central to the path-goal approach. The problem of causality, however, is very pertinent, since many of the investigations summarized above were static, cross-sectional studies. A longitudinal investigation by Greene (1979) provides evidence of the problems of assuming causal direction from cross-sectional studies with a particular focus on path-goal ideas. Greene studied sixty leader-subordinate dyads drawn from the financial and marketing divisions of a firm. Measures of IL and SL were developed from the Ohio Initiating Structure and Consideration sub-scales of the LBDQ-X11. Measurements of both leader behaviour and a number of dependent variables were gleaned on two occasions which were three months apart. Some of Greene's findings were supportive of path-goal theory. Both IL and SL were found to enhance subordinate satisfaction under different conditions of task structure. When task structure was low, IL was found to lead to greater intrinsic work satisfaction; when task structure was high, SL led to greater satisfaction. In each case, the leadership variable was found to be the causal variable. However, in medium and high structure conditions, subordinate performance was found to 'cause' IL. Only in the low task structure condition was there some evidence that IL induced higher performance. Furthermore, subordinate performance was found to 'cause' SL, almost irrespective of levels of task structure. It would seem that as in other studies, such as Barrow (1976) and Lowin and Craig (1968) subordinate performance is a more important determinant of leader behaviour than *vice versa*.

A problem with research relating to the path-goal theory until quite recently is that a great deal of it became rather stereotyped. Research tended to focus on the IL and SL dimensions of leader behaviour, even though other aspects of what leaders do could be seen as potentially important. For example, the study of leader reward behaviour along the lines developed by researchers like Sims and Szilagyi (1975) and Podsakoff *et al.* (1984) could provide insights into the impact of leaders on subordinates' beliefs that greater effort will result in desired rewards. Similarly, in spite of House's insistence that a range of moderating variables might be examined, there has been an overwhelming emphasis upon the role of task structure in this respect. Furthermore, the investigation of combinations of leadership behaviour has rarely been undertaken.

Two studies which go some way towards meeting these points can briefly be described. Firstly, a study by Griffin (1980) of 171 manual employees in a manufacturing firm examined all four types of leader behaviour proposed by House and Mitchell (1974). Further, instead of task structure he examined the moderating effects of 'individual-task congruence' which 'refers to the extent to which the growth needs of the individual match the motivational characteristics of the task being performed' (Griffin, 1980, pp. 665-6). In terms of this variable, a task may exhibit high or low levels of scope for employee growth, while the subordinate may exhibit high or low growth needs. This approach suggests a 2 × 2 scheme in which the two dichotomies present four possible individual-task combinations. It seems reasonable to assume that the extent to which an individual's 'growth needs' fit with the opportunities that the task offers for growth will affect his views about, for example, the likelihood that enhanced effort will lead to successful goal attainment. For example, SL may be highly desirable to subordinates with high growth needs but little scope for realizing them in their work. Supportive leadership could compensate for the disenchanting effects of such an experience. This particular notion received some support in that SL led to greater overall satisfaction, and satisfaction with both the job and supervisor, in such circumstances. Further, when people have low growth needs but high task scope, there was evidence that IL promotes satisfaction, presumably because it imposes a structure on the work of relatively unmotivated people. However, in neither case was better performance a consequence of the moderated effects of SL or IL, thereby echoing Mitchell's (1979) view that the evidence tends to be stronger when satisfaction measures, rather than performance indicators, constitute the dependent variable. This tendency is very troublesome to the path-goal approach which is ultimately seeking to explain the leadership circumstances which result in an enhanced preparedness to expend effort. Further, Griffin found that when individual growth needs and task scope are jointly high or low, there seems to be little that leaders can do to promote greater subordinate satisfaction. While the results of this research are slightly equivocal, particularly in relation to performance, it provides an alternative to the ubiquitous task structure as a mediating variable.

Another study which departs from established path-goal research practice is an investigation of clerical and managerial employees in a US public utility by Fulk and Wendler (1982). This study focused on four types of leader behaviour which the researchers deemed to be relevant to the path-goal approach, but only one of them (achievement-oriented behaviour) has been encountered above. The other three are: *contingent approval behaviour* – the use by the leader of positive feedback contingent upon good performance by the subordinate; *arbitrary and punishing behaviour* – autocratic behaviour which demands conformity to the leader's preferences about how work should be done and the use of punishment to increase production; and *leader upward influencing behaviour* – the maintenance of good relationships by the leader with his own superior and the ability to induce the latter to bestow favours on the leader's group. Each of these 'new' depictions of leader behaviour possesses an *a priori* justification for consideration within the path-goal framework. For example, arbitrary and punitive behaviour is likely to lead to confusion about the implications of one's effort for anticipated rewards, and also to occasion resentment. This study further departed from established methodology in that it examined the effects of combinations of the leader behaviour descriptions on subordinate outcomes, without an investigation of situational factors. Two patterns were revealed by the data analysis. One was to suggest that a combination of upward influencing, achievement orientation, contingent approval and low levels of arbitrary and punitive behaviour promotes satisfaction with supervision, a lower willingness to leave, greater role clarity and less anxiety. By contrast, a combination of arbitrary and punitive and achievement-oriented behaviour is deleterious to the first and third of these outcome variables. In a familiar fashion, neither combination exhibited a discernible impact on subordinate performance. This study is important for its suggestive inclusion of alternative conceptualizations of leader behaviour within a path-goal framework, but its static nature, its omission of situational factors, and the familiar lack of association of leadership with performance dampen one's enthusiasm somewhat.

More recently, House (House and Baetz, 1979) has suggested that future developments in path-goal research should seek to include a broader range of moderating variables. One cluster of variables he mentions relates to the extent to which the situation is stressful. One piece of research which has a bearing on this issue is a study of conflict within groups by Katz (1977). On the basis of a study of university teachers and two laboratory experiments, Katz found that greater Initiating Structure leads to greater subordinate satisfaction and performance when there is a high level of affective conflict, i.e. tension arising out of interpersonal relationships. When affective conflict is low, Initiating Structure either has less of an impact or can have a deleterious effect on performance. However, while there is the possibility of adding new situational factors, the early promise of path-goal theory seems to be abating. The discrepant findings, the problem of causality, and the failure of the theory to predict performance in many studies do not offer too much promise. Although a few of the more recent developments hold some promise, it seems likely that unless the basic theory receives more consistent empirical support than hitherto, it will lose its edge as a major focus for research interest in the field of leadership.

Hersey and Blanchard's Situational Leadership theory

The approach considered in this section is a highly prescriptive contingency theory of leader behaviour, which has undergone a number of revisions (Hersey and Blanchard, 1969, 1977, 1982; Hersey, Blanchard and Hambleton, 1980). Indeed, even the nomenclature of the perspective has undergone change, originally being called a 'life cycle theory of leadership'. Unlike the contingency theories associated with Fiedler, House and Vroom, the Situational Leadership theory has not generated a research tradition. To be more precise, there is virtually no evidence to substantiate its fundamental tenets. This absence is surprising in view of the wide popularity of the Situational Leadership theory among personnel managers and training directors, as well as the frequent reference to it in textbooks (Graeff, 1983).

For its description of leader behaviour, the approach draws heavily on the Ohio dimensions of Consideration and Initiating Structure (e.g. Hersey *et al.*, 1980, pp. 98-9). Following the Ohio school's preference for examining the effects of combinations of these two categories of leader behaviour, Hersey and Blanchard produce four basic leader behaviour styles. The latter are drawn from high and low combinations of the two dimensions in a manner similar to Figure 3.1 in Chapter 3. Instead of Initiating Structure, Hersey and Blanchard talk about 'task behaviour' which involves a directive approach by the leader toward each subordinate. The leader explains what, when, where, and how tasks are to be carried out. 'Relationship behaviour', Hersey and Blanchard's equivalent of Consideration, entails the provision of support for subordinates. More precisely, this aspect of leader behaviour involves 'opening up channels of communication, providing socioemotional support, "psychological" strokes, and facilitating behaviours' (Hersey and Blanchard, 1977, p. 104).

The other contingency approaches examined in this chapter propose quite a large number of situational factors which are likely to impinge upon the effectiveness of particular leadership styles. By contrast the Situational Leadership framework posits only one – the task-relevant 'maturity' of the leader's subordinates. This notion refers to 'the willingness and ability of a person to take responsibility for directing his or her own behaviour . . . in relation to a specific task to be performed' (Hersey *et al.*, 1980, p. 100). Maturity comprises two components – psychological and job maturity. The former denotes the subordinate's level of internalized motivation to accomplish the task. Job maturity refers to the subordinate's knowledge, ability and experience to accomplish a task without direction from others. According to Situational Leadership theory a leader needs to gauge the maturity of his or her subordinates before deciding which pattern of leadership behaviour is required. Figure 5.4 depicts the relationship between leader behaviour and psychological maturity of followers. The bell shaped curve indicates that as the level of maturity changes, a different leadership style is required. When maturity is low in terms of both of its constituent (MI) dimensions, style S1 is required in which task behaviour is emphasized while relationship behaviour is low. At the two intermediate maturity levels (M2 and M3), in which one of the aspects is high and the other is low, styles S2 and S3 respectively are required. Thus, when there is a high level of job maturity but little psychological maturity, a high relationship-low task behaviour is required. When maturity is high in both respects, there should be low levels of both task and relationship behaviour. The four styles S1, S2, S3 and S4 have been dubbed Telling, Selling, Participating and Delegating respectively.

Clearly, according to this approach it is vital for the leader to determine the maturity level of each subordinate before deciding which style should be adopted. To this end, Hersey and Blanchard have developed scales on which the leader is supposed to rate the maturity level of each subordinate and for the latter to rate himself. According to Hersey and Blanchard leadership styles may be negotiated by leader and subordinate. For example, when the two parties disagree over the subordinate's level of maturity, it may be necessary for the leader to defer to the subordinate's views and adopt a leadership style in accordance with this view. This possibility forces one to question how far the maturity level of subordinates is deterministic in this model, if a leader may have to adopt what he believes to be an inappropriate style in terms of his own assessments. As maturity improves, so greater latitude can be allowed to

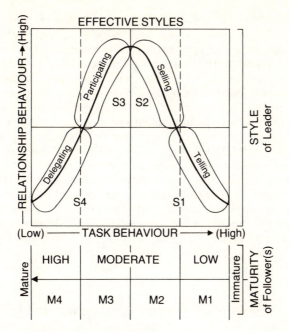

Figure 5.4 *Situational Leadership theory*

Source: P. Hersey/K.H. Blanchard, *Management of Organizational Behaviour: Utilizing Human Resources*, 3rd edn, © 1977, p. 170. Reprinted by permission of Prentice-Hall, Inc., Englewood-Cliffs, N.J.

the subordinate, so that leadership style is supposed to be highly responsive to new circumstances.

Hersey *et al.* (1980) provide the example of a restaurant chain in which supervisors and each manager, on the basis of the maturity scales, decided what the appropriate style should be. It was found that the S4 (delegating) style was generally adopted 'because both agreed that this manager was capable of working on his own' (Hersey *et al.*, 1980, p. 118). More supervisory styles tended to be adopted in relation to less experienced managers. Beyond such anecdotal evidence there seems to be little evidence that leaders are more effective when they take into account the maturity level of their followers. Given the considerable following that this approach has engendered, underlined by the hugely successful 'one minute manager' books (e.g. Blanchard and Johnson, 1982) which derive from it, the apparent absence of validation studies is surprising.

A number of conceptual confusions and deficiencies in the general approach have been identified by Graeff (1983). For example, there is no rationale for associating M2 and M3 and S2 and S3. Why could an S3 style not be equally appropriate where psychological maturity is high, but job maturity low (i.e. M2)? An aspect of the theory which has produced relatively little comment is the fact that the decision to adopt a particular style derives from an exchange between a leader and a particular subordinate. While this level of analysis is consistent with the Vertical Dyad Linkage notion of concentrating on leader-member exchanges (e.g. Graen and Cashman, 1975), it raises the possibility of leaders acting in quite diverse ways in respect of various subordinates in a group for which they have responsibility. The possibility of disaffection as a result of such differential treatment ought to be considered as a potential contaminant of the empirical relationships implicit in the model.

The main contribution of the Situational Leadership approach, as writers like Graeff (1983) and Yukl (1981) have suggested, is that it suggests that leaders need to be flexible in their behaviour. In addition, it underlines the importance of situational factors, thereby adding to the other approaches dealt with in this chapter. Beyond this, its concentration on just one situational variable, and the absence of a research tradition deriving from it, render it of limited utility for leadership researchers. Ironically, it may be the very simplicity of the model and the absence of negative evidence that has made it so popular within management circles!

The Vroom-Yetton contingency model

While the Vroom and Yetton (1973) contingency model shares some basic principles with the approaches adopted by writers such as Fiedler and House, it departs from them in a number of ways, one of the most fundamental of which is that it is more manifestly normative. The aim of the approach is to enable the leader to enhance both the quality of the decisions that he or she makes and also their acceptability to subordinates. In seeking to enhance these two outcomes, the model seeks to specify the impact of varying degrees of participative leadership on the quality and acceptability of decisions. The model explicitly suggests that a number of situational factors impinge on the likelihood that either an autocratic or a participative approach will be appropriate, in the light of these two criteria. The model has undergone a number of reformulations, one of the most important of which was a shift away from an exclusive focus upon group-level participative methods for dealing with problems. In a slightly later version (Vroom and Jago, 1974), participative approaches to dealing with problems which affect only one subordinate are addressed. However, in order to ease the exposition of a rather complex model, it is proposed to deal only with the group-level depiction of leader behaviour.

The starting point of the model is a problem for which a leader must seek out a solution. In order to deal with the problem different degrees of participative leadership are possible; in other words, the leader may share his decision-making with his subordinates to a greater or lesser extent. Five levels of participation are proposed which follow a code such that A = an autocratic process, C = a consultative process, and G = group decision making. More specifically, the five levels, which seem to owe a good deal to the Tannenbaum and Schmidt (1958) delineation of leadership styles,

Table 5.2   *Taxonomy of decision processes in the Vroom-Yetton model*

AI   You solve the problem or make the decision yourself using the information available to you at the present time.

AII   You obtain any necessary information from subordinates, then decide on a solution to the problem yourself. You may or may not tell subordinates the purpose of your questions or give information about the problem or decision you are working on. The input provided by them is clearly in response to your request for specific information. They do not play a role in the definition of the problem or in generating or evaluating alternative solutions.

CI   You share the problem with the relevant subordinates individually, getting their ideas and suggestions without bringing them together as a group. Then *you* make the decision. This decision may or may not reflect your subordinates' influence.

CII   You share the problem with your subordinates in a group meeting. In this meeting you obtain their ideas and suggestions. Then, *you* make the decision, which may or may not reflect your subordinates' influence.

GII   You share the problem with your subordinates as a group. Together you generate and evaluate alternatives and attempt to reach agreement (consensus) on a solution. Your role is much like that of chairman, coordinating the discussion, keeping it focused on the problem, and making sure that the critical issues are discussed. You can provide the group with information or ideas that you have but you do not try to 'press' them to adopt 'your' solution and are willing to accept and implement any solution that has the support of the entire group.

Source: V.H. Vroom and A. G. Jago, 'On the validity of the Vroom-Yetton model', *Journal of Applied Psychology*, Vol. 63, p. 152. Copyright (1978) by the American Psychological Association. Reprinted by permission of the publisher and authors.

are described in Table 5.2. These five approaches to leadership are on a continuum of participativeness with AI and GII at the extremes.

How does the leader decide which style to adopt? The model proposes seven 'rules' which allow the leader to eliminate step-by-step those styles which are not feasible. The idea is for the leader to follow through each rule in order to discover which style or styles is (or are) appropriate in view of the prevailing circumstances. Vroom and his co-authors use the term 'feasible set' to refer to the style or styles which it is appropriate for the leader to adopt when he or she has considered the implication of each rule for his or her circumstances. The seven rules are described in Table 5.3. The first three rules enable the leader to protect the quality of a decision; rules 4 to 7 protect the acceptance of a decision. The application of each rule enables a particular style or styles to be eliminated from the feasible set. According to the first rule, the Leader Information Rule, if a leader lacks sufficient knowledge or expertise to sort out a problem on his own, AI can be eliminated since the decision would be of poor quality if he failed to obtain information from subordinates. AI can then be eliminated from the feasible set. From this general approach, a decision-tree structure

Table 5.3 *Rules underlying the Vroom-Yetton model*

Rules to Protect the Quality of the Decision

1. The Leader Information Rule

   If the quality of the decision is important and the leader does not possess enough information or expertise to solve the problem by himself, then AI is eliminated from the feasible set.

2. The Goal Congruence Rule

   If the quality of the decision is important and subordinates are not likely to pursue the organization goals in their efforts to solve this problem, then GII is eliminated from the feasible set.

3. The Unstructured Problem Rule

   In decisions in which the quality of the decision is important, if the leader lacks the necessary information or expertise to solve the problem by himself, and if the problem is unstructured, the method of solving the problem should provide for interaction among subordinates likely to possess relevant information. Accordingly, AI, AII, and CI are eliminated from the feasible set.

Rules to Protect the Acceptance of the Decision

4. The Acceptance Rule

   If the acceptance of the decision by subordinates is critical to effective implementation and if it is not certain that an autocratic decision will be accepted, AI and AII are eliminated from the feasible set.

5. The Conflict Rule

   If the acceptance of the decision is critical, an autocratic decision is not certain to be accepted and disagreement among subordinates in methods of attaining the organizational goal is likely, the methods used in solving the problem should enable those in disagreement to resolve their differences with full knowledge of the problem. Accordingly, under these conditions, AI, AII, and CI, which permit no interaction among subordinates and therefore provide no opportunity for those in conflict to resolve their differences, are eliminated from the feasible set. Their use runs the risk of leaving some of the subordinates with less than the needed commitment to the final decision.

6. The Fairness Rule

   If the quality of the decision is unimportant but acceptance of the decision is critical and not certain to result from an autocratic decision, it is important that the decision process used generate the needed acceptance. The decision process used should permit the subordinates to interact with one another and negotiate over the fair method of resolving any differences with full responsibility on them for determining what is fair and equitable. Accordingly, under these circumstances, AI, AII, CI and CII are eliminated from the feasible set.

7. The Acceptance Priority Rule

   If acceptance is critical, not certain to result from an autocratic decision, and if subordinates are motivated to pursue the organizational goals represented in the problem, then methods that provide equal partnership in the decision-making process can provide greater acceptance without risking decision quality. Accordingly, AI, AII, CI and CII are eliminated from the feasible set.

Note: See Table 5.2 for a description of AI, AII, CI, CII and GII.
Source: V.H. Vroom and A.G. Jago, 'On the validity of the Vroom-Yetton model', *Journal of Applied Psychology*, Vol. 63, p. 153. Copyright (1978) by the American Psychological Association. Reprinted by permission of the publisher and authors.

emerges in which the leader follows through the implications of each of the seven rules for his style of leadership. The resulting structure can be found in Figure 5.5. From this analysis, twelve final feasible sets are derived. In some instances (e.g. 2, 5, 6a) only one style of leadership remains in the feasible set after the rules have been applied. On other occasions (e.g. 1, 3, 4) more than one style is left in the feasible set. Indeed, all five styles remain in sets 1 and 3, while only one has been eliminated from sets 4 and 8. How does the leader choose between the various possibilities when alternative styles appear to be equally viable? As Vroom (1976, p. 19) observes, for many feasible sets the model specifies how not to make decisions, rather than how they *should* be made. Two additional rules are proffered to guide the leader. One principle is the time required to make a decision. Since involving subordinates in decisions is time-consuming, autocratic methods ought to be chosen when time is precious (e.g. in an emergency) – or when the leader as a matter of preference believes that time is the chief consideration. This principle would help to guide the leader confronting the ranges of alternatives specified by the feasible sets numbered 1, 3, 4, 7 and 8. This principle reflects a priority being accorded to 'time-efficiency', whereas the second principle relates to 'time-investment'. It recognizes that 'participation contributes to individual and team development and is likely to result in more informed and responsible behaviour by subordinates in the future' (Vroom, 1976, p. 20). This principle implies a longer time perspective, in that the leader may have to trade off more immediate demands by acknowledging that participation is an investment in the future. If a leader seeks to adopt a time-investment strategy, he or she will emphasize more participative approaches within those feasible sets in which a choice exists.

According to the Vroom-Yetton model, a leader should be both autocratic and participative, varying his style according to various situational factors. The authors recognize that personal preferences are likely to impinge on the choice of style adopted, an obvious area being the choice of time-investment or time-efficiency criteria. However, the leadership training programme which derives from the model seeks to minimize the extent to which personal preferences impinge on the decision of which style to adopt. The leader is taught to gain insight into the nature of his leadership style and how it fits with the normative model (Vroom, 1976). In particular, leaders gain insight into the appropriateness of particular styles for the situational circumstances they face. Consequently, while the Vroom approach is in accord with Fiedler's in respect of the need to match the leader and the situation, the two models diverge over how this should be achieved. Fiedler's emphasis is upon changing the situation; Vroom's is on making the leader more aware of the implications of the situation for his behaviour.

The validity of the model

While the Vroom and Yetton (1973) book provided specific support for some of the ideas which make up their model, more general tests of the

A. Does the problem possess a quality requirement?
B. Do I have sufficient information to make a high-quality decision?
C. Is the problem structured?
D. Is acceptance of the decision by subordinates important for effective implementation?
E. If I were to make the decision by myself, am I reasonably certain that it would be accepted by my subordinates?
F. Do subordinates share the organizational goals to be attained in solving this problem?
G. Is conflict among subordinates likely in preferred solutions?

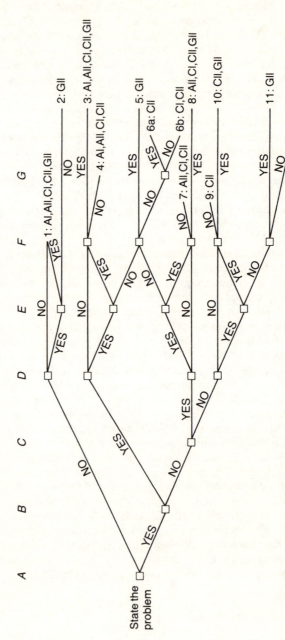

Figure 5.5   *The Vroom-Yetton decision process flowchart*

Reprinted from *Leadership and Decision-Making* by Victor H. Vroom and Phillip W. Yetton by permission of the University of Pittsburgh Press. © 1973 by University of Pittsburgh Press.

model have been less than numerous. Of greatest interest to the overall validity of the model is a study reported by Vroom and Jago (1978) in which ninety-six managers were asked to recall and to describe one successful and one unsuccessful decision-making situation that they had encountered. The managers were unfamiliar with the Vroom-Yetton model. They were asked to report on the decision-making processes that they had employed, as well as the overall effectiveness, quality and acceptability to subordinates of the decision. In 65 per cent of the cases described, the decision-making processes were in conformity with the feasible set of methods prescribed by the model. Very similar percentages had been achieved in studies reported in Vroom and Yetton (1973). Further, Vroom and Jago found that of the managers' accounts which conformed to the feasible set, 68 per cent were successful, whereas of the accounts which did not conform to the feasible set, only 22 per cent were successful. In other words, when managers' behaviour conformed to the dictates of the model, they were much more likely to reach successful decisions. Furthermore, among those accounts of decision-processes which fell outside the feasible set, the resulting decision was more likely to be regarded as successful when only one (or possibly two) rules had been violated. A similar study was carried out on forty-seven owner-managers of UK firms in the cleaning industry by Margerison and Glube (1979). All were franchisees of the same firm, thus enabling the researchers to hold constant a number of possible confounding variables. Leaders were confronted with thirty short cases which represented different problem types for which particular feasible sets were appropriate. A particular problem type might indicate a need for feasible set 4, suggesting a need for AI, AII, CI or CII. Leaders were dichotomized into those scoring above the mean for agreement with the feasible sets, and those below. The researchers found that the high scoring group, that is managers whose styles in response to the problems tended to conform to the model, had firms with higher productivity and workers who were more satisfied with supervision.

While this evidence seems to validate the model rather well, it is not without its problems. The Vroom and Jago study relies excessively on leaders' own reports of the quality and acceptability of decisions and as Vroom recognizes 'it is possible that the outcome of the decision, i.e. its success or lack of success, may influence one's recognition of either or both the process used in making it or the attributes of the situation in ways that might inflate the validity of the model' (Vroom, 1984, p. 25). This suggests that self-reports of decision success and the events which preceded them may be open to bias. While this problem does not apply to the Margerison and Glube study, it is important to realize that the outcome variables in their study (i.e. firm productivity and satisfaction with supervision) are fairly far removed from those to which the Vroom-Yetton model relates (i.e. the quality and acceptability of particular decisions). Nor is the use of the recall approach, as in the Vroom and Jago study, or the 'problem set' methodology used in the Margerison and Glube investigation without problems. It appears that subordinates see their superiors as using the AI style more frequently than their superiors claim to use it; and also, subordinates report less use of the GII style than superiors attribute to themselves (Jago and Vroom, 1975, pp. 113-114). Such findings suggest that there may be inaccuracies in managers' reports of the decision styles.

More recent validation studies have moved away from the methodologies reflected by these two investigations. Field (1982) has employed an experimental methodology, using Canadian business students as subjects. Subjects were allocated to decision-making groups comprising a 'leader', two subordinates, and an observer. Each group had to solve five decision-making problems and were told to use a particular decision process (i.e. AI, AII, CI, CII or GII) in so doing. Broad support for the model was found in that decisions reached through leadership styles within the appropriate feasible set were more likely to be effective than those gained by processes outside it. More specific findings suggested that decision quality is particularly adversely affected by the violation of the unstructured problem rule (rule 3); and that decision acceptance was adversely affected by the violation of rules 4, 6, and 7 (see Table 5.2). An experimental approach was devised for two investigations reported by Heilman, Hornstein, Cage and Herschlag (1984). In both experiments, the broad ideas of the Vroom-Yetton approach were introduced to subjects. In the first investigation, subjects adopted the perspective of the subordinate and were asked to evaluate the behaviour of leaders, as described by written cases, along a number of dimensions. Partial support for the model emerged. Subjects were asked about the likely quality of a decision and its effect on the organization ('task-related outcome') and the decision's likely acceptability and anticipated effect on morale ('socio-emotional outcome'). The researchers found that in accordance with the model, leaders who behaved autocratically when a participative style was called for received low ratings on both outcome measures. However, participative or consultative behaviour received high ratings even when an autocratic style was prescribed by the Vroom-Yetton model. As the authors succinctly put it: 'contrary to the contingency formulation, participative behaviour was seen as effective even when prescriptively inappropriate to the situation' (Heilman *et al.*, 1984, p. 56). A second and similar investigation was carried out on a different sample of subjects, but half took the subordinate perspective and half that of the boss. The authors found that when cast as bosses, the leaders depicted in the descriptions were evaluated in far greater conformity with the model. When autocratic behaviour is prescribed, a participative style gets lower task-related outcome ratings, though slightly higher socio-emotional ratings. When participative behaviour is called for, both outcomes get a much lower rating when the leader behaves autocratically. Such findings also suggest, however, that participativeness is nearly always preferred in socio-emotional terms. While subjects taking the boss's viewpoint will see contingently prescribed behaviour as appropriate in terms of task-relevance, there is a recognition that when the behaviour is autocratic it will not be liked.

General reflections

Overall, there is a fair amount of support for the Vroom-Yetton model, although the problem of the divergences of perspective between leaders and subordinates revealed by the Jago and Vroom (1975) and Heilman *et al.* (1984) studies are troublesome. In addition, there are other conceptual and empirical problems associated with the model, many of which Vroom (1984, pp. 24-5) has himself delineated. Unlike the path-goal approach, the Vroom-Yetton model focuses on the autocracy-participation dimension of leadership style, even though one might anticipate that other aspects of leader behaviour contribute to the adequacy of a decision. It focuses on a limited range of situational variables which impinge on the effectiveness of a particular leadership style, such as the personal attributes of subordinates and the formal organizational context. Further, the tendency to treat the situational factors in Yes/No terms is simplistic, since most of them are more accurately conceptualized as matters of degree. For example, problems vary in the degree of structure that they exhibit; they are not simply structured or unstructured. In addition, as Vroom (1984) has suggested, in many instances leaders may use a combination of decision styles in solving a problem, e.g. CI followed by GII.

The model also suffers in terms of some of the criteria which have been employed in assessing other approaches to the study of leadership in organizations. The issue of the direction of causality raises its head in that in many cases the past performance of subordinates in reaching good decisions may affect the style adopted by a leader. Research mentioned in previous chapters strongly suggests that AI or AII styles may be a response to past poor performance. Indeed, it may be that the past performance of subordinates should be included within the Vroom-Yetton model as a factor which impinges on decision quality. In addition, there is no reference to informal leadership in the model; indeed, in the light of its emphasis on formally designated leaders, it is not easy to see how informal processes could be incorporated into the model. Finally, the Vroom-Yetton model is similar to virtually every tradition covered thus far in that the research emanating from it does not entail the direct observation of leader behaviour, but relies on putative leaders' reports of their own behaviour or their responses to artificial vignettes of organizational predicaments.

Field (1979) has suggested that an additional problem with the model is that it lacks parsimony and is therefore 'too complex to use in actual practice' (1979, p. 254). This may be true though Vroom (1984) contends that 'it is best viewed not as a programme to be *used*, but rather as a stimulus for people to examine their own behaviour and to consider their own models' (Vroom, 1984, p. 28). Because of this view Vroom appears reluctant to add to the model's complexity by increasing the range of variables which may moderate the effectiveness of decision styles. An alternative view may be to consider an 'expert systems' approach which would render the complexity of the model less problematic. Such an approach would mean developing computer software which would ask the user (leader) for information about a range of situational contingencies and recommend answers. A very rudimentary start in this direction has been made by Peppenhorst (1983) who has written a simple computer program in a version of Microsoft BASIC which is based on the Vroom-Yetton model. The leader simply feeds in data on the situational conditions and the appropriate feasible set is listed. It may seem far-fetched to suggest that the choice of leadership styles can be reduced to a simple computer algorithm in view of the equivocal nature of so much of the research relating to the area, but the complexity of the models which it generates may not be a problem *per se*. In summary, the Vroom-Yetton approach has not suffered from as much disconfirming evidence as many other approaches to the study of leadership in organizations, but it shares with them many common problems while generating some alternative difficulties in its own right.

Overview

While the four approaches covered in this chapter share the basic structure depicted in Figure 5.1 there are some important differences between them. Firstly, they differ in the area of leadership style. Fiedler's model differs from the others, in that the absence of a prior conceptualization of leadership style makes the meaning of the LPC scale ambiguous in this context, since its implications for the study of leader behaviour are at best unclear. Further, it relies on a uni-dimensional conceptualization of leadership style (task- versus relationship-orientation), whereas the Hersey-Blanchard and path-goal approaches treat such ideas as separate dimensions. The Vroom-Yetton approach focuses on participative leadership alone. Secondly, the investigation of situational factors varies from a focus on one variable (subordinate maturity in the Hersey-Blanchard model) through three dimensions (Fiedler) to many more in the Vroom-Yetton and path-goal models. Thirdly, they diverge in their normative implications in that at the practical level the three boxes in Figure 5.1 would need to be rearranged as in Figure 5.6, except in the case of Fiedler's model. Figure 5.6 suggests that if we know which particular leadership style in a particular situation is most appropriate, the leader should adjust his behaviour to the situation in order to enhance performance, subordinate job satisfaction, etc. Fiedler's approach, by contrast, involves a matching of the leader to the situation largely by adjusting the situation to fit the leader's style which is less amenable to change. Thus, while there are basic similarities between the approaches, it is important to remember the differences too.

It is difficult not to feel slightly disenchanted with the fruits of the contingency approaches. The evidence for the Fiedler and path-goal models is equivocal, while there have not been enough tests of the Vroom-Yetton approach to come to a definitive conclusion, although there seems to be a fair degree of support. Indeed researchers may soon be questioning how far the effects of leader behaviour always are situationally contingent in the light of the research by Podsakoff *et al.* (1984) which points to the

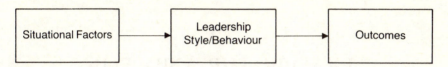

Figure 5.6 *The normative implications of contingency approaches*

largely non-contingent nature of the impact of reward behaviour (see previous chapter). The disappointment can be experienced at another level in that the conceptualization of leadership style employed by the contingency approaches has scarcely moved away from the person-orientation/task-orientation/participation trinity which under-pinned much of the earlier work on leadership styles (cf. Yukl, 1971). Furthermore, researchers within the contingency tradition have exhibited a similar level of uninterest in informal leaders to that of earlier generations of investigators.

The contingency approaches give rise to special problems too. Korman (1973) points to the problem of knowing in advance what critical values of a moderating variable are relevant to a particular leadership style-outcome relationship. In other words, whether a particular relationship is found to be moderated by a particular situational variable may depend on the choice of cut-off points used in examining the presence or absence of moderating effects. Korman (1973) also points to the problems of inferring an ordering of variables as in Figure 5.1 when the bulk of studies examining the implied relationships are static. Quite aside from the possibility of reverse causality (performance affects style) which has frequently been referred to, the ordering of the variables in time is difficult to deduce from static research since it may be that some of the leaders observed in a study have in fact adjusted their behaviour in the light of their perception or misperception of the situation. Furthermore, how does a leader deal with a context in which the implications of the situation for his behaviour are incongruent with one another? The possibility of conflicting situational factors has received some attention in the context of the contingency approach to the study of organizations (Child, 1984, pp. 228-9) but has received short shrift from leadership researchers. How should a leader respond when one aspect of the situation implies one style, while another aspect indicates that it would be quite inappropriate? It is also worth observing that the model of the normative implications of contingency ideas, as in Figure 5.6, assumes a much higher level of planning and intentionality on the part of leaders than people in leadership positions like managers exhibit, or have the opportunity to exhibit (Mintzberg, 1973).

6
LEADERSHIP AND THE
STUDY OF ORGANIZATIONS

This book deals with the literature on leadership in organizations. In spite of this fact, the organizational context of much leadership behaviour is a good deal less than fully explored by the researchers whose work has been examined. Indeed, the fact that leadership takes place within organizations is almost incidental to many studies. In large part this is because the general domain of research known as 'organization studies' or 'organizational analysis' has bifurcated into two sub-fields. One sub-field is known as 'organizational behaviour', which is primarily oriented to individual and small group level behaviour within the organization. Within this area of study is invariably found a concern for motivation, satisfaction, conflict and similar topics. The study of leadership in organizations is typically located within this sub-field. The second sub-field is often referred to as 'organization theory', and is typically concerned with attributes of the organization as such – its structure, its environment, and organizational change. At the extreme of this sub-field is the suggestion that organizations as such can act (Thompson, 1967). Of course, some overlap exists: textbooks on organizational behaviour typically contain a chapter or two on organizational context; those dealing with organization theory frequently deal with the implications of the structure for individual and group-level phenomena. Nonetheless a clear division exists. Many of the articles we have examined in this book thus far have been published in predominantly psychological journals like *Journal of Applied Psychology, Organizational Behaviour and Human Peformance,* and *Personnel Psychology.* Research emanating from organization theory has typically been published in *Administrative Science Quarterly, Organization Studies,* and sociology journals. The *Administrative Science Quarterly* and management journals like *Academy of Management Journal* publish articles from both sub-fields, but the former has become recognized as a major forum for the investigation of issues relating to organization theory.

To a certain degree, then, there is a division of labour within organization studies, with the study of leadership in organizations being located almost exclusively within the domain of organizational behaviour.

As a result we tend to find that, as Hunt and Osborn (1980, p. 48) have observed, most leadership researchers are psychologists and are trained by psychologists. In large part this is not surprising. The early trait approaches dealt with precisely the attributes (e.g. personality) that are conventionally studied by psychologists. The style approaches deal with the behaviour of leaders in relation to the group, an emphasis which is also evident in contingency approaches, so that a predominantly psychological (especially social psychological) emphasis was retained. Yet, in view of the very considerable interest in leadership within organizations, it is still somewhat surprising that the broader organizational context has not been a systematic concern. As a result, one author has concluded: 'Organization and leadership theory have largely developed without specialists in each area drawing on the literature of the other' (Melcher, 1977, p. 98).

There have been opportunities for cross-fertilization. The Ohio school was, as stated above, an interdisciplinary team. Indeed, in an early paper emanating from the Ohio group (published in a *sociology* journal), Morris and Seeman (1950) sought to articulate a paradigm for the investigation of leadership. Within this approach a number of factors were identified which impinge on leader behaviour, and with which organization theory is strongly associated: organization history, formal organization structure, informal organization structure, communication systems, organization ideologies, and external situational factors. As we have seen, these variables received little systematic attention in the bulk of Ohio research which seems in fact to have provided (in concert with the early Michigan approach) a paradigm for a predominantly social psychological framework for the investigation of leadership.

To be sure, leadership researchers have frequently addressed the impact of organizational factors on leader behaviour, as well as their role in mediating leadership style-outcome relationships. The position power of the leader has been emphasized by writers like Pelz (1951) and Fiedler. The organizational climate was investigated as a possible determinant of the four leadership dimensions developed by the later Michigan researchers (e.g. Taylor and Bowers, 1972). Within both path-goal theory and the Vroom-Yetton decision-making approach organizational factors are seen as impinging on the relationship between leadership style and outcome. In their study of managers, Bass *et al.* (1975) found that the amount of clarity of organizational arrangements had an impact on the style adopted. The results of this investigation are somewhat difficult to determine in that greater clarity was associated with *both* greater direction and participation in leader style. Ford's (1981) research on employees in a university, a bank, and a book publishing company, found that the amount of environmental uncertainty external to the organization (a prominent topic among organization theorists) was negatively related to leader Initiating Structure. Departmental size was found to be negatively associated with Consideration. Miles and Petty (1977) in a study of social service agencies in the USA found that organizational size was an important moderating variable in respect of leader behaviour outcome relationships. For example, more Consideration (as measured by the Ohio SBDQ) was associated with greater work satisfaction in large agencies only; Initiating Structure was positively associated with work satisfaction in small agencies, but negatively in large ones. Insofar as larger organizations are more formalized and bureaucratized than smaller ones (Child, 1973), it would seem that the degree of bureaucratization moderates the relationship between leadership style and various outcomes.

Clearly, then, leadership researchers have not been insensitive to the impact of organizational attributes on their domain of study. What has been lacking in the bulk of these examples (including to some extent the contingency theories) has been a systematic theoretical treatment of the interrelationships between leadership and organizational factors. In many instances there is little rationale for the inclusion of a particular attribute other than a hunch that it might be important. Such an approach is too arbitrary, relying excessively on what happens to occur to researchers, on which organizational attributes they happen to have collected data on, and on which attributes emerge with statistically interesting effects in a general trawl for mediating variables. This cynical view is not without foundation in that it is virtually impossible to discern a theoretical rationale to the inclusion of many of the organizational factors which leadership researchers have examined. The path-goal approach seems to come close to a theoretical rationale but much of it has emerged after a number of studies had identified moderating effects of organizational characteristics. There are, however, some exceptions to the separation of organization theory from leadership theory. In such cases, the investigation of the impact of particular organizational factors on leadership processes and outcomes is based on a theoretical justification which is provided in advance of empirical exploration. Two frameworks to be examined will be the macro-oriented approach (sometimes called 'adaptive-reactive') associated with Hunt and Osborn, and the 'substitutes for leadership' approach associated with Kerr and Jermier.

A macro-oriented model

This approach has undergone a number of formulations upon whose differences it is not intended to dwell excessively (see Hunt and Osborn, 1982, for a brief history). Central to the approach is a distinction between discretionary and non-discretionary leadership. The former is a mode of influence which is under the leader's control – he or she *chooses* to engage in leader behaviour (e.g. greater Initiating Structure) of a particular kind; non-discretionary leadership is engaged in as a consequence of the organizational context, that is, the leader has to engage in a particular pattern. The basic point that Hunt and Osborn make in connection with this distinction is that the subordinates will respond differently to their leaders according to whether their behaviour is perceived to be by choice or of necessity.

A study (Osborn and Hunt, 1975) of sixty chapters of a nationwide, undergraduate, professional business fraternity examined how far the distinction was relevant to the examination of Consideration and Initiating Structure (as measured by the Ohio LBDQ-Form X11). This study pointed to two clusters of variables which enhance or detract from the leader's discretion to act in a particular way. Firstly, they distinguished environmental factors which limit discretion. Focusing in particular on the complexity of the immediate environments of the chapters, Osborn and Hunt examined the degree to which factors like the predictability and volatility of the environment affected the amount of discretion at the leader's disposal. Secondly, organizational characteristics were identified as possible factors which inhibit discretion. Organizational (i.e. chapter) size and technology were the main characteristics addressed; the latter variable has been identified as a variable of major importance in the determination of organizational structures and processes (e.g. Woodward, 1965), though the evidence has been contested (e.g. Hickson, Pugh and Pheysey, 1969). Briefly, chapter size was not found to be an important variable in terms of their theory. However, their results for environmental complexity pointed to subordinates responding (in terms of levels of job satisfaction and performance criteria) differently according to whether the leadership behaviour was discretionary or non-discretionary. In particular, the research suggests that subjects exhibited greater satisfaction and performance in response to discretionary than to non-discretionary leadership.

One of the better known studies within this tradition is a study of white collar employees and managers from an engineering division of a large US public utility (Hunt, Osborn and Schuler, 1978). The leadership behaviour dimensions investigated were: leader contingent approval (i.e. contingent on performance), leader consideration, leader contingent disapproval, and leader ego deflation (i.e. behaviour on the part of the leader which disparages a subordinate). This study was much more systematic about the examination of organizational characteristics which might impinge on the leader's discretion. Twelve categories were examined, examples of which are: formalization, upward information requirements, chain of command, inter-group cooperation, etc. Their data suggested that non-discretionary leadership (for each of the four categories of leader behaviour) is a better predictor of overall satisfaction (with work, supervision, etc.) than discretionary leadership. The opposite was the case for performance, though the associations between discretionary leadership and performance were weak. Of the twelve organizational characteristics, only five were clearly of importance to the discretionary/non-discretionary distinction. These items were to do with 'promoting clarity and clear standards and enhancing communications' (Hunt *et al.*, 1978, p. 518).

The third study to be discussed (Hunt and Osborn, 1982) was carried out on US telecommunications units. Yet another set of leader categories was used: *support* – how far the job is made pleasant by the leader; *role clarification* – the extent to which clear explanations of their roles are conveyed to subordinates; *work assignments* – whether subordinates are placed on specific jobs; and *rules and procedures* – how far the leader tells subordinates how to carry out their jobs. Ratings were made in respect of each leadership style in terms of how far the associated behaviour was discretionary, an important improvement over the earlier studies. Three clusters of 'macro' factors (i.e. organizational characteristics) were employed: environmental complexity, contextual complexity (including size and technological sophistication and variability) and structural complexity (including specialization, diversity, and control and coordination). It was found that discretionary leadership was generally associated with greater work unit performance, job satisfaction, job involvement, a disinclination to leave, and other outcomes. Further, Hunt and Osborn found that in general when the environmental, contextual and structural complexity is considerable, discretionary leadership has a stronger impact on work unit outcomes than non-discretionary leadership.

This approach strongly suggests that it is necessary to include organizational characteristics as central rather than subsidiary foci in leadership investigations by dint of their relevance for the discretionary/non-discretionary distinction which seems in turn to have implications for subordinates' perceptions. The latest findings indicate that: 'Leader action attributed to the superior is expected to have a more dramatic impact on subordinate affective states than that action attributed to role requirements' (Hunt and Osborn, 1982, p. 203). When leader behaviour is seen as discretionary it is seen as more crucial by subordinates in solving their particular job and organizational problems, though the Hunt *et al.* (1978) study does not confirm this. A problem with the evidence is that the use of different categorizations of leader behaviour and organizational characteristics across investigations renders comparisons somewhat difficult. Also the employment of perceptual measures of organizational characteristics is also a problem, since they exhibit a poor correspondence with measures derived from interviews with key informants (Pennings, 1973). There is also a tendency to treat the 'macro' organizational factors as inert entities to which leaders must adapt, when the successful leader may be the one who refuses to accept them as constraints and acts back on the context in which he finds himself. In so doing, leaders may be able to establish areas of discretion where *prima facie* none exist. Such an emphasis would dovetail well with some of the prevailing approaches within organization theory which emphasize the 'political' dimension of life in organizations (see below). According to this view, organizational characteristics are emergent properties emanating from the ebb and flow of the squabble for power and resources that takes place. Nonetheless, the macro-oriented approach is highly suggestive, and points to a need to take into account the organizational context as a prominent element in leadership studies.

Substitutes for leadership

The idea of 'substitutes for leadership' was formulated most explicitly by Kerr and Jermier (1978) to draw attention to the possibility that many of the situational factors which moderate leadership-outcome relationships do so by 'tending to negate the leader's ability to either improve (sic) or impair subordinate satisfaction or performance' (p. 377). This can occur because particular situational factors neutralize the effects of leadership style. Thus a company which is tightly structured, provides clear role definitions, and plans ahead, may neutralize the effects of Initiating Structure, as the organization is providing this role and work clarifying function. Kerr and Jermier distinguish between two general types of leader behaviour: relationship-oriented/supportive/people-centred leadership and task-oriented/instrumental/job-centred leadership. The former pattern comprises notions of Consideration, support, and interaction facilitation; the latter comprises Initiating Structure, goal emphasis, and work facilitation. According to Kerr and Jermier substitutes for leadership can best be grouped into three headings: subordinate, task, and organizational characteristics. The full scheme is presented in Table 6.1. Within this scheme, organizational characteristics are highly prominent. The table should be interpreted as indicating that, say, 'formalization' (substitute number 9) will tend to neutralize the effects of task-oriented behaviour because it renders this style redundant. Measures were developed for the possible substitutes.

Kerr and Jermier report a study of city police in which the relative effects of the substitutes and both instrumental and supportive leader behaviour were examined to discern their relative impact on police officers' organizational commitment and role ambiguity. Three measures of instrumental leader behaviour were employed: role clarification (clarifying what is expected of subordinates), work assignment (assigning specific tasks), and specification of procedures (development of procedures to aid task accomplishment). The Kerr and Jermier (1978) paper reports an analysis of these data for 'selected' (ten) substitutes for leadership and leader behaviour variables in terms of their relative impact on organizational commitment and role ambiguity. They found that the impact of leader behaviour on these two outcome variables was small. The role clarification style was the only one to have a significant effect in that it enhanced organizational commitment and reduced role ambiguity. The two 'substitute' variables of intrinsically satisfying tasks and task feedback clearly enhanced organizational commitment; role ambiguity was reduced by greater task routineness, intrinsically satisfying tasks, and organizational formalization. In the case of both of these outcome variables, none of the other 'substitute' measures had a considerable impact. Thus it would seem that the leader's supportive behaviour as well as two aspects of his instrumental behaviour (work assignment and specification of procedures) had no effect on these outcomes, presumably because of their negation by the substitutes.

While these findings are taken as providing broad support for their approach, the fact that few of the substitutes had a strong effect on the outcomes renders an interpretation of the lack of influence of the leader behaviours somewhat indeterminate. If so few have an effect, in what sense are they substitutes for leadership? Further, some leadership behaviour (i.e. role clarification) did have an impact on these two outcomes, and in the case of role ambiguity it exhibited a stronger relationship than any other variable. A very similar study was conducted

Table 6.1 *Substitutes for leadership*

| | Will tend to neutralize | |
| | Relationship-Oriented, Supportive, People-Centred Leadership: Consideration, Support, and Interaction Facilitation | Task-Oriented, Instrumental, Job-Centred Leadership: Initiating Structure, Goal Emphasis, and Work Facilitation |
Characteristic		
of the subordinate		
1. ability, experience, training, knowledge		X
2. need for independence	X	X
3. 'professional' orientation	X	X
4. indifference toward organizational rewards	X	X
of the task		
5. unambiguous and routine		X
6. methodologically invariant		X
7. provides its own feedback concerning accomplishment		X
8. intrinsically satisfying	X	
of the organization		
9. formalization (explicit plans, goals, and areas of responsibility)		X
10. inflexibility (rigid, unbending rules and procedures)		X
11. highly-specified and active advisory and staff functions		X
12. closely-knit, cohesive work groups	X	X
13. organizational rewards not within the leader's control	X	X
14. spatial distance between superior and subordinates	X	X

Source: S. Kerr and J.M. Jermier, 'Substitutes for leadership: their meaning and measurement', *Organizational Behaviour and Human Performance*, vol. 22, 1978, p. 378. Reproduced with permission of Academic Press and the authors.

on hospital employees by Howell and Dorfman (1981) using the same leader behaviour and substitutes scales. The two outcome variables investigated were organizational commitment and job satisfaction. In this study the only clear definitive evidence for the Kerr and Jermier approach was that organizational formalization combined with task routineness substituted for work assignment behaviour in respect of organizational commitment only. In other words, this exception aside, leader behaviour was not being substituted by the variables addressed by Kerr and Jermier – they still made a difference to the outcomes investigated. Thus, according to Howell and Dorfman's data, a leader's supportive behaviour still makes a difference to organizational commitment and job satisfaction even when tasks are intrinsically satisfying or when there are cohesive work groups, two variables which, according to the original formulation, are supposed to negate such leader behaviour.

Finally, the research reported in Chapter 4, by Podsakoff *et al.* (1984) also investigated the impact of the substitutes for leadership scales on the effects of the four reward and punishment behaviours they distinguished. In this study, the effects of leader reward behaviour were examined on subordinate performance and five measures of satisfaction. As was reported in Chapter 4, Podsakoff *et al.* were primarily concerned with the possible moderators of leader reward behaviour-outcome relationships and the substitutes were investigated for this reason. In fact, very little evidence was found for the substitutes for leadership approach. This is surprising since two of the posited substitutes – 'indifference to rewards' and 'rewards not controlled by leader' – relate very directly to a leader's reward behaviour. It might be expected that when subordinates are indifferent to rewards or when they are outside the leader's control, a leader's reward behaviour would be neutralized. The only evidence for such a conclusion was a rather weak tendency for indifference to organizational rewards to reduce the impact of contingent reward behaviour on performance (Podsakoff *et al.*, 1984, p. 56). No such effect seems to have been noted in connection with the five satisfaction measures.

Kerr and Jermier's interesting notion of substitutes for leadership was included in this chapter because of the heavy emphasis on variables associated with the work of organization theorists. It seems, however, that the first tranche of results is none too encouraging. It may be that a concentration of a wider range of leader behaviours and substitutes in relation to each other will bear fruit. There is also evidence that the Kerr and Jermier measures of the substitutes are less than adequate (see Podsakoff *et al.*, 1984, pp. 41–2). It may also be that greater attention will be needed to the distinction made by Kerr and Jermier between 'substitutes' and 'neutralizers'. The latter counteract the influence of leadership in that they render it impossible for a particular leadership style to make a difference. 'Substitutes' make a particular style unnecessary as well as impossible. Some conceptual clarification of this potentially useful distinction might provide a useful way forward. Moreover, the idea that organizational arrangements may act as substitutes for leadership is occasionally employed as an explanation of discrepant findings. For example, in Chapter 4, reference was made to a study of management styles by Chitayat and Venezia (1984) which found that the correlation between a manager's power was positive in business organizations, but negative in non-business contexts. In order to explain this finding, the researchers drew attention to the pervasiveness of rules and procedures in the non-business organizations they examined, namely military and government agencies. It may be that where there is a high level of routinization and an emphasis on procedures, a directive style is deemed less appropriate since such organizational arrangements serve the same kind of function as directive leadership. However, we are still left with a similar problem to that encountered in connection with the 'macro' approach of the previous section, namely that leadership, particularly good leadership, may inhere in the blunt refusal to take too much as given. The ability to winkle out room for manoeuvre by the judicious and often political deployment of strategies of independence is somewhat understated in the implicit views about the interaction between organizational and leadership variables revealed by both the 'macro' and 'substitutes' perspectives.

Leadership research and organization theory

The two foregoing approaches are significant in the context of the present discussion for their systematic inclusion of organizational attributes in the study of leadership. In the contingency theories of leadership, organizational attributes seem, on the whole, to be entertained in a rather piecemeal fashion. There is a further interesting feature about these two domains of study when considered in relation to each other. This feature is simply that there is something of a symmetry in their respective developments.

In the first chapter the following characterization of the development of leadership research was presented:

This simplified account is implicit in the treatment of research provided in this book. It *is* a simplification because there are no absolute ruptures in the development of the research, as the continued presence of trait studies since its apparent demise in the late 1940s would imply. In broad terms, this model of the development of leadership research merely brings out the relative emphasis on particular approaches over the years. This development closely parallels that of organization studies. This is especially the case in respect of the two later phases of leadership research. In just the same way that there was a heavy emphasis on generally applicable leadership styles during the 1950s and 1960s in particular, organization theory went through a period (albeit earlier and over a longer period of time) in which universal principles of organization and administration were sought after and often advocated. The two main examples of this trend are the so-called Classical Management theory and the work of Max Weber.

Early developments in organization theory

The Classical Management theorists were practitioners of management who sought to apply broad principles of organization to a wide variety of contexts.[1] The kind of organizational design which they tended to advocate was a rigidly structured one which minimized discretion, stipulated clear channels of authority and communication, and tight central control and coordination. Such principles were advocated more or less irrespective of the context in which a particular organization operates. In the work of Max Weber, a German sociologist, we find the suggestion that the bureaucratic form of organization is universally superior to non-bureaucratic forms in modern societies. This bureaucratic form of organization resembles that advocated by the Classical Management theorists quite closely. It is fundamentally a highly structured type of organization with advanced specialization, closely defined job descriptions, clearly articulated authority channels, and the like. Weber saw bureaucracy as an increasingly prominent mode of organization in capitalist societies, the reasons for which are:

> The decisive reason for the advance of the bureaucratic organization has always been its purely technical superiority over any other form of organization. (Weber, 1948, p. 214)

Although there seems to be a clear claim in such a statement for the general superiority of bureaucracy in terms of technical efficiency, Weber differed from the Classical Management theorists in that he was not an advocate of the principles he discerned as contributing to its superiority; indeed, he was critical of a number of its effects on modern society and on the administrators who inhabit it.

From the late 1950s, the universal approach gradually drifted out of fashion as a consequence of greater recognition that organizations need to respond to the contexts in which they find themselves. In her research on technology, Woodward (1965) noted that the principles of Classical Management theory were not generally appropriate to her sample of British manufacturing firms. The modes of production technology seemed to act as a determinant of the kind of organization that was adopted. Moreover, the more successful firms seemed to have developed organization structures that were appropriate to their production technologies. In other words the closer the 'fit' between a firm's technology and its organization structure the more successful it seemed to be. A finding such as this would seem to go against the grain of the advocacy of universal principles of organizational design. Research by Burns and Stalker (1961) echoed this orientation in that they pinpointed the necessity for organizations to have internal structures and processes in synchrony with their environments. In stable environments a 'mechanistic' structure is appropriate, in which tasks are well defined, clearly articulated rules and authority channels and the like are in evidence, in the manner of the Weberian notion of bureaucracy. When environments are volatile, an 'organismic' structure, which exhibits a highly fluid and loosely structured design, is superior by virtue of its greater adaptability. The importance of the environment as a determinant of organizational structures and their relative effectiveness was also evident in the work of Lawrence and Lorsch (1967). Other writers stressed the importance of an organization's size to its internal structure (e.g. Pugh, Hickson, Hinings and Turner, 1969; Child, 1973). This general approach was also dubbed the 'contingency' approach to the study of organizations so as to draw attention to its systematic inclusion of situational factors in the assessment of the appropriateness of structures for performance.

There appears to be a symmetry with the gradual disenchantment among leadership researchers with general, universal principles and a growing preoccupation with the situational factors which have an impact on the appropriateness of particular organizational structures or leadership styles as the case may be. Indeed, in summarizing a number of trends which seemed to point at the time to a contingency approach to the study of organizations, Lawrence and Lorsch (1967, pp. 206–7) mentioned Fiedler's research on leadership as a highly congruent development. It is not possible to deduce whether developments in organization theory in the direction of a contingency orientation influenced leadership researchers or *vice versa*. It is nonetheless striking that since the late 1940s, the two fields of study have trodden remarkably similar paths. This comment applies less comfortably, however, to more recent years. A fairly detailed treatment of these more recent developments will now be undertaken.

Some recent developments in organization theory

The work of both 'universalist' writers like the Classical Management theorists and Weber and the 'it-all-depends' writers is underpinned by what is conventionally referred to as a 'rational system model', a notion which has received the attention of a number of writers like Gouldner (1959) and Scott (1981).[2] The fundamental orientation of this model is that of viewing organizational structures and processes as geared to the attainment of goals. Thus an organization's structure is viewed as a means to an end, irrespective of whether the approach is that of a universalist writer or one oriented to situational circumstances. Organizations are viewed as seeking to enhance the appropriateness of their structures in order to enhance performance. As Scott (1981) has observed, the only difference between the universalist and the contingency approaches is that the former tended to conceive of the organization as a closed system. The contingency researchers, by encapsulating contextual factors like the environment and technology within their purview, viewed the organization as an open system. At the more microscopic level, the rational system model has tended to possess a corresponding image of the individual decision-maker as a calculative individual who weighs up alternative possible lines of action with a particular goal in mind, albeit with a recognition of his or her likely inability, for example, to conceive of the full range of alternatives and to possess sufficient knowledge to make completely informed choices (e.g. Simon, 1957).

This broad orientation seems equally to underpin leadership research with its quest for effective leadership styles. The highly goal-directed behaviour that leaders are perceived as exhibiting is redolent of the rational system model and, in many respects, is a symptom of it. Leaders are perceived as highly purposive, seeking to produce particular effects with their actions. Indeed, many of the definitions of leadership encountered in Chapter 1 reveal this orientation in that the leader is typically perceived as a person who influences his subordinates towards the achievement of group goals. Subordinates too are viewed in these terms, this being particularly evident in path-goal theory's assumption that they are highly instrumental seekers of appropriate means to attain their personal goals. It would seem, then, that much of the research that has been addressed thus far shares similar presuppositions of the rational system model of organizations.

More recently, as writers like Scott (1981) and Bryman (1984a) have observed, there has been a very considerable drift away from the assumptions of the rational system model within organization studies. Three different perspectives can be used as examples of this tendency. The first is the 'garbage can' model initially outlined in a paper by Cohen, March and Olsen (1972). According to this view many organizations are organized anarchies which bear little resemblance to the image portrayed by the rational system model. According to Cohen *et al.*, an organization can often be viewed more fruitfully as

> a collection of choices looking for problems, issues and feelings looking for decision situations in which they might be aired, solutions looking for issues to which they might be the answer, and decision-makers looking for work. (Cohen *et al.*, 1972, p. 2)

The image provided by the rational system model, of organizational structures being synchronized to pre-ordained goals and of decision-makers calculating the relative utility of various means in relation to these goals, recedes from view in a quite dramatic fashion. Organizational life seems to be much more fluid than it appears in the eyes of writers associated with the rational system model. Not all organizations are organized anarchies, however, in that such attributes are most likely to obtain where there are problematic goals, unclear technologies (in a general sense – not only production technologies), and fluid participation. Cohen and March (1974) suggest that, in these terms, colleges and universities are protypical organized anarchies. Such educational establishments, for example, are invariably unclear about their goals and about how their raw materials (i.e. students) should be fashioned. The implicit point to which the organized anarchy perspective draws attention is that the rational system model cannot adequately embrace such organizations. The premises on which it is based do not readily provide for a meaningful analysis of the internal life of organized anarchies. If it is indeed the case that in organized anarchies 'the flow of individual actions produces a flow of decisions that is intended by no one and is not related in a direct way to anyone's desired outcomes' (March and Olsen, 1976, p. 19), then it is little wonder that the rational system model, with its pervasive assumption of rational decision-making, fits uneasily in such milieux.

A fairly congruent perspective to the garbage can model is the image of educational organizations as loosely coupled systems portrayed by Weick (1976). Weick argues that such organizations are better viewed as ones in which there is only a loose correspondence between means and ends, between system parts, between intention and action, and so on. To assume that 'unity, integration, co-ordination and consensus' (Weick, 1976, p. 4) pervade all organizations may be misguided. Weick proposes the idea that organizational elements and the components of decision-making and action in educational organizations are not tightly coordinated and integrated. Consequently, the rational system model is inappropriate in such circumstances, so that Weick offers the principle of loose coupling as an alternative hypothesis. While the ideas of Weick and the garbage can theorists seem to have been developed largely in the context of educational organizations, it is worth noting that studies of managers and their work in industry and elsewhere frequently point to the possibility that the rational systems model relates poorly to what managers do. In summarizing her own work as well as that of Mintzberg (1973), Stewart (1983) has observed that the assumption that managerial work involves 'rationality, planning, and pursuit of organizational goals' (p. 82) is misguided. In fact, research points to managerial work being much more disjointed and fragmented, reactive and instinctive, and involving a substantial orientation to personal and parochial departmental goals, than is often supposed.[3] While such evidence cannot be taken as proof of the views of Cohen *et al.* and Weick, its emphasis on the lack of internal consistency that pervades much organizational activity is broadly consistent with them.

Stewart's (1983) reference to the political activity which permeates managerial work usefully introduces a second set of ideas which seem to clash with the rational system model. The term 'political' is used to denote the presence, if not prevalence, within organizations of conflicting interests and dissension over resources. A number of writers have drawn attention to the importance of the political dimension of organizations (e.g. Hickson *et al.*, 1971; Pettigrew, 1973; Pfeffer, 1978, 1981a). The political perspective points to the way in which members of organizations seek to gain advantage for themselves and for their groups and departments. Managers are seen as seeking to expand the resources of their section over and against the ravenous urges of their competitors. The literature on the internal politics of organizations is now replete with the plays and tactics that are mustered in order to carve out additional increments of power. High visibility, enhancing status, the jealous guarding of information at one's disposal, creating uncertainty for others, controlling the agenda, doing 'the right things', and the like, have all been identified as parts of the arsenal to be deployed directly or indirectly against one's competitors.

Such a view of organizations creates difficulties for the rational system model. It suggests that there exists a multiplicity of interests within organizations to which members orientate themselves. As such, people's political stratagems may take the organization's over-arching goals only tangentially if at all, as a point of reference. The rational system model, by contrast, tends to emphasize that the organization has goals or clusters of goals to which people address themselves. There is a further clash between the political and rational system emphases in terms of their accounts of organizational structure. The rational system model sees it as intentionally designed to enhance the attainment of the organization's goals. By contrast, the political perspective seems to imply that organization structure is, at least in part, a product of the political machinations of managers and others, since the tendency for relative power to ebb and flow will have implications for the internal structure. Like the previous assault on the rational system edifice, the emphasis on the political dimension of organizations creates a number of difficulties for the emphasis on rationality, largely because of its suggestion that people do not consistently take the organization and its goals as a constant reference point for their actions.

Finally, the institutional approach to the study of organizations has led to a questioning of some of the precepts of the rational model. An article by Meyer and Rowan (1977) exemplifies these ideas well. According to these authors, organizations seek to be seen as legitimate in the eyes of the wider society; as a result, they adopt rationalized work and organizational structures not in order to enhance efficiency (as the rational system model might lead one to predict), but to be seen as adopting the procedures and practices which are deemed desirable in modern society. Like Cohen *et al.* and Weick, Meyer and Rowan suggest that this quest for what they call 'ceremonial conformity' with the beliefs held by the wider society is most likely to occur in educational and some service organizations. This ceremonial conformity arises because organizations need to exhibit the trappings of legitimacy, in order to ensure a flow of resources to them either from other organizations or from the State, or both. The adoption of rationalized work structures, even though unnecessary in terms of organizational efficiency, conveys the impression of a bona fide organization worthy of continued or even additional support and resources. Not to adopt the trappings of rationality may risk associating an organization with poor management and lack of coordination and control. The implications of this approach, then, are that organizational arrangements may be adopted in order to impress, or as Tolbert and Zucker (1983, p. 26) succinctly put it: 'In order to survive, organizations conform to what is societally defined as appropriate and efficient, largely disregarding the actual impact on organizational performance.' Thus the adoption of

such trappings may have minimal implications for organizational operations and their efficiency. Support for many of these ideas has been
discerned in the context of schools (Meyer, Scott and Deal, 1981) and of
civil service reforms in the USA (Tolbert and Zucker, 1983), and further
theoretical elaboration can be found in Di Maggio and Powell (1983).

Possible implications for leadership research

Collectively, these recent developments and trends in organization theory
represent a sharp retreat from the rational system model, albeit in different
ways and with divergent implications for theory and research. The rational
system model's preoccupation with means-ends theorizing appears less
tenable in the light of these varied ideas. As yet, there appears to be little
evidence of parallel developments among leadership researchers who still
seem to be wedded to the fundamental tenets of rational model ideas.
Could it be that the developments reported in connection with organization
theory are of relevance to that field alone, and so have few implications for
the study of leadership? *Prima facie* there is a case for rejecting such a
proposition on the grounds that the area of study covered by this book has
been that of leadership that takes place *in* organizations. On this basis
alone, it would seem premature, if not foolhardy, to imply that the fruits
of recent organization theory are of little relevance to leadership research.
Furthermore, if one takes each of the three recent developments in turn,
they appear to be suggestive of new departures for leadership researchers.
    The 'garbage can', 'organized anarchies', and 'loose coupling' ideas
have been broadly applied to the study of leadership in a study of
American college presidents by Cohen and March (1974). Taking as their
starting point the idea that colleges and universities are organized
anarchies, they analysed the status and power of presidents. In their view,
an aspect of the leadership of these organizations is that of recognizing and
acknowledging that they are organized anarchies and so not imposing an
excessive and possibly inappropriate bureaucratic structure on them.
Cohen and March point to a number of ambiguities and dilemmas built
into the presidential role. For example, presidents tend to feel that they
have many pressures on them which tend to render them unable to allocate
time and energy as they see fit. As a result they are often under pressure to
do things which they feel are 'trivial' or mundane. Why do they persist
with such a state of affairs? The answer proffered by Cohen and March is
that they are forced to submit to the expectations of colleagues and others.
Again, we might ask why. Precisely because colleges are organized
anarchies with ambiguous goals and unclear technologies 'there is no way
that a president can demonstrate either to others or to himself, that an
alternative pattern of attention would (or did) result in improved
performance' (Cohen and March, 1974, p. 149). In an organization that
does not have clearly articulated goals, the problem of having to
demonstrate means-ends relationships in connection with what he does or
wants to do haunts the college president. As such:

The college president is an executive who does not know exactly what he should be doing and does not have much confidence that he can do anything important anyway. (Cohen and March, 1974, p. 151)

In what sense, then, can a leader lead in an organized anarchy? This issue is more than that denoted by apparently similar ideas like the discretionary/non-discretionary leadership distinction of Hunt and his colleagues introduced above. The dilemmas of leadership imposed on the college president derive from forces above, below and around him, and permeate every fibre of the institution he attempts to lead.

· This suggestive piece of research is one of very few seeking to address some of the implications of the ideas initially put forward in the Cohen *et al.* (1972) garbage can model. It entices us to examine the meaning that could be attributed to studies attempting to relate leadership style to outcomes in these settings. It suggests that one would have to question how far the leadership style is supposed to have an impact on the posited outcomes. By drawing attention to the disjunctures that frequently occur between choice and action and between intention and outcome writers like Weick (1976) and Cohen *et al.* render the meaning of the leadership style-outcome relationships discerned in many organizations somewhat ambiguous.

The political approach to the study of organizations developed by Pfeffer and various others raises somewhat different possibilities for the study of leadership which have already been hinted at. Rather than treat the organizational context as a given, as an inert entity to which the leader merely responds (as do the contingency, 'macro' and 'substitutes' approaches), this perspective may be taken as suggesting that successful leaders may be able to 'enact' (Weick, 1969) the organizational milieux that confront them. This idea is based on the dictum that: 'The human actor does not *react* to an environment, he *enacts* it' (Weick, 1969, p. 64). While there is a case for being wary of drifting into a position of viewing everything as capable of being changed, the point is that the individual is capable of effecting desired alternatives. This basic idea is also present in the so-called 'resource dependence' model, which views the organization as not simply reactive to its external environment but also capable of exerting influence over it (e.g. Aldrich and Pfeffer, 1976). Notions such as these raise the possibility that leaders may be able to massage and manipulate their organizational milieux, the very attributes of which so many leadership researchers treat as contextual givens to which the leader must respond. The example of position power is a case in point. Pelz (1951), Fiedler and others have shown that the amount of power that leaders possess by virtue of their organizational position mediates the effects of their behaviour on subordinates. The latter seem to be more responsive, and better disposed, to leaders who are able to do things for them within the organization. But position power is both an achieved and an ascribed status. It may be that strong leaders are the ones who successfully ingratiate themselves and carve out extra increments of wider influence. Power is not simply a given, so that subordinates' views about a leader's position power may not derive solely from that power, but from a recognition of the leader's preparedness to be a political animal and expand his area of influence.

A political perspective also invites the researcher to consider the impact of the leader's attention to rather narrow parochial issues on how he behaves and the effect on his subordinates. This theme raises the possibility that much leader behaviour may be oriented to more self-interested goals rather than those associated with the organization as such. Stewart's (1983) summary of research on managers, which was mentioned above, pointedly suggests that their behaviour is not governed by a constant recourse to organizational goals. By contrast, measures of leadership style typically assume that group or broader organization goals are at the forefront of the leader's thinking. If much leader behaviour is not oriented to such goals, but has a more personal focus, then it is small wonder that the correlations between leadership style and performance are so often small and inconsistent.

There is some evidence of increasing interest in the political devices of leaders. An example is an investigation by Mowday (1978) of a sample of school principals in the USA which sought to determine their tactics of upward influence in a number of areas. Five influence methods were delineated: threats; legitimate authority (e.g. invoking regulations and policies); persuasive arguments; rewards or exchange of favours; and manipulation, i.e. 'providing information in such a way that the recipient is not aware that he or she is being influenced' (Mowday, 1978, pp. 142–3). The data suggest that the type of decision involved and the stage of the decision process (whether early or late) had an effect on the choice of influence method(s). However, it was also found that those principals who were rated by their own superiors as exhibiting higher levels of influence effectiveness than their peers were more likely to employ the tactic of manipulation. Such findings point to the possibility that the political acumen of leaders may be an important source of their effectiveness and of the affective responses of their subordinates (cf. Pelz, 1951). What is missing from such analyses is any theoretical or empirical purchase on the implications of the lateral aspects of political striving within organizations for the study of leadership. Researchers concerned with leadership in organizations seem to be obsessed with its vertical aspects, thereby having little regard for the horizontal exercise of leadership among peers.

The institutional approach of Meyer and Rowan (1977) has implications for the study of leadership too. While their focus was mainly upon the symbolizing and signalling functions served by bureaucratic structures, they draw attention to the ceremonial nature of such rationalized designs. This point raises the possibility that some aspects of leadership behaviour may be ceremonial as well. To some extent this was apparent when it was noted in the discussion of the later Michigan research that managerial leadership was considerably affected by the climate of the organization (Taylor and Bowers, 1972; Franklin, 1975). Similarly, in a study of supervisors, Fleishman, Harris and Brutt (1955) found that it was difficult to effect long-term change in leadership behaviour through training programmes when the nature of the changed behaviour clashes with the organizational climate. It would seem that the behaviour of leaders conforms to the values which prevail in their organizations. How much of this conformity is ceremonial is difficult to estimate, but there is at least a possibility that leaders are unwilling to act in a way which is inconsistent with the ethos of the organization. However, Meyer and Rowan's focus was centred upon the possibility that rationalized work structures are often in ceremonial conformity with the values of the wider society, whereas these findings relate to the climate of the organizations.

But leadership practices too may be refractions of societal values. Participation is a case in point. It is often observed that participative leadership and practices dovetail well with the value that many Western industrial societies place on individual self-determination and democracy. Consequently, the question of whether participation is desirable may be construed as an ethical issue rather than a strictly practical one.[4] In this way it is feasible that the fairly widespread deployment of participative practices is a product of leaders' perceptions of what is acceptable to their subordinates and to their own superiors. Further, the dramatic reorganization of a firm which propels it in a more participative direction may have a lot to do with the quest for organizational legitimacy. It may 'signal' (Meyer, 1979) a change of direction, a change of policy, and a quest for greater efficiency (since participative systems are often *believed* to be more efficient, cf. Ouchi, 1982, p. 36). Participative systems may act as signalling devices to existing and potential employees, as well as shareholders, customers, and so on, of the 'cooperative intent of the firm' (Ouchi, 1982, p. 66). If participative styles of leadership are in part ceremonial, then it may be arguable whether a primary aim of their adoption is to enhance efficiency. If so, then the many participation-productivity studies which have been referred to would not be easy to interpret, even if their results had been less inconsistent. Greater productivity or effectiveness resulting from enhanced participation would have to be seen as a by-product rather than an intended effect. In a manner similar to that adopted by Meyer and Rowan (1977) in connection with the study of organizations, deliberations such as these raise the possibility that leadership styles may serve a ceremonial rather than an efficiency-enhancing function as is commonly assumed.

Greater attention to the ceremonial nature of organizational practices is of potential interest in connection with some of the material addressed in Chapter 2. It appears that there is little unequivocal evidence about the personal characteristics and traits which denote the effective leader. Yet the selection procedures employed for recruiting people with such potential are in large part predicated upon the belief that there are identifiable traits, even though the predictive accuracy of these methods is likewise dubious (Hubbard, 1985). Why, then, do such practices persist? According to one view, the continued use of such selection techniques 'may depend on their symbolic value as ceremonials rather than any demonstrable utility as selection devices' (Trice, Belasco and Alutto, 1969).

Selection practices invest successful applicants with a sense of early achievement and provide early pointers to their competence. The scientific aura of tests is important too in that those responsible for recruitment can claim to be adopting a rational approach to the selection process, thereby celebrating and reflecting the ideological predilections of modern society.

Conclusion

By and large, the foregoing remarks constitute general reflections about some of the implications of ideas drawn from recent developments in organization theory. Nor has the full range of possibilities been exhausted, though an attempt has been made to deal with three particularly significant strands in the study of orgnizations. It is also worth observing that the three strands are by no means entirely congruent in their implications for leadership studies, which was also the case in their original context of research on organizations. One might justifiably question whether the above exercise is worthwhile. Why should leadership research slavishly follow students of organizations, especially since the latter, while disillusioned with rational approaches like the contingency theory of organizations, seem frequently to want to retain many of its tenets with a view to refining them (e.g. Tosi and Slocum, 1984)? The simple answer is that they do not have to, but since the research with which we are concerned in this book is to do with leadership in the context of organizations, developments in respect of organization studies may provide clues which can be followed to some advantage.

7

RECENT DEVELOPMENTS

In this chapter some of the more significant developments of interest to the student of leadership in organizations will be examined. It was observed in the first chapter that this is not an easy undertaking when a field is spawning so many new and alternative approaches. As a result, a choice was made to mention a small number of them with a particular view to their prospective importance. In addition, newer developments in the study of leadership have on occasions been encountered and examined *en passant*. A notable example of this is the Vertical Dyad Linkage approach which received a fairly detailed treatment in Chapters 3 and 4. It could just as easily and appropriately have been dealt with in the current chapter but was appraised in the context of its implications for the study of leadership style because of its specific relevance to that topic. It is hoped that this chapter will provide the reader with a flavour of the unsettled (and perhaps unsettling) nature of the study of leadership, as well as the more positive effect of introducing some interesting developments.

The application of attribution theory to leadership

Attribution theory is an approach to, or possibly a branch of, psychology which takes as its subject matter the causal explanations that people offer for events in everyday life. Its major focus is well summarized by the editors of a major symposium:

> Attribution theory deals with the rules the average individual uses in attempting to infer the causes of observed behaviour. Thus it concerns what Heider has called 'naive psychology' – the cause-effect analyses of behaviour made by the 'man in the street'. (Jones *et al.*, 1972, p. x)

This approach has attracted a good deal of attention in recent years with many conceptual elaborations having been developed and much empirical research emanating from it (see Kelley and Michela, 1980, for a review). The more specific application of these ideas to leadership is of fairly recent origin and revolves around two main issues. Firstly, researchers have been interested in the causal attributions made by leaders, such as the perceived causes of poor subordinate performance. Secondly, they have been concerned to examine people's perceptions of leadership, that is, the theories that people carry around about what leadership and effective leadership are. These two areas of interest do not exhaust the full range of possibilities for the application of attribution theory to leadership, but they constitute the ones which have been submitted to a good deal of theoretical and empirical elaboration.

The first of the chief areas of interest in the application of attribution theory to leadership processes has been the nature of leaders' responses to different levels of (in particular, poor) subordinate performance. These interests are in a fairly direct line of succession to the earlier work of researchers like Lowin and Craig (1968) and Farris and Lim (1969) whose experimental investigations pointed to the influence of subordinate performance on leader behaviour. The more recent work discussed in this section deals with a broader range of responses by leaders to good and poor performance, in particular how the poor performer is perceived by the leader. One of the major strands explores the idea that when a subordinate performs at a certain level, the leader gathers information about his or her behaviour. On the basis of these bits of information the leader makes 'causal attributions' about the subordinate's behaviour, i.e. what factors seem to have engendered a particular performance level. On the basis of the explanation(s) that the leader decides upon, he or she then effects a response. In this way, a leader faced with a poor performing subordinate (the chief focus for most of the research in this area) seeks to determine the causes of that poor performance, and adjusts his or her behaviour accordingly. A simple model is suggested from these considerations (Green and Mitchell, 1979) as indicated in Figure 7.1.

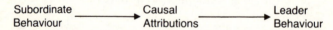

Subordinate Behaviour ⟶ Causal Attributions ⟶ Leader Behaviour

Figure 7.1 *The impact of subordinate behaviour on leader behaviour (following attribution theory)*

While this is an excessively simple model which has been greatly elaborated (Mitchell, Green and Wood, 1981) it can stand as it is for the discussion below since it provides a succinct statement of the chief foci for researchers.

An obvious consideration for researchers relates to the causal attribution process, that is, the criteria which leaders take into account when seeking to comprehend the causes of poor performance. The conceptual work of Weiner *et al.* (1972) has provided a bedrock for many researchers, even though there is a recognition that the scheme is not without problems (e.g. Mitchell *et al.*, 1981, pp. 200–1). According to this conceptual scheme, four causes are typically proffered for success or failure: ability, effort, task difficulty and luck:

That is, in attempting to explain the prior success or failure at an achievement-related event, the individual assesses his or her level of ability, the amount of effort that was expended, the difficulty of the task, and the magnitude and direction of experienced luck. (Weiner, 1979, p. 4)

In his earlier work, Weiner saw these four ascribed causes as being underpinned by two dimensions: stability and locus of control (see Table 7.1). The internal versus external locus of control issue denotes whether the causes of, say, poor performance are attributable to the individual or to factors not strictly within his or her control. The stable-unstable dimension points to whether the causes of poor performance are deemed to be relatively permanent or temporary. More recently, a third dimension has been appended to the model to indicate whether a cause is perceived as being 'subject to volitional control' (Weiner, 1979, p. 6), but since, at the time of writing, only one investigation of the causal attributions invoked by leaders has dealt with it (James and White, 1983), the elements of the simpler model evident in Figure 7.1 will provide the major focus for the discussion of research findings.

Table 7.1 *Classification scheme for the determinants of achievement behaviour*

STABILITY	LOCUS OF CONTROL	
	Internal	*External*
Stable	Ability	Task difficulty
Unstable	Effort	Luck

In addressing these broad ideas, investigators have tended to employ experimental or quasi-experimental research designs in which variations in subordinate performance form the primary experimental treatments. For example, subjects (either real or pseudo leaders) are often presented with details of subordinate performance and their causal attributions and behavioural responses are then examined. While much of the research has been carried out on American college students, some evidence has also been obtained from studies of nurses and US Navy personnel. To a certain extent, the fundamental methodology is similar to the early work of Lowin and Craig (1968), but the emphasis differs on at least two accounts. Firstly, the research emanating from the ideas of attribution theory is much more concerned with the processes which link subordinate performance and leader behaviour. Indeed, some investigations do not deal with leader behaviour, and are only concerned with the effects of subordinate performance on leaders' causal attributions. Secondly, there is an increasing interest in the various situational factors which may moderate the empirical relationships explored. Since the investigations which are relevant to this section employ quite complicated research designs, the bare bones of the findings will be summarized. Since a start has been made in this context by Mitchell *et al.* (1981), their résumé will be elaborated upon below:

1   Leaders and subordinates differ in their views of the causes of poor subordinate performance. Leaders tend to make internal attributions, whereas subordinates offer external attributions (Mitchell and Wood, 1980; and unpublished research by Soulier – reported in Mitchell *et al.*, 1981; Ilgen *et al.*, 1981). If a subordinate has a poor work history the likelihood of an internal attribution is greater (Mitchell and Wood, 1980). If the effects of poor performance are serious or harmful, an internal attribution is even more likely (Mitchell and Wood, 1980; Mitchell and Kalb, 1981). If subordinates make excuses for, or apologise for, poor performance, the leader is less likely to make internal attributions (Wood and Mitchell, 1981).

2   When leaders make internal attributions of poor subordinate performance, the former's behavioural response is likely to be punitive (Green and Liden, 1980) and to engender closer supervision (Ilgen *et al.*, 1981). The nature and severity of the leader's response is affected by the quality of the subordinate's work history, whether the effects of poor performance are serious, and whether an apology or an excuse is offered. However, a study of Navy personnel by James and White (1983) strongly suggests that poor performance *per se* affects leader behaviour. For example, the poorer the performance, the less likely leaders were to provide opportunities for participation, but were more likely to supervise closely. These relationships were direct and only rarely moderated by the nature of the causal attributions made. This finding suggests that the simple causal attribution model specified by Green and Mitchell needs to be qualified, in that it should not be too readily assumed that the subordinate performance-leader behaviour relationship is indirect.

3   A leader's rating of a subordinate who performs poorly is affected by a number of factors. Ilgen *et al.* (1981) found that leaders responded more positively to the poor performing subordinate when their own rewards were affected by his or her performance. When such interdependence was evident, the ability of the poor performer was more likely to be rated highly, training was more likely to be recommended, and an attempt was more likely to be made to search for a new bonus scheme. In addition, research by Mitchell and Liden (1982) suggests that poor performing subordinates stand a better chance of being highly rated by their leaders when the latter believe them to have social (e.g. popularity) and leadership skills

The foregoing résumé does not do justice to the sophisticated research designs from which the findings emerged. Taken together the various findings provide insights into the implications of varied subordinate performance levels for leaders' perceptions of and behaviour towards the people for whom they are responsible. In addition, some of the situational factors which impinge upon both perceptions and behaviour have been explored by these writers. The findings are of general interest in that the divergent perceptions exhibited by leaders and followers of poor performance on the part of the latter may be an important source of friction within organizations. In this context, Mitchell *et al.* (1981) have suggested that there may be important practical implications of the research, in that an important component of leadership training may be that of enhancing leaders' awareness of the causes of their perceptions and actions, and alerting them to the possibility that their responses may be occasionally inappropriate and unjust. Such sensitization would also draw to the attention of leaders the likelihood that very often their own and a subordinate's perceptions of the latter's performance may diverge, possibly inducing friction and disillusionment.

There is, however, another strand to the interest in the implications of attribution theory for the study of leadership. In the writings of Calder (1977) and Pfeffer (1977) it is the attributions that people make in 'recognizing' leaders and leadership which is of key interest. 'Leadership' is an everyday construct which has widespread usage, but when and under what circumstances people attribute it to the behaviour of others, provides an important focus of interest. According to Calder, leadership is a label which is applied to other people's (and occasionally one's own) behaviour. It is assumed in everyday discourse that leadership qualities engender certain effects. Or as Calder puts it:

> the belief that a certain leadership quality produces a certain behaviour is transformed into the expectation that an instance of the behaviour implies the existence of the quality. (Calder, 1977, p. 198)

The implication for research of such a suggestion is that one needs to examine the factors people take into account when attributing certain outcomes to leadership, or more specifically to a particular quality of leadership. People may, of course, be wrong in their belief that a particular pattern of leadership produces a certain effect. Indeed, if they *were* right, one might cynically suggest that they have done much better than the army of leadership 'experts' who have accumulated so much equivocal evidence. The main point is that people *believe* that it has certain effects. Organizations may capitalize on these everyday notions by firing prominent leaders who have been unsuccessful and in so doing give notice that the failure was attributable to the person (e.g. lack of leadership qualities), not the organization. Further, as Pfeffer (1977) observes, leaders themselves will often be aware of the taken-for-granted indicators of good leadership, and so ensure that they are associated with organizational successes and disentangle themselves from failures. Yet another implication is that people who aspire to positions of leadership may seek to emphasize precisely those attributes or ways of behaving which are indicative of leadership ability and effectiveness in their milieu. Thus in their experimental study, Staw and Ross (1980) found that the image of the effective leader was enhanced by exhibiting full commitment and steadfastness to a course of action even in the face of suggestions that it may not be the best choice. If leaders recognize this attribution they will model their own behaviour on it in order to be perceived more favourably.

Research in the context of this second strand has not developed into a systematic programme in the manner of the investigations dealing with leaders' responses to subordinate performance. There is a growing interest in the impact of knowledge of group performance on people's perceptions of the leader. In such research, subjects are allocated to different stories or videotapes which diverge *inter alia* in respect of implied differences in group performance. Subjects then indicate their perceptions of the leader under different experimental conditions. Such evidence would suggest a sequence of the kind indicated in Figure 7.2, which is analogous to that provided in Figure 7.1. It also points to the kinds of leader behaviour that are deemed to be associated with effective leadership.

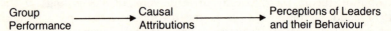

Figure 7.2 *The impact of group performance on the perception of leader behaviour (following attribution theory)*

There is evidence from laboratory experiments that when confronted with evidence of good and poor group performance, people tend to believe that success is associated with greater Consideration and Initiating Structure (Mitchell, Larson and Green, 1977). Another experimental study (Butterfield and Powell, 1981) found that leaders were evaluated more highly (in terms of group productivity, promotability, etc.) when group performance was good, irrespective of the leadership style they employed. Further, leaders were seen as exhibiting more Consideration and Initiating Structure when group performance was good, again independently of the styles which they were portrayed as exhibiting in the 'stories' with which subjects were presented. There is a slight problem with findings such as these. In Chapter 3, reference was made to the growing evidence that people have implicit leadership theories which act as cognitive simplifications for understanding and apprehending matters relating to leadership. Research within this framework has also demonstrated that the group performance cues manipulated by researchers have an impact on how leaders are deemed to behave (e.g. Rush, Thomas and Lord, 1977; Larson, 1982). When performance cues indicate good performance, greater Consideration and Initiating Structure are perceived. However, an experimental study by Phillips and Lord (1981) suggests that the role of causal attributions in this process may not be very important. It was found that performance cues had an impact on the perceived behaviour of the leader, in large part independently of the causal attributions to the leader. The impact of performance on leadership perceptions was only partially affected by people's beliefs about whether the leader was an important contributory factor to good or bad performance. As a consequence,

Phillips and Lord favour an interpretation of such results in terms of the cognitive simplifications (implicit theories) which people employ, rather than one which postulates causal attributions as moderators of the relationship between group performance and the perception of the leader's behaviour (as in Figure 7.2).

However, there may be a case for suggesting that the application of experimental and other quantitative approaches to this topic may be premature, and that a more subtle, qualitative approach might be employed to discern the range of criteria that people take into account in attributing leadership qualities to people or events. It might also be more insightful to suspend one's beliefs about what these qualities might be, and to investigate what kinds of phenomena people are referring to when talking about leadership. Such questioning may enable researchers to thresh out the concepts and ideas that people carry around which relate to leadership and which might provide a foundation for subsequent investigations in the somewhat more familiar quantitative mould. While the investigations reported in this section obviously tell us quite a lot about people's notions of leadership, by dint of using experimental or quasi-experimental research designs there is an excessive reliance on researchers' perceptions of what is important. In addition, they tell us too little about the circumstances under which 'leadership' is invoked as an explanation for events (and the reasons for it) which was the main focus of the articles of both Calder and Pfeffer. In other words, much of the research seems to have lost sight of some of the more interesting questions which an attribution approach suggests. These questions have much more to do with the everyday circumstances in which leadership is used as an explanation for events and with what is meant by leadership when such attributions are made. Both of the two strands of research identified in this review have focused on interesting issues, but their preoccupation with subordinate or group performance and with very familiar manifestations of leader behaviour have acted as a barrier to the investigation of the broader range of issues with which Calder and Pfeffer were concerned.

Leadership and organizational culture

At this point, the reader would do well to return to Chapter 1 and to scrutinize the quotations from Zaleznik and Bennis which were offered as significant attempts to distinguish leadership from management. Both quotations share a common theme in viewing leadership as essentially to do with the creation of values which inspire, provide meaning for, and instil a sense of purpose to the members of an organization. The leader is the person who actively moulds the organization's image for both internal and external consumption and who suffuses it with a sense of direction. In the words of Selznick (1957, p. 28) leadership is to do with 'the promotion and protection of values' and defining 'the mission of the enterprise' (p. 26). Selznick is in many respects the progenitor of this approach, though the significance of his ideas have lain dormant to a large extent for around two decades. The following quotations from some of the recent literature give a sense of the conceptions of leadership which converge around these ideas:

> The object of leadership is the stirring of human consciousness, the interpretation and enhancement of meanings, the articulation of key cultural strands, and the linking of organizational members to them. (Sergiovanni, 1984, p. 8)

> leaders will try to convince others to the values they themselves believe are good. (Greenfield, 1984, p. 166)

> Leaders help to define reality for others; they interpret actions, give meaning and perspective to events. (Morley, 1984, p. 269)

Further, business leaders often see themselves in a similar light. John Opel, chairman of IBM, sees himself as the custodian and promoter of the value system created by the company's founder. Opel's views are demonstrated by the following: 'I have an absolute conviction that our beliefs, our commitment to our beliefs, our ethics are imperatives'; and continues that they have been 'chipped into the marble of our conscience' (quoted in Taylor, 1983, p. 15).

This revision of the concept of leadership has occurred more or less simultaneously with a great deal of interest in business and academic circles in what is referred to as 'organizational culture' or 'corporate culture'. While a number of definitions have been proffered for these concepts they share a basic concern for the values which an organization holds dear. Examples are commitments to 'customer service' and 'teamwork' at Delta, 'financial discipline' in ITT, 'service' at IBM, 'competitiveness and innovation' at ATT, 'entrepreneurship' at Atlantic Richfield, 'productivity through people' at Dana, and so on (Anon., 1980; Bryman, 1984b, p. 23; Siehl and Martin, 1984, p. 228). Organizational cultures provide people with direction, a framework within which to interpret events, inspiration, a sense of unity, and an opportunity to transcend the routine of their work lives. Such cultures may be transmitted through a variety of media, which include: (1) clear statements of philosophy and beliefs disseminated in company documents and journals (such as *Understanding Our Philosophy* at Tandem Computers, Magnet, 1982) as well as annual statements and reports; (2) a special argot which enshrines and conveys the axioms of life in a particular organization; (3) legends and stories which are absorbed into organizational mythology, such as the spectacle of Porsche's chief executive officer strutting the pits at Le Mans after his company's surprise success (Tinnin, 1982); (4) rites, rituals and ceremonies (Deal and Kennedy, 1982, ch. 4); (5) physical settings (Martin and Siehl, 1983; Deal and Kennedy, 1982); and (6) company training programmes (Siehl and Martin, 1984).

Culture is not an esoteric area of study according to many management theorists, but one of the areas out of which success or failure are effected and a very potent one at that. In particular, it has been suggested that companies with clearly articulated cultures ('strong' cultures) tend to be more successful. Peters and Waterman (1982) examined a number of America's best-run companies and concluded:

> Without exception, the dominance and coherence of culture proved to be an essential quality of the excellent companies. . . . In these companies, people way down the line know what they are supposed to do in most situations because the handful of guiding values is crystal clear. (pp. 75-6)

Similarly, a study of 'high-performing systems' by Vaill (1984) found that members of organizations so described were imbued with a clear sense of direction by dint of the ideals and meanings which surrounded them. Similarly, Bennis (1984) concluded from his research on eighty chief executive officers drawn from a variety of contexts that the better leaders infused their organizations with a sense of vision and purpose which entices commitment and excellence. Many of the issues relating to organizational culture are more complex than this brief summary of the chief issues implies. In particular, there is a recognition that simply possessing a strong, coherent culture cannot guarantee success since strong cultures may on occasions be counter-productive (Bryman, 1984b). Indeed, much of the more recent focus within this area has been on programmes for changing corporate cultures which are inappropriate (Uttal, 1983) particularly in the light of a recognition that cultural change is difficult to effect because of people's attachments to entrenched values and their manifestations.

A fascinating example of these ideas and processes (albeit a rather extreme one) is provided by Tandem Computers and its Chief Executive Officer, Jim Treybig (Magnet, 1982; Deal and Kennedy, 1982, pp. 8-13). While this firm has all of the organizational prerequisites of companies operating in high-technology environments (e.g. few controls, flexibility, partially defined hierarchies, fluid roles), the structure is underpinned by a strong corporate culture which was the brain-child of Treybig and his associates. The culture is transmitted through orientation lectures, newsletters, magazines, a large volume called *Understanding Our Philosophy* which all staff receive, and a two-day course. The values which constitute the culture promote a wide-ranging understanding of the firm and its purpose, as well as dictates about how to treat fellow employees. The company inculcates an attitude of respect for employees at all levels. It has its rituals too, for example, in the form of Friday afternoon 'beer-busts' which not only facilitate catharsis at the end of a busy week, but also permit informal mingling across all levels. The culture pervades the nooks and crannies of the organization and instils a sense of purpose. Whether the company's great success can be attributed to its strident culture cannot be ascertained, although Magnet's (1982) report is certainly consistent with Peters and Waterman's (1982) enthusiasm for strong cultures. Of course, as implied above, in many companies Tandem's culture and its attendant organizational structure would be catastrophic. Cultures need to be appropriate as well as strong. The art of leadership would seem to be not just the inbuilding of purpose, as Selznick called it, but a recognition of the appropriate values which should be forged.

However, the main point which ought to be registered for the present discussion is that there is a clear congruence between the idea of a corporate culture and the conceptualization of the leader as a purveyor of values.[1] In the eyes of Peters and Waterman (1982, p. 75) leadership is to do with forging the meanings which form the bedrock of organizational culture. This emphasis is still highly programmatic, however, in that a full-blooded research tradition has yet to develop around it in spite of the widespread interest that the ideas have produced. The Peters and Waterman book is highly anecdotal in nature, a description which often applies to some of the theoretical statements of a number of writers too.

It is apparent that the preoccupation with the implications of the notion of the leader as visionary is rapidly being aligned with ideas of organizational effectiveness. This is evident in the Peters and Waterman and Bennis research briefly cited above. Similarly, at the end of an article on the imagery of bank managers, the authors promise that they 'plan to use these constructs to compare the imagery of high- and low-performing bank managers as identified by a performance index' (Moore and Beck, 1984, p. 252). It is easy to envisage this nascent tradition converging with the leader behaviour approach of earlier years, such that particular cultural attributes would be investigated as possible predictors of organizational effectiveness. There may be a case for suggesting that were this to happen, researchers may be running before learning to walk. Researchers' efforts may well be better directed at attempting to define and conceptualize more precisely than hitherto the nature of organizational culture and its attributes.

A more positive reaction to the ideas which have been discussed is to observe that they seem to go some way towards meeting Dubin's (1979) criticism of much research on leadership in organizations, namely, that it concentrates too much upon leadership *in* organizations (e.g. foremen, supervisors) and too little on leadership *of* organizations. The level of analysis implied by the research of Peters and Waterman and Bennis is that of the leader *of* organizations. The leaders to whom they refer are people at the very top of their respective organizations. This emphasis is different from the somewhat small-scale approach of the vast majority of the studies covered in the preceding chapters, in which the focus is upon the leader influencing a group of subordinates towards the attainment of a goal. The emphasis in both the theoretical and empirical endeavour relating to the view of the leader as a creator of culture is to focus on the organization as a whole, and leadership *of* it. It remains to be seen whether work in this tradition will persist with the emphasis on top leaders, since interviewing and observation are made more difficult by their greater inaccessibility and the considerable time constraints to which they are subject. Bennis's (1984) research, however, suggests that it is feasible to construct such research. But while an emphasis on very senior personnel is a useful corrective to the plethora of studies on leadership *in* organizations (that is, among people in a variety of supervisory positions), it is important not to neglect the possible significance of subcultures in organizations (e.g. Martin and Siehl, 1983) and leadership in relation to them.

One of the main contributions that this general approach may make is that of disentangling the idea of leadership from that of management, of saying something about what it is and how it differs from kindred notions. There is a clear desire in the work of Bennis (1984, p. 66) and Peters and Waterman (1982) to clarify such issues. Indeed, there is the possibility of reading into what they write a suggestion that if a leader does not explicate a cluster of values to define the purpose of an organization he or she is not acting as a leader. Such an orientation would clearly facilitate a distinction between leadership as headship (the incumbency of an office to which authority pertains) and leadership as a qualitatively distinct activity. According to this latter view, it is not so much the behaviour of leaders that is important (and which has been the central focus for over three decades) but the images and impressions they invoke.[2] Equally, there is a recognition in the literature that frequently leaders are not allowed to lead, and that instead they are pressured into being managers. Bennis (1976), in particular, has bemoaned the tendency for leaders to become enmeshed in the bureaucratic routine of organizational life, which frequently threatens to submerge them. When this occurs, the leader has neither the time nor the opportunity to raise his or her head above an inexorable tide of humdrum tasks which, while necessary for the smooth running of the organization, often inhibit the leader's scope for instilling purpose and creating a culture: the leader becomes a manager.

Other developments

The foregoing developments – the application of attribution theory and the emphasis on the leader as the creator of organizational culture – are particularly prominent foci in the recent literature, in addition to the ones encountered in the previous chapters. The rest of this chapter will address some recent tendencies (as against identifiable clusters) in the literature.

1 The observation of leader behaviour

There seems to be a growing disenchantment with questionnaire and (although probably to a lesser extent) with experimental studies of leaders and their behaviour. The accumulating evidence on implicit leadership theories (e.g. Phillips, 1984) has severely affected the faith of many researchers in some of the standard questionnaire instruments. Further, the widespread interest among leadership researchers in the studies of managers *au naturel* by writers like Mintzberg (1973) may have had an effect in this respect too. Indeed, such research has often fomented unease among leadership researchers, since the image of the manager which such observation studies have painted is at some variance with the assumptions frequently held about leaders and their behaviour (see Chapter 6). In particular, the representation of the work of managers as imbued with orderliness, rationality, and an emphasis on planning, has been seriously undermined by such research. This recognition has been taken to have implications for the study of leadership which has tended to operate with a similar battery of assumptions. Consequently, researchers have been directing their attentions increasingly to the observation of leadership. In addition to the work of Bussom *et al.* (1982), which was briefly encountered in Chapter 3, there are some further examples.

One recent case in point is the development of a Leader Observation System (LOS) by Luthans and Lockwood (1984). Unlike the works of writers like Mintzberg who adopted a strongly qualitative orientation to the investigation of managers, the LOS seeks to quantify leader behaviours. Initially, graduate students conducted a total of 440 hours of unstructured observation of forty-four leaders. On the basis of their logs and records an attempt was made to render down the observations into categories. Finally, twelve categories were derived, all of which are fairly self-explanatory: planning/cooperating, staffing, training/developing, decision-making/problem-solving, processing paperwork, exchanging routine information, monitoring/controlling performance, motivating/reinforcing, disciplining/punishing, interacting with outsiders, managing conflict, and socializing/politicking. From this classification, the authors derived the LOS instrument which enables the recording of either the presence or absence of each behavioural category in a random ten-minute time-slot.

While an instrument such as this is valuable and a useful corrective to the perceptual nature of questionnaires, a major problem for the student of leadership is indicated by a passing comment: 'it appears to be difficult to separate "leadership behaviour" per se from the larger domain of managerial activities, and the LOS reflects this difficulty' (Luthans and Lockwood, 1984, p. 121). A similar observation was made by the author in Chapter 3 in connection with the Bussom *et al.* (1982) approach. The difficulty for the leadership researcher is that of uncoupling the leadership component of managerial behaviour in the context of either structured or unstructured observation. Can leadership as such be studied in such contexts when, as Mintzberg suggests, it pervades all managerial activity? While the work of Mintzberg (1973) and Stewart (1967) has quite properly been taken to have implications for the study of leadership, they were not attempting to study leadership *per se*. Indeed, the list of LOS categories produced by Luthans and Lockwood does not differ greatly from the ten-fold list of managerial roles Mintzberg provided, but has the disadvantage of not demarcating a leader role! In short, can leadership be observed?

Another recent piece of research which employs observational methods is a study of school principals by Martinko and Gardner (1984). The researchers adopted a social learning theory approach as the general orientation to the investigation. According to their application of the approach, the environments both external and internal to the school affect the likelihood of managerial behaviour being effective. Principals are viewed as processors of these environmental stimuli, who then decide what kinds of behaviour are likely to be effective in the prevailing circumstances, and behave in accordance with their hunches. Trained observers collected their data through direct, non-participant observation (over nine days) which entailed using a coding form. The data recording involved both narrative descriptions of the behaviour of school principals and subsequent documentation of specific details such as the medium of communication of specific events, their duration, and the like. Martinko and Gardner were interested not just in generating broad descriptions of these educational managers, but also in the implications of variations in practices for performance. The researchers were able to distinguish high-performing from moderate-performing principals on the basis of a range of performance criteria (e.g. superintendents' ratings of both the schools and the principals). They found, among other things, that high performers spend more time in unscheduled meetings (and less time in scheduled ones) than moderate performers. Of particular interest to the study of leadership is the finding that high performing principals adopted a task-oriented style in their interactions with both teachers and students more frequently than moderate performers who were more likely to employ a 'human-relations' orientation.

This research is of interest because it seeks to thresh out the leadership component of managerial behaviour (while being interested in the latter in its own right too) and because it relates variations in leadership style and other aspects of managerial behaviour to performance. The examination of the implications of variations in observed leader and managerial behaviour for performance has been missing from studies like those of Mintzberg (1973), Bussom *et al.* (1982), and Luthans and Lockwood (1984). Consequently, Martinko and Gardner have harnessed an observation approach to the study of designated leaders (in contrast to a questionnaire study or an experimental approach) in addressing a topic that has preoccupied generations of leadership researchers – namely the effect of leadership style on performance. In finding that a task-oriented style enhances performance, their findings are in broad synchrony with the early Ohio State findings (e.g. Halpin, 1957). Unfortunately, their presentation of the data analysis does not permit any inferences to be drawn about the implications of an emphasis on *both* the task and 'human relations'. A major limitation of the research is that it is based on only twenty-one principals (only seven of whom were moderate performers), so that caution needs to be exercised in attaching too much significance to the findings. Further, in seeking to make a contribution to the study of leadership, the researchers have been seduced by the very familiar task-versus-people dichotomy as its main manifestation. Where people of some seniority are concerned, other components of leadership would be just as, if not more, interesting. For example, how principals handle the job of being in charge of organizations with ambiguous goals and technologies (following Cohen and March, 1974 – see Chapter 6) would have been of great interest; so too would an emphasis on the cultures they help to create and their divergent implications for performance.

There seems to be, then, a growing interest in the direct observation of the behaviour of leaders. As has already been suggested, the method is not without its problems, if only because the problem of disentangling the leadership component of managerial behaviour is troublesome. It may be that instilling a qualitative component into such research will provide a basis for unravelling the leadership element, for although the data derived from the studies reviewed in this section are qualitative, they have rapidly been harnessed to the quantitative approach to data analysis which has been pervasive in the past.[3]

2　Leadership as a process

The bulk of leadership research in organizations has involved a static conception of its subject matter: this assertion applies not only to the correlational designs which have been reviewed but even to the longitudinal studies and many of the experiments examined in previous chapters. Leadership has been seen as something that is done to others, so that changes in the behaviour of leaders and leadership processes over time have been treated somewhat cursorily. Yet theory and research have often shown such foci to be important, but have had scant effect on prevailing conceptions and research designs. Examples of an awareness of leadership processes which have been encountered are: Hollander's (1978) notion of leadership as an exchange process in which leaders and followers are reciprocally interdependent; the somewhat congruent Vertical Dyad Linkage Model (Danserau *et al.*, 1975) which views leader-follower relations as changing over time in terms of the kinds of relationships that prevail, although one may wish to question how permanent the differentiation of followers into In and Out Groups is; evidence that leadership style is not fixed but changes over time in response to variations in context (see Chapter 4); and the growing interest in the observation of leader behaviour enhances the researcher's ability to gain empirical leverage on changes in leadership processes.

A further instance of a greater sensitivity to the processual element in leadership is the application of social learning theory. The Martinko and Gardner (1984) article, which was referred to in the previous section, is one example of the application of these ideas in a context relevant to the study of leadership. Similarly, Luthans (1979, pp. 204-5) argues that social learning theory implies a perspective in which 'a leader's behaviour is explained as a reciprocal interaction of personal, environmental, and behavioural determinants'. Such a perspective suggests a more dynamic orientation being injected into the study of leadership, in which environmental circumstances are not simply moderating variables in the manner of contingency approaches, but are mercurial phenomena to whose changing implications the leader must constantly adjust. The Leader Observation System developed by Luthans and Lockwood was prepared with this broad orientation in mind. However, the tendency for the proponents of this approach to vacillate between talking about leadership (Luthans, 1979) and managerial behaviour (Davis and Luthans, 1980) renders the interpretation of its relevance for the study of leader behaviour somewhat problematic. Nonetheless, it provides an interesting example of the infusion of processual elements into the study of leader behaviour, though the theory and sparse research are still quite a way from constituting a research tradition.

Another indication of the interest in leadership processes is provided by the work of Zahn and Wolf (1981) who take the view that: 'More process-oriented models are required to capture the fluid nature of leadership' (p. 26). Their model builds on the idea of superior-subordinate relationships as involving an exchange, and suggests that such relationships go through cycles. Zahn and Wolf argue that two important elements in such dyadic relationships are the resources exchanged and communication functions. The first aspect – resources exchanged – can be conceptualized in terms of task resources (which contribute to or detract from task attainment in varying degrees) and relationship resources (which contribute to the creation and maintenance of the dyad). Secondly, the communication process can be taken to comprise initiations (which start a cycle of communication) and responses (which may terminate it). These two dichotomies imply four types of behaviour: task initiation, task response, relationship initiation, and relationship response. The model assumes that it is not only designated leaders who initiate action, but subordinates too. Thus one cycle may go roughly as follows: the superior threatens (task initiation by superior) → the subordinate rejects the threats (task response by the subordinate) → the subordinate sabotages the task (task initiation by subordinate) → the superior punishes (task response by superior). Other parallel cycles suggested are: superior instructs → subordinate legitimizes → subordinate performs dependably → superior acknowledges; or superior offers participation → subordinate agrees to participate → subordinate cooperates → superior listens. While the full model is much more complex than this brief description implies, this very cursory treatment of it highlights how much is omitted or taken as given in conventional, non-processual models of leadership. It still awaits empirical treatment, however.

The ideas which have been addressed in this section not only manifest a more pronounced concern for leadership as a process: they also imply that the leader/follower distinction is often not as stark as it is sometimes depicted. Leadership entails a sensitivity to the needs and values of followers which implies that it is not simply a matter of doing things to subordinates. As suggested in Chapter 1, conceptions of leadership which concentrate excessively on the leader-follower relationship in terms of power or influence seem to omit the notion of leadership as involving the motivation of others. But motivation is unlikely to occur unless the leader takes the needs and values of followers into account. As a prominent writer on leadership has put it:

> I define leadership as leaders inducing followers to act for certain goals
> that represent the values and motivations – the wants and needs, the
> aspirations and expectations – *of both leaders and followers*. And the
> genius of leadership lies in the manner in which leaders see and act on
> their own and their followers' values and motivations. (Burns, 1978,
> p. 19)

The interpenetration of leaders and followers has been a neglected area but
is one which the more recent emphasis on leadership processes may help to
rectify. Furthermore, as the quotation from Burns implies, in order to
understand the motivational component in leadership, it is necessary to
conceptualize it as a process in which the reciprocal interdependence of
leaders and followers is a highly salient ingredient.

3   Does leadership change make a difference?

Over the years that researchers have been emphasizing the contribution of
leader behaviour to organizational effectiveness, there have been a number
of writers concerned with a different kind of question: what contribution
does a change in leadership make to the subsequent performance of an
organization? It would be inaccurate to refer to writers who have
addressed this question as forming a research tradition, in that the
publication of material relating to it has been highly spasmodic. However,
there has been a surge of interest in the issue. It is appropriate to examine
this literature, not because the empirical data emanating from it are
particularly interesting, but because it raises fundamental issues about
theory and research relating to the study of leadership.

An early study by Gamson and Scotch (1964) found that changing the
coaches of basketball teams had little effect on subsequent team
performance. According to these researchers the firing of coaches is a form
of scapegoating, that is a means of publicly attributing blame for
performance which is below expectations. Lieberson and O'Connor
examined the effects of changes in top management on subsequent
performance in 167 large corporations over twenty years. In addition to
leadership changes, the authors also examined the effects of the state of the
economy, the industrial sector in which each firm was located, and the
company's position within the industrial sector. The authors found that
the two latter variables had a stronger effect on company sales and
earnings than did changes in leadership. However, leadership was found to
have a significant impact on profit margins. Lieberson and O'Connor take
these findings to suggest that:

> in emphasizing the effects of leadership we may be overlooking far
> more powerful environmental influences. Unless leadership is studied as
> part of a total set of forces, one cannot gauge its impact. (Lieberson and
> O'Connor, 1972, p. 129)

Such findings suggest that the amount of discretion available to top leaders is constrained by forces internal and external to the organization, a point that was also made in Chapter 6. In like fashion, Salancik and Pfeffer (1977) have observed that the ability of mayors in the USA to have an impact on city budgets is affected by the presence of organized interest groups. Mayors had little discretion over budgets in cities with higher median incomes, higher levels of unionization, and higher proportions of persons in professional and managerial positions.

There has even been the suggestion from a study of major-league basketball teams over fifty years that changes in leadership during a season may result in a deterioration in performance, suggesting that the disruption occasioned by succession has a detrimental effect on performance (Allen, Panian and Lotz, 1979). This finding was not supported by Brown's (1982) analysis of data on National Football League teams in the USA, though the suggestion that changes in leadership may enhance performance was not sustained either. Brown concludes that changing football coaches should be seen as a ritual which conforms to and reinforces the popular belief that they really do make a difference.

Studies such as these imply that leadership is not as important as many people take it to be. Changing top leaders seems to make little difference to subsequent performance. In part this may be because leaders are often severely constrained; in part it may be that researchers and lay people alike habitually overstate the importance of leadership. While it is certainly feasible and appropriate to draw these rather pessimistic conclusions from the foregoing summary of research, the studies are of interest at another level. As Pfeffer (1981b) has observed, top leaders act as powerful symbols of their organizations, as well as of successes and failures. When things go awry, as Gamson and Scotch (1964) realized, such leaders provide ideal scapegoats for past failure. By removing a top leader from office the organization is able to attribute blame, to signal its commitment to removing the source of past infelicity, and in the appointment of a successor to herald renewal and change. The search for and appointment of a successor may be undertaken in a highly public way, with no expense spared, in order to reinforce the break with the past. Further, as Pfeffer has observed:

> Ceremonies of firing and replacement . . . can help to placate groups
> from which the organization needs support as well as to signal changes
> in policies and practices to those who work within the organization.
> (Pfeffer, 1981b, p. 40)

This approach to understanding the nature and significance of leadership succession is highly congruent with the 'institutional' approach to the study of organizations (see Chapter 6). This perspective views organizational practices as often deriving from a quest for legitimacy rather than efficiency (Meyer and Rowan, 1977). In other words, the fact that leadership seems to make little difference in terms of performance outcomes is unimportant, since it is the *belief* that it matters that is of interest. This suggestion also brings us back to the emphasis within the attribution approach on the perception of the causation of events and the role of leaders in relation to it. The tendency to attribute failure to personal rather than environmental factors is likely to ensure that leaders will tend to be scapegoats; but the same proclivity in everyday life for personal rather than environmental causation is likely to ensure the continuation of the belief that replacing leaders will make things better. However, as was suggested in connection with attribution theory earlier in this chapter, very little is known about the nature of the beliefs that people hold about leaders and leadership, a lacuna that will have to be assailed before this line of thinking can be taken much further.

Ironically, more recent researchers have generated findings which indicate that, after all, leadership changes *do* make a difference. An examination by Weiner and Mahoney (1981) of data on 193 manufacturing firms over twenty years suggests that changes in top leadership make more of a difference to company performance than Lieberson and O'Connor found. Further, two leadership strategies were investigated: a capital structure strategy (debt to equity ratio) and a retained earnings strategy (per cent of net earnings retained). The former was found to have a strong inverse effect on a number of performance indicators – in particular stock prices. A retained earnings strategy had little effect on performance. Findings such as these suggest that top leaders can make a difference to organizational performance although Weiner and Mahoney somewhat disconcertingly attribute part of the difference between their results and those of Lieberson and O'Connor to contrasting research designs and approaches to data analysis.

A study by Smith, Carson and Alexander (1984) provides a particularly interesting example of research which suggests that leadership can make a difference. The authors examined the careers of senior ministers in the United Methodist Church over twenty years. This church regularly (roughly every five years) reassigns ministers as a matter of policy, so that movement from congregation to congregation is largely unaffected by the minister's performance. The pivotal contribution of this research is the identification of a sub-sample of particularly effective ministers. By identifying such a group, the researchers would be able to compare the impact of effective ministers on organizational performance with that of their less effective counterparts. The researchers were able to determine such a group on the basis of their having consistently received high salaries across their careers. In the view of Smith *et al.*, this is an adequate means of identifying effective leaders, because congregations determine salary levels which are likely to reflect the leader's past, present, or prospective performance. It was found that changes in leadership among this group of effective leaders had a significant impact on five out of six indicators of organizational performance. The five indicators were: weekly attendance, number on membership rolls, value of church property, the amount given to the General Assembly, and the church's charitable income for a year. When Smith *et al.* examined the effect of leadership changes on organizational performance for all of the ministers in their sample, no substantial evidence for leadership making a difference was discerned. It would seem that effective leaders do make a difference to the performance of their new organizations; leaders as a whole do not. As the authors recognize, however, while their findings offer a possible reason for the failure to find that leadership changes have an effect on performance (namely, they lump together effective and ineffective leaders), we still do not know what it is about the effective leaders that makes them effective. In a clear attempt to draw their study closer to the research traditions encountered in earlier chapters of this book, they suggest: 'Perhaps it is time to go beyond describing leader activities or behaviour and concentrate on identifying effective or influential behaviours' (Smith *et al.*, 1984, pp. 775-6). In fact, it would be exceedingly difficult to accommodate this recommendation. Their data were based on a twenty-year period, so that inferences about what kinds of activities distinguish effective from ineffective leaders would have to be considered retrospectively. This procedure would be less than desirable, and yet long time spans are necessary in order to establish whether or not leadership makes a difference. Three further problems remain. One is that effective leaders and their less effective peers may differ from each other in ways other than their effectiveness and leader behaviour. Secondly, many social scientists and ministers would dispute the employment of financial indicators of performance, rather than spiritual ones.

Finally, while of great interest, all of the studies of leadership succession reviewed here beg the question of what they have to do with the study of leadership. Fundamentally, they are referring to 'headship' (see Chapter 1) – the incumbency of an office. The inclusion of 'leadership strategy' in the Weiner and Mahoney (1981) research does little to remedy this problem, since it departs substantially from any notion of leadership as it is conventionally understood. Their two dimensions of leadership strategy denote approaches to corporate financial management that people in leadership positions can be conceptualized as adopting and have little to do with leadership as an influence process or as a motivational force. We still know far too little about whether the people to whom the studies assessed in this section refer really are leaders rather than either managers or powerful office holders. It is assumed that such people are leaders and that they exhibit leadership, whereas many writers have striven (apparently unsuccessfully) to suggest that headship is different from leadership, as some of the discussion in Chapter 1 indicated.

A final overview

The foregoing explication and examination of recent developments in the study of leadership in organizations has not done full justice to the range of new departures. Undoubtedly, the author's omissions will be a source of ire, but it is hoped that readers will have developed a sense of the proliferation of new approaches that has occurred in recent years. There can be little doubt that this trend has been prompted by the disappointment with the overall thrust of leadership research. As one writer has recently put it:

> As we all know, the study, and more particularly, the results produced by the study, of leadership has been a major disappointment for many of us working within organizational behaviour. (Cummings, 1981, p. 366)

The developments referred to in this chapter are ones about which many writers on leadership are displaying a good deal of enthusiasm and may well alleviate the disappointment that pervades the field. The interest in viewing leadership in terms of the creation of values which instil a sense of purpose is likely to be fuelled by the fascination over corporate culture with which many practitioners and researchers are currently infused. The recognition that organizations are not simply structures, but socially created realities imbued with heavy doses of symbolism, has been a major conceptual advance in which leadership researchers are sharing. In the past, the study of leadership in organizations and research on organizations have often operated as separate fields, with little dovetailing of ideas. The emphasis on organizational cultures, along with some of the departures mentioned in Chapter 6, are going some way towards alleviating this tendency. However, as was noted earlier in this book, there may be other developments in the study of organizations in which leadership researchers might share. In addition, the growing interest in the application of attribution theory has also been reviewed and there are clear signs that fruitful lines of enquiry are emanating from it. Unfortunately, it has not gone far enough. We need to know far more about leadership as an everyday construct – what people mean by it and how they recognize it. This suggests that it will be necessary to conduct systematic questioning of people regarding their perceptions of leadership in a variety of milieux.

It may be that the various new departures mentioned in this and previous chapters, as well as those not treated within these covers, are merely examples of researchers clutching at straws, and that Miner's (1975) suggestion that the concept of leadership should be abandoned is the more appropriate way forward. Of course, only time will tell. But of one thing this author is absolutely certain: there will always be doubt about the utility of the concept of leadership, and the desirability of examining aspects of it, as long as researchers are imprecise about what it denotes. Throughout this book reference has been made to the tendency for researchers to use the term 'leadership' synonymously with management and supervision. Many of the dimensions of leader behaviour measured by researchers could just as easily be referred to as managerial or supervisory behaviour. Indeed, whether the aspects of behaviour are referred to in many publications as, for example, leadership or managerial or supervisory style seems to have much more to do with the predilections of researchers rather than anything denoted by the behaviour and its conceptualization. To a very large extent, this problem arises because of the tendency to investigate leadership as that which is exhibited by a person in a position of leadership, i.e. the incumbent of an office. This propensity prevails in spite of the fact that there is a widespread acknowledgment that leadership is not simply the occupation of a position, but something rather more. We still know far too little about this 'something rather more'.

Books conventionally end with conclusions, but in the author's view a final, pithy conclusion would be gratuitously arbitrary. The study of leadership in organizations is a field in flux, with many cherished assumptions, theories and methodological proclivities under siege. More conventional research interests and strategies co-exist with the emerging products of the waves of new orientations and perspectives. If anything is to be concluded from these manifold trends it is that the concept of leadership is an elusive one. Not only are there difficulties attached to distinguishing it from neighbouring ideas and concepts, but research designs so frequently fail to capture its distinctiveness. Future generations of researchers may lose heart and decide that the conceptual and methodological problems associated with the concept of leadership are too intractable, but this is an unlikely eventuality. The theory and research which have been confronted in this book have led to interesting insights into organizational behaviour, though their implications for the study of leadership as such are often less than obvious. Insofar as 'leadership' has been the focus for these interests such endeavour is likely to continue. On the other hand, the groping towards new directions, many of which are sensitive to the conceptual and methodological tribulations of past researchers, is cause for much optimism.

NOTES

1 The idea of leadership and the methodology of leadership research

1 The other managerial roles delineated by Mintzberg (1973) are: 1 *figurehead* – formally representing the organization; 2 *liaison* – maintaining outside contacts to secure favours and information; 3 *monitor* – the manager receives and collects information about the organization; 4 *disseminator* – transmits accumulated information internally; 5 *spokesman* – information about the organization is disseminated to its environment; 6 *entrepreneur* – initiator of change; 7 *disturbance handler* – dealing with unanticipated problems affecting the organization; 8 *resource allocator* – deciding how organizational resources ought to be distributed; and 9 *negotiator* – conducts negotiations on the organization's behalf.

2 The problem of social desirability effects has been addressed in Phillips (1973).

3 Campbell (1957) refers to internal validity as the extent to which the experimental stimulus (i.e. participative leadership) really does make a difference to the presumed effect. Essentially, it refers to the degree to which extraneous factors which may affect internal validity are eliminated. Campbell distinguishes this issue from 'external validity' which refers to the generalizability of a finding.

4 The alternative that is often used is that of matching group members on known characteristics.

5 The absence of pre-testing may be advantageous, however, in that it may reduce the degree of sensitization to the experimental variable.

6 The 'critical incident' method is a technique which has attracted some attention. The basic idea is to collect from both leaders and other respondents examples of effective and ineffective leadership which are then distilled to provide fundamental components of leader behaviour. Yukl (1981, p. 104) cites fourteen studies of leaders using this technique and has since published an article (Yukl and van Fleet, 1982) which relies in part on data derived from two critical incidents data collection exercises. This article is referred to briefly in Chapter 4. One of the data collection exercises involved asking respondents (members of the Texas A & M University Corps of Cadets) to write short descriptions of especially effective and especially ineffective leadership behaviour. A total of 3,111 incidents were collected. Only the 1,511 positive incidents were analysed and were rendered down according to a conceptual

scheme for classifying leader behaviours which Yukl has developed. The technique suffers from a problem of knowing how far respondents are in agreement over what leadership means. It also relies heavily on the skills of those who distil the data. There are signs that the technique is becoming more popular, though it may be that it will tend to be used as an adjunct to more conventional techniques like questionnaires, as in the Yukl and van Fleet article. Compared to the use of questionnaires and experiments, the critical incident technique is nonetheless a minority method.

2 Traits and abilities

1 This methodologial stance was not by any means the only one employed by researchers working within the trait tradition. It was, however, a very prominent one and seems to have been responsible for some of the more classic studies associated with this genre.

2 The idea of charismatic leadership is one of a number of 'metaphors of leadership' employed in popular speech (Dubin, 1979). The idea of someone 'having charisma' is a popular explanation of a person's success as a leader. As such, the idea tends to be invoked in such a way that charisma is an attribute which a person possesses. This popular treatment of the idea differs from that of Weber (1947) who did much to popularize it within academic circles. According to Weber the follower is an important ingredient:

> The term 'charisma' will be applied to a certain quality of an individual personality by virtue of which he is set apart from ordinary men and endowed with supernatural, superhuman, or at least specifically exceptional powers or qualities. . . . What is alone important is how the individual is actually regarded by those subject to charismatic authority, by his 'followers' or 'disciples'. . . . It is recognition on the part of those subject to authority which is decisive for the validity of charisma. (Weber, 1947, pp. 358-9)

Such a view emphasizes the perception of the charismatic leader and his or her qualities, rather than treating charisma as a personal attribute. Similarly, Burns (1978), who prefers the term 'heroic leadership', because the idea of charisma has been somewhat exploited, remarks: 'Heroic leadership is not simply a quality or entity possessed by someone; it is a type of relationship between leader and led' (Burns, 1978, p. 244). House's (1977) approach to the idea of charismatic leadership in terms of the 'charismatic effects' that such leaders have on others, seems to encapsulate the element of 'followership' to which Burns implicitly refers. According to House, such leaders *inter alia* articulate ideological goals and 'arouse motives relevant to the accomplishment of mission' (House, 1977, p. 203) in greater degree than do non-charismatic leaders. These speculations imply that charisma may be better viewed, not as a personal trait, which is the conventional interpretation, but as denoting a certain kind of leader-follower relationship.

3 One aspect of trait research which has been neglected is the contribution, not of traits as such, but of the perception of traits by followers. A study of boys and girls at a summer camp by Clifford and Cohn (1964) emphasized the contribution of the personal attributes perceived by followers to the attribution of leadership. This study also found that the perception of the appropriate characteristics differed from situation to situation. This aspect of trait research

has been surprisingly overlooked. Its omission is at least in part a function of the neglect of the follower in much leadership research.

3 Leadership style I: early approaches and normative programmes

1 Whether the three leadership climates in the Iowa research denote three experimental treatments is a moot point. One of the 'leaders' did not act according to his script and failed to provide leadership of either a democratic or autocratic kind. This style of leadership was retrospectively dubbed *laissez-faire* (Albanese and van Fleet, 1983, p. 294).

2 In addition to Initiating Structure, Consideration and Production Emphasis, the sub-scales are: (i) *representation* – representing and acting on behalf of the group; (ii) *demand reconciliation* – the reconciliation of conflicting demands; (iii) *tolerance of uncertainty* – the ability to cope with uncertain situations; (iv) *persuasiveness* – the ability to deploy persuasive arguments; (v) *tolerance of freedom* – permitting scope for subordinates' initiative and action; (vi) *role assumption* – the active exercise of leadership rather than abrogating it to others; (vii) *predictive accuracy* – the ability to have foresight; (viii) *integration* – the maintenance of group cohesion; and (ix) *superior orientation* – the maintenance of good relations with the leader's own supervisors. There is some variation from study to study in the number of sub-scales discerned by statistical analysis (Stogdill, Goode and Day, 1962, 1963a, 1963b, 1964). It is worth observing that 'tolerance of freedom' bears a strong resemblance to the idea of 'participative leadership' which will be a prominent theme in Chapters 4 and 5.

3 Those items with 'Reverse' after them are scored in reverse order from the others. A person who agrees with this item is describing his or her leader as lacking Consideration; the other items are indicative of Consideration when the respondent agrees with them. Consequently, items with 'Reverse' in brackets are scored in the opposite direction from the rest.

4 'Cognitive complexity' means the extent to which an individual differentiates between the diverse elements in his or her environment. Individuals who are cognitively complex might have exhibited a less pronounced reliance on implicit leadership theories. In fact, this possibility was not supported by Weiss and Adler's (1981) evidence.

5 In fact, the symmetry between Initiating Structure/Consideration and Concern for Production/People is not as obvious as is often assumed. In many respects, Concern for Production is closer to the Ohio factor called 'Production Emphasis'.

4 Leadership style II: participation, rewards, motivation and control

1 On the basis of detailed observation of interaction within leaderless problem-solving groups, Bales (e.g. Bales and Slater, 1955) drew a distinction between leaders who fulfil a group's task-related needs and those who satisfy its social-emotional needs. These descriptions bear a resemblance to the Initiating Structure/Consideration dichotomy discussed in detail in the last chapter. However, whereas the Ohio State researchers felt that it was perfectly feasible to describe a focal leader in terms of both dimensions, Bales seems to have seen them as mutually exclusive. Bales's work has been enormously influential and it

was tempting to allocate more space to it. However, as Limerick (1976) has observed, Bales's work has not been very influential in connection with research into leadership in formal organizations. In part, this is due to the tendency for the conceptualization of the two types of leader as opposites to be unfashionable; indeed, as Limerick observes, Bales was not entirely successful in his attempt to isolate two distinct patterns of behaviour associated with each leader. Further, the location of Bales's research in laboratories may have limited its appeal to students of formal organizations.

2 Further problems regarding the Coch and French study have been raised by Bartlem and Locke (1981). They observe that the experimental groups had only relatively insignificant opportunities for participation (i.e. minor proposals for changes in work design). Bartlem and Locke also believe that the experiment was confounded by: (a) the explanation employed to justify the job changes; (b) the methods for timing and setting rates for the new jobs; and (c) the provision of extra training. The authors argue that an alternative interpretation of the experiment is that the 'perceived fairness of the (new) pay rates' (p. 564 was a major factor in determining the results.

3 The authors of reviews of the literature on participation diverge over the interpretation of some studies. An example of this tendency is a study of the opportunity for managers to participate in setting the goals of an appraisal system to examine their performance (French, Kay and Meyer, 1966). Both Yukl (1981) and Filley *et al.* (1976) assert that greater participation led to greater productivity when comparison is made with the control groups. Locke and Schweiger (1979, pp. 310 and 315) portray the research as not demonstrating that participation led to greater productivity. The divergence in interpretation is due to Locke and Schweiger's recognition that contextual factors (e.g. whether subjects were used to participation) impinged upon the participation-productivity relationship. Where contextual variables were found by researchers to have a moderating effect, Locke and Schweiger take the view that the positive effects of participation have not been demonstrated. This tendency among reviewers to interpret the meaning of evidence differently from each other applies equally to studies of participation in non-organizational settings and to the correlational research.

4 Interestingly, Nightingale (1981) formed a different conclusion about the substantive significance of finding that 42 per cent of structure-style pairings were incongruent. He concluded that 'in general, organizational structure and supervisory style tend toward congruence' (Nightingale, 1981, p. 1127). The problem is: how large is large? In this author's view 42 per cent represents a lot of incongruence, too much to draw the conclusion formulated by Nightingale.

5 The reader may quite appropriately ask why the literature on participative systems was included at all in the light of the author's clear misgivings. Two responses can be made in this context. Firstly, the study of participative systems has a bearing on the study of participative leadership, in that it investigates the possibility that allowing people greater latitude at work enhances their involvement, performance, etc. The fruits of such scrutiny are bound to be relevant to the study of participative leadership. Secondly, the author has striven to provide a portrayal of the literature on leadership in organizations as it is conventionally apprehended, without, it is to be hoped, succumbing to sycophancy. Hence, insofar as research on participative systems is routinely included within the purview of the study of leadership in organizations (e.g. Filley *et al.*, 1976; Yukl, 1981) there was a further justification for including it.

5 Contingency approaches to the study of leadership

1 The three components of situational favourableness (control) are differentially weighted, thus: Situational Favourableness = 4 (leader-member relations) + 2 (task structure) + (positive power).

2 The reasons for the pattern of empirical relationships revealed by Figure 5.3 are not always apparent. An explanation which relies on the early 'task versus relationship' interpretation of the LPC scale runs as follows:

> In very favourable conditions . . . the group is ready to be directed how to go about its task. Under a very unfavourable condition, however, the group will fall apart unless the leader's active intervention and control can keep members on the job. In moderately unfavourable conditions, a relationship-oriented, nondirective, permissive attitude may reduce member anxiety or intra-group conflict, and this enables the group to operate more effectively. (Fiedler, 1978a, p. 183)

With the emergence of the 'motivational hierarchy' interpretation of the LPC scale the explanation has become more complex (see Fiedler and Chemers, 1984, pp. 22-5).

3 There is yet another interpretation of the LPC scale, which was in fact the first one proposed by Fiedler. Initially, it seems to have been seen as indicative of social and psychological distance among leaders. Low LPC leaders are more distant from group members; high LPC leaders tend to be more socially and emotionally involved (see Rice, 1978a, pp. 1202-3). Furthermore, Rice has suggested an alternative interpretation on the basis of a thorough examination of the relevant literature. He calls it the 'value-attitude interpretation' because it 'views the LPC scale as a measure of *attitudes* that reflect basic difference in the *values* of persons scoring high or low on the scale' (Rice, 1978a, p. 1215). Accordingly, low LPC people *value* task success which affects their *attitudes* to themselves, the environment and others; high LPC people *value* interpersonal success which affects their *attitudes*. This interpretation seems to place a greater emphasis upon the perceptual ramifications of the values associated with high and low scoring LPC respondents than on the behavioural aspects of such distinctions. Like other approaches to the interpretation of the scale, the meaning of the middle-scoring LPC person in this light is not without difficulties.

4 Adequate tests are those which (a) do not entail gross departures from the methods and procedures associated with Fiedler's methodology; (b) were conducted on groups whose characteristics were not congruent with the necessary preconditions specified by Fiedler (e.g. groups members were not 'interacting', or were selected by virtue of their similarity to each other); and (c) may have had their results confounded by other factors (e.g. if leaders were the source of descriptions of the situation or performance). Studies which contain practices such as these are regarded by Hosking (1981) as questionable in terms of their relevance for the empirical validity of Fiedler's model.

6 Leadership and the study of organizations

1 The names conventionally associated with the Classical Management tradition are Fayol, Urwick, Follett, Gulick and Taylor. While their writings are

obviously not identical, they share common preoccupations. In particular, they tended to focus on the refinement of organizational blueprints which were presented as general principles. Most of the literature emerging from the tradition was published in the first half of the century. By the early 1950s it was going out of fashion in management circles. The 'human relations' writers (see Chapter 3) were early protagonists of Classical Management theory by virtue of their emphasis on informal processes in organizations. Useful discussions of Classical Management theory may be found in Filley, House and Kerr (1976, ch. 1) and Mouzelis (1967, ch. 4).

2 Weber's views on bureaucracy are often distorted by organization theorists, a tendency which is reinforced by their inclination to dovetail his writings with those emerging from the Classical Management School (e.g. Gouldner, 1959). Quotations like the one supplied in the text certainly imply a congruence between Weber and the Classical Management approach. However, Weber was not only not an advocate of the characteristics of bureaucracy, he was also primarily interested in bureaucracy in historical terms, i.e. as a distinctive form of organization associated with modern capitalism (although he does provide examples of pre-capitalist instances). Although Weber and the Classical Management writers share certain common elements, which together are taken to denote the 'rational system model', the broader differences in orientation ought not to be ignored.

3 This point has been underlined by an observational study of twelve very senior executives by Isenberg (1984). According to this investigator, senior executives

> seldom think in ways that one might simplistically call 'rational' i.e. they rarely systematically formulate goals, assess their worth, evaluate the probabilities of alternative ways of reaching them, and choose the path that maximizes expected return. Rather, managers frequently bypass rigorous, analytical planning altogether, particularly when they face difficult, novel or extremely entangled problems. (Isenberg, 1984, p. 82)

When viewed retrospectively, their decision-making may have the semblance of rationality; but when examined concurrently, executives' cognitive processes provide little evidence of rationality.

4 This is not the only aspect of the ethical implications of participation. For example, Sashkin (1984) has argued that people have strong needs for autonomy, meaningful work, and social interaction at work. When these needs are not met, their physical and psychological health is jeopardized. Since participative management goes a long way towards allowing these needs to be met, Sashkin contends that there is a strong ethical argument for its introduction in organizations.

7 Recent developments

1 One major problem with the notion of organizational culture is that it is riddled with conceptual ambiguity. In this sense, too, it is highly consonant with the idea of leadership! 'Organizational culture' has become a dumping ground for a wide array of attributes. In response to this problem, Trice and Beyer (1984) have sought to inject greater precision into the concept. At the very least, they observe, it is necessary to distinguish the ideas, meanings, and values associated with organizational cultures from their expressions and

manifestations (i.e. rites, ceremonies, legends, and the like). Many writers drift rather imprecisely between these two levels of analysis.

2 However, as so often occurs in the study of leadership, there is no thoroughgoing consensus on this issue. Writers like Pfeffer (1981b) view 'management' in exactly the same way that Bennis (1976) and Zaleznik (1977) describe leadership (when trying to distinguish it from management): 'the activity of management is viewed as making what is going on in the organization meaningful and sensible to the organizational participants, and furthermore developing a social consensus and social definition around the activities being undertaken' (Pfeffer, 1981b, p. 21). The article by Siehl and Martin (1984) operates within a similar frame of reference. These authors oscillate between talking about both management *and* leadership as entailing the provision of meaning systems within organizations. It is not necessarily inappropriate to conceptualize the managerial task in this way, but such discussions reinforce the difficulty of distinguishing leadership from management. As long as writers take the view that the study of leadership entails the study of designated leaders (i.e. headship), the tendency to be unclear about, and possibly indifferent to, the distinctiveness of leadership and neighbouring notions like management will persist.

3 Most leadership research has been conducted within a positivist model of enquiry, the manifestations of which – the emphasis on causality, the quest for quantifiable indicators, and the like – have been recurring features of the studies which have been summarized in this book. This often unquestioning reliance on the paraphernalia of positivism has probably hampered the incursion of qualitative research into the study of leadership, largely because the somewhat intuitive nature of qualitative methods has often been taken to be incongruent with the conventional (i.e. positivist) attitude to methodological issues. However, the extent to which particular techniques are necessarily entwined with prior epistemological positions is often exaggerated (see Bryman, 1984c, for a discussion of this issue).

BIBLIOGRAPHY

Adair, J. (1983) *Effective Leadership*, London: Pan.

Albanese, R. and Van Fleet, D.D. (1983) *Organizational Behaviour*, Chicago: The Dryden Press.

Aldrich, H.E. and Pfeffer, J. (1976) 'Environments of organisations', *Annual Review of Sociology*, 2, 79-105.

Allen, M.P., Panian, S.K. and Lotz, R.E. (1979) 'Managerial succession and organizational performance: a recalcitrant problem revisted', *Administrative Science Quarterly*, 24, 167-80.

Anon. (1980) 'Corporate culture: the hard-to-change values that spell success or failure', *Business Week*, 27 October, 148-60.

Anthony, W.P. (1978) *Participative Management*, Reading, Mass.: Addison-Wesley.

Argyle, M., Gardner, G. and Cioffi, F. (1958) 'Supervisory methods related to productivity, absenteeism, and labour turnover', *Human Relations*, 11, 23-40.

Ashour, A.S. (1973) 'The contingency model of leadership effectiveness: an evaluation', *Organizational Behaviour and Human Performance*, 9, 339-55.

Bales, R.F. and Slater, P.E. (1955) 'Role differentiation in small decision-making groups', in T. Parsons and R.F. Bales (eds), *Family, Socialization and Interaction Process*, New York: Free Press.

Barrow, J.C. (1976) 'Worker performance and task complexity as causal determinants of leader behaviour style and flexibility', *Journal of Applied Psychology*, 61, 433-40.

Barrow, J.C. (1977) 'The variables of leadership: a review and conceptual framework', *Academy of Management Review*, 2, 231-51.

Bartlem, C.S. and Locke, E.A. (1981) 'The Coch and French study: a critique and reinterpretation', *Human Relations*, 34, 555-66.

Bass, B.M. (1981) *Stogdill's Handbook of Leadership*, New York: Free Press.

Bass, B.M., Burger, P.C., Doktor, R. and Barrett, G.V. (1979) *Assessment of Managers: An International Comparison*, New York: Free Press.

Bass, B.M. and Valenzi, E.R. (1974) 'Contingent aspects of effective management styles', in J.G. Hunt and L.L. Larson (eds), *Contingency Approaches to Leadership*, Carbondale, Illinois: Southern Illinois University Press.

Bass, B.M., Valenzi, E.R., Farrow, D.L. and Solomon, R.J. (1975) 'Management styles associated with organizational, task, personal and interpersonal contingencies', *Journal of Applied Psychology*, 60, 720-9.

207

Baumgartel, H. (1956) 'Leadership, motivations, and attitudes in research laboratories', *Journal of Social Issues*, 12, 24-31.

Beer, M. and Kleisath, S.N. (1975) 'The effects of the Managerial Grid Lab on organizational and leadership dimensions', in E.F. Huse, J.L. Bowditch and D. Fisher (eds), *Readings on Behaviour in Organizations*, Reading, Mass.: Addison-Wesley.

Bennis, W.G. (1959) 'Leadership theory and administrative behaviour: the problem of authority', *Administrative Science Quarterly*, 4, 259-301.

Bennis, W.G. (1976) *The Unconscious Conspiracy: Why Leaders Can't Lead*, New York: AMACOM.

Bennis, W.G. (1984) 'Transformative power and leadership', in T.J. Sergiovanni and J.E. Corbally (eds), *Leadership and Organizational Culture*, Urbana: University of Illinois Press.

Bernardin, H.J. and Alvares, K.M. (1976) 'The managerial grid as a predictor of conflict resolution method and managerial effectiveness', *Administrative Science Quarterly*, 21, 84-94.

Bird, C. (1940) *Social Psychology*, New York: Appleton-Century.

Blake, R.R. and Mouton, J.S. (1964) *The Managerial Grid*, Houston: Gulf Publishing Co.

Blake, R.R. and Mouton, J.S. (1982) 'Theory and research for developing a science of leadership', *Journal of Applied Behavioural Science*, 18, 275-91.

Blake, R.R., Mouton, J.S., Barnes, J.S. and Greiner, L.E. (1964) 'Breakthrough in organizational development', *Harvard Business Review*, 42, 133-55.

Blanchard, K. and Johnson, S. (1982) *The One Minute Manager*, New York: Morrow.

Blau, P.M. (1956) *Bureaucracy in Modern Society*, New York: Random House.

Blumberg, M. and Pringle, C.D. (1983) 'How control groups can cause loss of control in action research: the case of Rushton coal mine', *Journal of Applied Behavioural Science*, 19, 409-25.

Bowers, D.G. (1975) 'Hierarchy, function, and the generalizability of leadership practices', in J.G. Hunt and L.L. Larson (eds), *Leadership Frontiers*, Kent, Ohio: Kent State University Press.

Bowers, D.G. and Seashore, S.E. (1966) 'Predicting organizational effectiveness with a four-factor theory of leadership', *Administrative Science Quarterly*, 11, 238-63.

Bragg, J. and Andrews, I.R. (1973) 'Participative decision making: an experimental study in a hospital', *Journal of Applied Behavioural Sciences*, 9, 727-35.

Bray, D.W., Campbell, R.J. and Grant, D.L. (1974) *Formative Years in Business: A Long Term AT & T Study of Managerial Lives*, New York: Wiley.

Brown, M.C. (1982) 'Administrative succession and organizational performance: the succession effect', *Administrative Science Quarterly*, 27, 1-16.

Brownell, P. (1983) 'Leadership style, budgetary participation and managerial behaviour', *Accounting, Organizations and Society*, 8, 307-21.

Bryman, A. (1976) 'Structure in organisations: a reconsideration', *Journal of Occupational Psychology*, 49, 1-9.

Bryman, A. (1984a) 'Organization studies and the concept of rationality', *Journal of Management Studies*, 21, 391-408.

Bryman, A. (1984b) 'Leadership and corporate culture: harmony and disharmony', *Personnel Review*, 13, 19-24.

Bryman, A. (1984c) 'The debate about quantitative and qualitative research: a question of method or epistemology?', *British Journal of Sociology*, 35, 75-92.

Burns, J.M. (1978) *Leadership*, New York: Harper & Row.

Burns, T. and Stalker, G.M. (1961) *The Management of Innovation*, London: Tavistock.

Bussom, R.S., Larson, L.L. and Vicars, W.M. (1982) 'Unstructured, non-participant observation and the study of leaders' interpersonal contacts', in J.G. Hunt, U. Sekaran and C.A. Schriesheim (eds), *Leadership: Beyond Establishment Views*, Carbondale, Illinois: Southern Illinois University Press

Butler, M.C. and Jones, A.P. (1979) 'Perceived leader behaviour, individual characteristics, and injury occurrence in hazardous work environments', *Journal of Applied Psychology*, 64, 299-304.

Butterfield, D.A. and Powell, G.N. (1981) 'Effect of group performance, leader sex, and rater sex on ratings of leader behaviour', *Organizational Behaviour and Human Performance*, 28, 129-41.

Calder, B.J. (1977) 'An attribution theory of leadership', in B.M. Staw and G.R. Salancik (eds), *New Directions in Organizational Behaviour*, Chicago: St Clair.

Cammalleri, J.A., Hendrick, H.W., Pittman, W.C., Blout, H.D. and Prather, D.C. (1973) 'Effects of different leadership styles on group accuracy', *Journal of Applied Psychology*, 57, 32-7.

Cammann, C., Fichman, M., Jenkins, G.D. and Klesh, J.R. (1983) 'Assessing the attitudes and perceptions of organizational members', in S.E. Seashore, E.E. Lawler, P.H. Mirvis and C. Cammann (eds), *Assessing Organizational Change: A Guide to Methods, Measures and Practices*, New York: Wiley.

Campbell, D.T. (1957) 'Factors relevant to the validity of experiments in social settings', *Psychological Bulletin*, 54, 297-311.

Campbell, J.P., Dunnette, M.D., Lawler, E.E. and Weick, K.E. (1970) *Managerial Behaviour, Performance and Effectiveness*, New York: McGraw-Hill.

Carey, A. (1967) 'The Hawthorne Studies: a radical criticism', *American Sociological Review*, 32, 403-16.

Carter, L.F. and Nixon, M. (1949) 'An investigation of the relationship between four criteria of leadership ability for three different tasks', *Journal of Psychology*, 27, 245-61.

Cartwright, D. and Zander, A. (1960) *Group Dynamics: Research and Theory*, New York: Harper & Row.

Cattell, R.B. and Stice, G.F. (1954) 'Four formulae for selecting leaders on the basis of personality', *Human Relations*, 7, 493-507.

Chemers, M.M. and Skrzypek, G.J. (1972) 'An experimental test of the contingency model of leadership effectiveness', *Journal of Personality and Social Psychology*, 24, 172-7.

Child, J. (1973) 'Predicting and understanding organization structure', *Administrative Science Quarterly*, 18, 168-85.

Child, J. (1984) *Organization: A Guide to Problems and Practice*, London: Harper & Row (2nd edn).

Chitayat, G. and Venezia, I. (1984) 'Determinants of management styles in business and nonbusiness organizations', *Journal of Applied Psychology*, 69, 437-47.

Clifford, C. and Cohn, T.S. (1964) 'The relationship between leadership and personality attributes perceived by followers', *Journal of Social Psychology*, 64, 57-64.

Coch, L. and French, J.R.P. Jr (1948) 'Overcoming resistance to change', *Human Relations*, 1, 512-32.

Cohen, M.D. and March, J.G. (1974) *Leadership and Ambiguity: The American College President*, New York: McGraw-Hill.

Cohen, M.D., March, J.G. and Olsen, J.P. (1972) 'A garbage can model of organisational choice', *Administrative Science Quarterly*, 17, 1-25.

Cooper, R. (1966) 'Leader's task relevance and subordinate behaviour in industrial work groups', *Human Relations*, 19, 57-84.

Csoka, L.S. (1975) 'Relationship between organizational climate and the situational favourableness dimension of Fiedler's contingency model', *Journal of Applied Psychology*, 60, 273-7.

Cummings, L.L. (1975) 'Assessing the Graen/Cashman model and comparing it with other approaches', in J.G. Hunt and L.L. Larson (eds), *Leadership Frontiers*, Kent, Ohio: Kent State University Press.

Cummings, L.L. (1981) 'Organizational behaviour in the 1980's', *Decision Sciences*, 12, 365-77.

Cummings, T.G., Molloy, E.S. and Glen, R. (1977) 'A methodological critique of fifty-eight selected work experiments', *Human Relations*, 30, 675-708.

Cummins, R.C. (1972) 'Leader-member relations as a moderator of the effects of leader behaviour and attitude', *Personnel Psychology*, 25, 655-60.

Danserau, F., Cashman, J. and Graen, G. (1973) 'Instrumentality theory and equity theory as complementary approaches in predicting the relationship of leadership and turnover among managers', *Organizational Behaviour and Human Performance*, 10, 184-200.

Danserau, F., Graen, G. and Haga, W.J. (1975) 'A vertical dyad linkage approach to leadership within formal organizations', *Organizational Behaviour and Human Performance*, 13, 46-78.

Davis, T.R.V. and Luthans, F. (1980) 'Managers in action: a new look at their behaviour and operating modes', *Organizational Dynamics*, 9, 64-80.

Day R.C. and Hamblin, R.L. (1964) 'Some effects of close and punitive styles of supervision', *American Journal of Sociology*, 69, 499-510.

Deal, T.E. and Kennedy, A.A. (1982) *Corporate Cultures*, Reading, Mass.: Addison-Wesley.

Dessler, G. (1982) *Organization and Management*, Reston, Va.: Reston.

Dessler, G. and Valenzi, E.R. (1977) 'Initiation of structure and subordinate satisfaction: a path analysis test of path-goal theory', *Academy of Management Journal*, 20, 251-9.

Deutscher, I. (1966) 'Words and deeds: social science and social policy', *Social Problems*, 13, 235-54.

Diener, E. and Crandall, R. (1978) *Ethics in Social and Behavioural Research*, Chicago: University of Chicago Press.

Di Maggio, P.J. and Powell, W.W. (1983) 'The iron cage revisited: institutional isomorphism and collective rationality in organizational fields', *American Sociological Review*, 48, 147-60.

Dossett, D.L., Latham, G.P. and Mitchell, T.R. (1979) 'The effects of assigned versus participatively set goals, KOR, and individual differences in employee behaviour when goal difficulty is held constant', *Journal of Applied Psychology*, 64, 291-8.

Dowling, W.F. (1973) 'Conversation with Rensis Likert', *Organizational Dynamics*, 1, 32-50.

Dowling, W.F. (1975) 'At General Motors: System 4 builds performance and profits', *Organizational Dynamics*, 3, 23-38.

Drory, A. and Gluskinos, U.M. (1980) 'Machiavellianism and leadership', *Journal of Applied Psychology*, 65, 81-6.

Dubin, R. (1979) 'Metaphors of leadership: an overview', in J.G. Hunt and L.L. Larson (eds), *Crosscurrents in Leadership*, Carbondale, Illinois: Southern Illinois University Press.

Durand, D.E. and Nord, W.R. (1976) 'Perceived leader behaviour as a function of personality characteristics of supervisors and subordinates', *Academy of Management Journal*, 19, 427-38.

Eden, D. and Leviatan, U. (1975) 'Implicit leadership theory as a determinant of the factor structure underlying supervisory behaviour scales', *Journal of Applied Psychology*, 60, 736-41.

England, G.W. (1975) *The Manager and His Values: An International Perspective*, Cambridge, Mass.: Ballinger.

Etzioni, A. (1961) *A Comparative Analysis of Complex Organizations*, New York: Free Press.

Etzioni, A. (1965) 'Dual leadership in complex organizations', *American Sociological Review*, 30, 688-98.

Farris, G.F. (1975) 'Chickens, eggs, and productivity in organizations', *Organizational Dynamics*, 3, 2-15.

Farris, G.F. and Lim, F.G. (1969) 'Effects of performance on leadership cohesiveness, influence, satisfaction, and subsequent performance', *Journal of Applied Psychology*, 52, 490-7.

Fiedler, F.E. (1965) 'Engineer the job to fit the manager', *Harvard Business Review*, 43, 115-22.

Fiedler, F.E. (1967) *A Theory of Leadership Effectiveness*, New York: McGraw-Hill.

Fiedler, F.E. (1971) 'Validation and extension of the Contingency Model of Leadership effectiveness: a review of empirical findings', *Psychological Bulletin*, 76, 128-48.

Fiedler, F.E. (1972) 'Personality motivational systems, and behaviour of high and low LPC persons', *Human Relations*, 25, 391-412.

Fiedler, F.E. (1973) 'The contingency model - a reply to Ashour', *Organizational Behaviour and Human Performance*, 9, 356-68.

Fiedler, F.E. (1977) 'A rejoinder to Schriesheim and Kerr's premature obituary of the contingency model', in J.G. Hunt and L.L. Larson (eds), *Leadership: The Cutting Edge*, Carbondale, Illinois: Southern Illinois University Press.

Fiedler, F.E. (1978a) 'A contingency model of leadership effectiveness', in L. Berkowitz (ed.), *Group Processes*, New York: Academic Press.

Fiedler, F.E. (1978b) 'Recent developments in research on the Contingency Model', in L. Berkowitz (ed.), *Group Processes*, New York: Academic Press.

Fiedler, F.E. (1978c) 'The Contingency Model and the dynamics of the leadership process', *Advances in Experimental Social Psychology*, 11, 59-112.

Fiedler, F.E. and Chemers, M.M. (1974) *Leadership and Effective Management*, Glenview, Illinois: Scott Foresman.

Fiedler, F.E. and Chemers, M.M. (1984) *Improving Leadership Effectiveness: The Leader Match concept*, New York: Wiley, 2nd edn.

Field, R.H.G. (1979) 'A critique of the Vroom-Yetton contingency model of leadership behaviour', *Academy of Management Review*, 4, 249-57.

Field, R.H.G. (1982) 'A test of the Vroom-Yetton Normative model of Leadership', *Journal of Applied Psychology*, 67, 523-32.

Filley, A.C., House, R.J. and Kerr, S. (1976) *Managerial Process and Organizational Behaviour*, Glenview, Illinois: Scott Foresman.

Finkle, R.B. (1976) 'Managerial assessment centres', in M.D. Dunnette (ed.), *Handbook of Industrial and Organizational Psychology*, Chicago: Rand McNally.

Fleishman, E.A. (1953) 'The description of supervisory behaviour', *Personnel Psychology*, 37, 1-6.

Fleishman, E.A. (1973) 'Twenty years of consideration and structure', in E.A. Fleishman and J.G. Hunt (eds), *Current Developments in the Study of Leadership*, Carbondale, Illinois: Southern Illinois University Press.

Fleishman, E.A. and Harris, E.F. (1962) 'Patterns of leadership behaviour related to employee grievances and turnover', *Personnel Psychology*, 15, 43-56.

Fleishman, E.A., Harris, E.F. and Burtt, H.E. (1955) *Leadership and Supervision in Industry*, Columbus: Bureau of Educational Research, Ohio State University.

Foa, U.G., Mitchell, T.R. and Fiedler, F.E. (1971) 'Differentiation matching', *Behavioural Science*, 16, 130-42.

Ford J.D. (1981) 'Departmental context and formal structure as constraints on leader behaviour', *Academy of Management Journal*, 24, 274-88.

Franke, R.H. and Kaul, J.D. (1978) 'The Hawthorne Experiments: first statistical interpretation', *American Sociological Review*, 43, 623-42.

Franklin, J.L. (1975) 'Relations among four social-psychological aspects of organizations', *Administrative Science Quarterly*, 20, 422-33.

French, J.R.P., Israel, J. and As, D. (1960) 'An experiment on participation in a Norwegian factory', *Human Relations*, 13, 3-19.

French, J.R.P., Kay, E. and Meyer, H.H. (1966) 'Participation and the appraisal system', *Human Relations*, 19, 3-20.

French, J.R.P., Ross, I.C., Kirby, S., Nelson, J.R. and Smyth, P. (1958) 'Employee participation in a program of industrial change', *Personnel*, 35, 16-29.

French, J.R.P. and Snyder, R. (1959) 'Leadership and interpersonal power', in D. Cartwright (ed.), *Studies in Social Power*, Ann Arbor: Institute for Social Research, University of Michigan.

Fulk, J. and Wendler, E.R. (1982) 'Dimensionality of leader-subordinate interactions: a path-goal investigation', *Organizational Behaviour and Human Performance*, 30, 241-64.

Gamson, W.A. and Scotch, N. (1964) 'Scapegoating in baseball', *American Journal of Sociology*, 70, 69-72.

Ghiselli, E.E. (1971) *Explorations in Managerial Talent*, Pacific Palisades, Calif.: Goodyear.

Gibb, C.A. (1947) 'The principles and traits of leadership', *Journal of Abnormal and Social Psychology*, 42, 267-84.

Gibb, C.A. (1969) 'Leadership', in G. Lindzey and E. Aronson (eds), *The Handbook of Social Psychology*, Vol. 4, Reading, Mass.: Addison-Wesley.

Gouldner, A.W. (1959) 'Organizational analysis', in R.K. Merton, L. Brown and L.S. Cottrell (eds), *Sociology Today*, New York: Basic Books.

Graeff, C.L. (1983) 'The situational leadership theory: a critical view', *Academy of Management Review*, 8, 285-91.

Graen, G. and Cashman, J.F. (1975) 'A role making model of leadership in formal organizations: a developmental approach', in J.G. Hunt and L.L. Larson (eds), *Leadership Frontiers*, Carbondale, Illinois: Southern Illinois University Press.

Graen, G., Novak, M.A. and Sommerkamp, P. (1982) 'The effects of leader-member exchange and job design on productivity and satisfaction: testing a dual attachment model', *Organizational Behaviour and Human Performance*, 30, 109-31.

Green, S.G. and Liden, R.C. (1980) 'Contextual and attributional influences on control decisions', *Journal of Applied Psychology*, 65, 453-8.

Green, S.G. and Mitchell, T.R. (1979) 'Attributional processes of leaders in leader-member interactions', *Organizational Behaviour and Human Performance*, 23, 429-58.

Greene, C.N. (1975) 'The reciprocal nature of influence between leader and subordinate', *Journal of Applied Psychology*, 60, 187-93.

Greene, C.N. (1979) 'Questions of causation in the path-goal theory of leadership', *Academy of Management Journal*, 22, 22-41.

Greene, C.N. and Podsakoff, P.M. (1981) 'Effects of withdrawal of a performance-contingent reward on supervisory influence and power', *Academy of Management Journal*, 24, 527-42.

Greenfield, T.B. (1984) 'Leaders and schools: order in organizations', in T.J. Sergiovanni and J.E. Corbally (eds), *Leadership and Organizational Culture*, Urbana: University of Illinois Press.

Greenwood, R.G., Bolton, A.A. and Greenwood, R.A. (1983) 'Hawthorne a half century later: relay assembly participants remember', *Journal of Management*, 9, 217-31.

Griffin, R.W. (1980) 'Relationships among individual, task design, and leader behaviour variables', *Academy of Management Journal*, 23, 665-83.

Hall, J. and Donnell, S.M. (1979) 'Managerial achievement: the personal side of behavioural theory', *Human Relations*, 32, 77-101.

Halpin, A.W. (1957) 'The observed leader behaviour and ideal leader behaviour of aircraft commanders and school superintendents', in R.M. Stogdill and A.E. Coons (eds), *Leader Behaviour: Its Description and Management*, Columbus: Ohio State University, Bureau of Business Research.

Halpin, A.W. and Winer, B.J. (1957) 'A factorial study of the leader behaviour descriptions', in R.M. Stogdill and A.E. Coons (eds), *Leader Behaviour: Its Description and Measurement*, Columbus: Ohio State University, Bureau of Business Research.

Heilman, M.E., Hornstein, H.A., Cage, J.H. and Herschlag, J.K. (1984) 'Reactions to prescribed leader behaviour as a function of role perspective: the case of the Vroom-Yetton model', *Journal of Applied Psychology*, 69, 50-60.

Heller, F. (1971) *Managerial Decision Making: A Study of Leadership Style and Power Sharing Among Senior Managers*, London: Tavistock.

Heller, F.A. and Wilpert, B. (1977) 'Limits to participative leadership: task, structure and skill as contingencies - a German-British comparison', *European Journal of Social Psychology*, 7, 61-84.

Heller, F.A. and Wilpert, B. (1981) *Competence and Power in Managerial Decision-Making*, Chichester: Wiley.

Heller, F. and Yukl, G.A. (1969) 'Participation, managerial decision making, and situational variables', *Organizational Behaviour and Human Performance*, 4, 227-41.

Hemphill, J.K. (1955) 'Leadership behaviour associated with the administrative reputations of college departments', *Journal of Educational Psychology*, 46, 385-401.

Hemphill, J.K. and Coons, A.E. (1957) 'Development of the Leader Behaviour Description Questionnaire', in R.M. Stogdill and A.E. Coons (eds), *Leader Behaviour: Its Description and Measurement*, Columbus: Ohio State University, Bureau of Business Research.

Hersey, P. and Blanchard, K.H. (1969) *Management of Organizational Behaviour*, Englewood Cliffs, N.J.: Prentice-Hall.

Hersey, P. and Blanchard, K.H. (1977) *Management of Organizational Behaviour: Utilizing Human Resources*, Englewood Cliffs, N.J.: Prentice-Hall, 3rd edn.

Hersey, P. and Blanchard, K.H. (1982) *Management of Organizational Behaviour: Utilizing Human Resources*, Englewood Cliffs, N.J.: Prentice-Hall, 4th edn.

Hersey, P., Blanchard, K.H. and Hambleton, R.K. (1980) 'Contracting for leadership style: a process and instrumentation for building effective work relationships', in P. Hersey and J. Stinson (eds), *Perspectives in Leader Effectiveness*, Columbus, Ohio: Centre for Leadership Studies.

Hickson, D.J., Hinings, C.R., Lee, C.A., Schneck, R.E. and Pennings, J.M. (1971) 'A strategic contingencies theory of intra-organizational power', *Administrative Science Quarterly*, 16, 216-29.

Hickson, D.J., Pugh, D.S. and Pheysey, D.C. (1969) 'Operations technology and organization structure: an empirical reappraisal', *Administrative Science Quarterly*, 14, 378-95.

Hill, W.A. (1973) 'Leadership style: rigid or flexible?', *Organizational Behaviour and Human Performance*, 9, 35-47.

Hill, W.A. and Hughes, D. (1974) 'Variations in leader behaviour as a function of task type', *Organizational Behaviour and Human Performance*, 11, 83-96.

Hinton, B.L. and Barrow, J.C. (1976) 'Personality correlates of the reinforcement propensities of leaders', *Personal Psychology*, 29, 61-6.

Hollander, E.P. (1978) *Leadership Dynamics: A Practical Guide to Effective Relationshps*, New York: Free Press.

Hollander, E.P. and Julian, J.W. (1969) 'Contemporary trends in the analysis of leadership processes', *Psychological Bulletin*, 71, 387-97.

Hollander, E.P. and Julian J.W. (1978a) 'Studies in leader legitimacy, influence, and innovation', in L. Berkowitz (ed.), *Group Processes*, New York: Academic Press.

Hollander, E.P. and Julian, J.W. (1978b) 'A further look at leader legitimacy, influence and innovation', in L. Berkowitz (ed.), *Group Processes*, New York: Academic Press.

Hosking, D.-M. (1981) 'A critical evaluation of Fiedler's contingency hypothesis', in G.M. Stephenson and J.M. Davis (eds), *Progress in Applied Social Psychology*, Vol. 1, New York: Wiley.

Hosking, D.-M. and Morley, I. (1982) 'Leadership and organization: the negotiation of order', University of Aston Management Centre Working Paper, No. 249.

Hosking, D.-M. and Schriesheim, C.A. (1978) 'Review essay: improving leadership effectiveness: the leader match concept', *Administrative Science Quarterly*, 23, 496-505.

House, R.J. (1973) 'A path-goal theory of leadership effectiveness', in E.A. Fleishman and J.G. Hunt (eds), *Current Developments in the Study of Leadership*, Carbondale, Illinois: Southern Illinois University Press.

House, R.J. (1977) 'A 1976 theory of charismatic leadership', in J.G. Hunt and L.L. Larson (eds), *Leadership: The Cutting Edge*, Carbondale, Illinois: Southern Illinois University Press.

House, R.J. and Baetz, M.L. (1979) 'Leadership: some empirical generalizations and new research directions', in B.M. Staw (ed.), *Research In Organizations Behaviour Volume 1*, Greenwich, Conn.: JAI Press.

House, R.J. and Dessler, G. (1974) 'The path-goal theory of leadership: some post hcc and a priori tests', in J.G. Hunt and L.L. Larson (eds), *Contingency Approaches to Leadership*, Carbondale, Illinois: Southern Illinois University Press.

House, R.J. and Mitchell, T.R. (1974) 'Path-goal theory of leadership', *Journal of Contemporary Business*, 3, 81-97.

Howell, J.P. and Dorfman, P.W. (1981) 'Substitutes for leadership: test of a construct', *Academy of Management Journal*, 24, 714-28.

Hubbard, G. (1985) 'How to pick the personality for the job', *New Scientist*, No. 1441, 31 January, 12-15.

Huck, J.R. (1977) 'The research base', in J.L. Moses and W.C. Byham (eds), *Applying the Assessment Centre Method*, New York: Pergamon.

Hunt, J.G., Hosking, D.-M., Schriesheim, C.A. and Stewart, R. (1984) *Leaders and Managers: International Perspectives on Managerial Behaviour and Leadership*, New York: Pergamon.

Hunt, J.G., Osborn, R.N. and Schuler, R.S. (1978) 'Relations of discretionary and non-discretionary leadership to performance and satisfaction in a complex organization', *Human Relations*, 31, 507-23.

Hunt, J.G. and Osborn, R.N. (1980) 'A multiple-influence approach to leadership for managers', in P. Hersey and J. Stinson (eds), *Perspectives in Leadership Effectiveness*, Columbus, Ohio: Centre for Leadership Studies, Ohio University.

Hunt, J.G. and Osborn, R.N. (1982) 'Toward a macro-oriented model of leadership: an odyssey', in J.G. Hunt, U. Sekaran and C.A. Schriesheim (eds), *Leadership: Beyond Establishment Views*, Carbondale, Illinois: Southern Illinois University Press.

Hunt, J.G., Sekaran, U. and Schriesheim, C.A. (1982) *Leadership: Beyond Establishment Views*, Carbondale, Illinois: Southern Illinois University Press.

Ilgen, D.R., Mitchell, T.R. and Fredrickson, J.W. (1981) 'Poor performers: supervisors' and subordinates' responses', *Organizational Behaviour and Human Performance*, 27, 386-410.

Isenberg, D.J. (1984) 'How senior managers think', *Harvard Business Review*, 62, 81-90.

Jackson, S.A. (1983) 'Participation in decision making as a strategy for reducing job-related strain', *Journal of Applied Psychology*, 68, 3-19.

Jacobs, T.O. (1971) *Leadership and Exchange in Formal Organizations*, Alexandria, Virginia: Human Resources Research Organization.

Jago, A.G. and Vroom, V.H. (1975) 'Perceptions of leadership style: superior and subordinate descriptions of decision-making behaviour', in J.G. Hunt and L.L. Larson (eds), *Leadership Frontiers*, Carbondale, Illinois: Southern Illinois University Press.

James, L.R. and White, J.F. (1983) 'Cross-situational specificity in managers' perceptions of subordinate performance, attributions, and leader behaviours', *Personnel Psychology*, 36, 809-56.

Janda, K.F. (1960) 'Towards the explication of the concept of leadership in terms of the concept of power', *Human Relations*, 13, 345-63.

Jenkins, G.D. and Lawler, E.E. (1981) 'Impact of employee participation in pay plan development', *Organizational Behaviour and Human Performance*, 28, 111-28.

Jenkins, W.O. (1947) 'A review of leadership studies with particular reference to military problems', *Psychological Bulletin*, 44, 54-79.

Johnson, A.L., Luthans, F. and Hennessey, H.W. (1984) 'The role of locus of control in leader influence behaviour', *Personnel Psychology*, 37, 61-75.

Jones, A.P., James, L.R. and Bruni, J.R. (1975) 'Perceived leadership behaviour and employee confidence in the leader as moderated by job involvement', *Journal of Applied Psychology*, 60, 146-9.

Jones, E.E., Kanouse, D.E., Kelley, H.H., Nisbett, R.E., Valins, S. and Weiner, B. (1972) *Attribution: Perceiving the Causes of Behaviour*, Morristown, N.J.: General Learning.

Jones, G.R. (1983) 'Forms of control and leader behaviour', *Journal of Management*, 9, 159-72.

Kabanoff, B. (1981) 'A critique of leader match and its implications for leadership research', *Personnel Psychology*, 34, 749-64.

Kahn, R.L. (1956) 'The prediction of productivity', *Journal of Social Issues*, 12, 41-9.

Kahn, R.L. (1958) 'Human relations on the shop floor', in E.M. Hugh-Jones (ed.), *Human Relations and Modern Management*, Amsterdam: North-Holland Publishing Co.

Kahn, R.L. and Katz, D. (1953) 'Leadership practices in relation to productivity and morale', in D. Cartwright and A. Zander (eds), *Group Dynamics*, New York: Harper & Row.

Katerberg, R. and Hom, P.W. (1981) 'Effects of within-group and between-groups variation in leadership', *Journal of Applied Psychology*, 66, 218-23.

Katz, D. (1951) 'Survey Research Center: an overview of the human relations program', in H. Guetzkow (ed.), *Groups, Leadership and Men*, Pittsburgh: Carnegie Press.

Katz, D. and Kahn, R.L. (1951) 'Human organization and worker motivation', in L.R. Tripp (ed.), *Industrial Productivity*, Madison, Wisc.: Industrial Relations Research Association.

Katz, D. and Kahn, R.L. (1978) *The Social Psychology of Organizations*, New York: Wiley (2nd edn).

Katz, D., Maccoby, N., Gurin, G. and Floor, L. (1951) *Productivity, Supervision and Morale Among Railroad Workers*, Ann Arbor: Survey Research Center, University of Michigan.

Katz, D., Maccoby, N. and Morse, N. (1950) *Productivity, Supervision, and Morale in an Office Situation*, Ann Arbor, Michigan: Institute for Social Research.

Katz, R. (1977) 'The influence of group conflict on leadership effectiveness', *Organizational Behaviour and Human Performance*, 20, 265-86.

Keller, R.T. and Szilagyi, A.D. (1978) 'A longitudinal study of leader reward behaviour, subordinate expectancies, and satisfaction', *Personnel Psychology*, 31, 119-29.

Kelley, H.H. and Michela, J.L. (1980) 'Attribution theory and research', *Annual Review of Psychology*, 31, 457-501.

Kennedy, J.K. (1982) 'Middle LPC leaders and the contingency model of leadership effectiveness', *Organizational Behaviour and Human Performance*, 31, 1-14.

Kerr, S. and Jermier, J.M. (1978) 'Substitutes for leadership: their meaning and measurement', *Organizational Behaviour and Human Performance*, 22, 375-403.

Kerr, S., Schriesheim, C.A., Murphy, C.J. and Stogdill, R.M. (1974) 'Toward a contingency theory of leadership based upon the consideration and initiating structure literature', *Organizational Behaviour and Human Performance*, 12, 62-82.

Kochan, T.A., Schmidt, S.M. and De Cotiis, T.A. (1975) 'Superior-subordinate relations: leadership and headship', *Human Relations*, 28, 279-94.

Korman, A.K. (1966) '"Consideration", "initiating structure", and organizational criteria – a review', *Personnel Psychology*, 19, 349-61.

Korman, A.K. (1968) 'The prediction of managerial performance: a review', *Personnel Psychology*, 21, 295-322.

Korman, A.K. (1971) *Industrial and Organizational Psychology*, Englewood Cliffs, N.J.: Prentice-Hall.

Korman, A.K. (1973) 'On the development of contingency theories of leadership: some methodological considerations and a possible alternative', *Journal of Applied Psychology*, 58, 84-7.

Landsberger, H.A. (1958) *Hawthorne Revisited*, Ithaca, N.Y.: New York State

School of Industrial and Labour Relations.

La Piere, R.T. (1934) 'Attitudes vs. actions', *Social Forces*, 13, 230–7.

Larson, J.R. (1982) 'Cognitive mechanisms mediating the impact of implicit theories of leader behaviour on leader behaviour ratings', *Organizational Behaviour and Human Performance*, 29, 129-40.

Larson, L.L., Hunt, J.G. and Osborn, R.N. (1976) 'The great hi-hi leader behaviour myth: a lesson from Occam's razor', *Academy of Management Journal*, 19, 628-41.

Larson, L.L. and Rowland, K.M. (1974) 'Leadership style and cognitive complexity', *Academy of Management Journal*, 17, 37-45.

Latham, G.P. and Marshall, H.A. (1982) 'The effects of self-set, participatively set and assigned goals on the performance of government employees', *Personnel Psychology*, 35, 399-404.

Latham, G.P. and Saari, L.M. (1979a) 'The effects of holding goal difficulty constant on assigned and participatively set goals', *Academy of Management Journal*, 22, 163-8.

Latham, G.P. and Saari, L.M. (1979b) 'Importance of supportive relationships in goal setting', *Journal of Applied Psychology*, 64, 151-6.

Latham, G.P., Steele, T.P. and Saari, L.M. (1982) 'The effects of participation and goal difficulty on performance', *Personnel Psychology*, 35, 677-86.

Lawrence, P. (1984) *Management in Action*, London: Routledge & Kegan Paul.

Lawrence, P.R. and Lorsch, J.W. (1967) *Organisation and Environment*, Homewood, Ill.: Irwin.

Lewin, K., Lippitt, R. and White, R.K. (1939) 'Patterns of aggressive behaviour in experimentally created social climates', *Journal of Social Psychology*, 10, 271-99.

Liden, R.C. and Graen, G. (1980) 'Generalizability of the Vertical Dyad Linkage model of leadership', *Academy of Management Journal*, 23, 451-65.

Lieberson, S. and O'Connor, J.F. (1972) 'Leadership and organizational performance: a study of large corporations', *American Sociological Review*, 37, 117-30.

Likert, R. (1961) *New Patterns of Management*, New York: McGraw-Hill.

Likert, R. (1967) *The Human Organization: Its Management and Value*, New York: McGraw-Hill.

Likert, R. (1977) 'Management styles and the human component', *Management Review*, 66, 23-8, 43-5.

Likert, R. (1979) 'From production- and employee-centredness to Systems 1-4', *Journal of Management*, 5, 147-56.

Limerick, D.C. (1976) 'Authority: an axis of leadership role differentiation', *Psychologia Africana*, 16, 153-72.

Locke, E.A. (1981) 'Comments on Neider: the issue of interpretation of experiments', *Organizational Behaviour and Human Performance*, 28, 425-30.

Locke, E.A., Feren, D.B., McCaleb, V.M., Shaw, K.N. and Denny, A.T. (1980) 'The relative effectiveness of four methods of motivating employee performance', in K.D. Duncan, M.M. Gruneberg and D. Wallis (eds), *Changes In Working Life*, Chichester: Wiley.

Locke, E.A. and Schweiger, D.M. (1979) 'Participation in decision-making: one more look', in B.M. Staw (ed.), *Research in Organizational Behaviour, Volume 1*, Greenwich, Conn.: JAI Press.

Lowin, A. (1968) 'Participative decision-making: a model, literature critique, and prescriptions for research', *Organizational Behaviour and Human Performance*, 3, 68-106.

Lowin, A. and Craig, C.R. (1968) 'The influence of performance on managerial style: an experimental object lesson in the ambiguity of correlational data', *Organizational Behaviour and Human Performance*, 3, 440-58.

Lowin, A. Hrapchak, W.J. and Kavanagh, M.J. (1969) 'Consideration and initiating structure: an experimental investigation of leadership traits', *Administrative Science Quarterly*, 14, 238-53.

Luthans, F. (1979) 'Leadership: a proposal for a Social Learning Theory base and observation and functional analysis techniques to measure leader behaviour', in J.G. Hunt and L.L. Larson (eds), *Crosscurrents in Leadership*, Carbondale, Illinois: Southern Illinois University Press.

Luthans, F. and Lockwood, D.L. (1984) 'Toward an observation system for measuring leader behaviour', in J.G. Hunt, D.-M. Hosking, C.A. Schriesheim and R. Stewart (eds), *Leaders and Managers: International Perspectives on Managerial Behaviour and Leadership*, New York: Pergamon.

McClelland, D. (1975) *Power: The Inner Experience*, New York: Irvington.

McGregor, D. (1960) *The Human Side of Enterprise*, New York: McGraw-Hill.

Magnet, M. (1982) 'Managing by mystique at Tandem Computers', *Fortune*, 28 June, 84-91.

Mann, F.C. (1965) 'Toward an understanding of the leadership role in formal organization', in R. Dubin (ed.), *Leadership and Productivity*, San Francisco: Chandler.

Mann, R.D. (1959) 'A review of the relationship between personality and performance in small groups', *Psychological Bulletin*, 56, 241-70.

March J.G. and Olsen, J.P. (1976) *Ambiguity and Choice in Organisations*, Bergen: Universitetsførlaget.

March, J.G. and Simon, H.A. (1958) *Organizations*, New York: Wiley.

Margerison, C. and Glube, R. (1979) 'Leadership decision-making: an empirical test of the Vroom and Yetton model', *Journal of Management Studies*, 16, 45-55.

Marrow, A.J., Bowers, D.G. and Seashore, S.E. (1967) *Management by Participation*, New York: Harper & Row.

Martin, J. and Siehl, C. (1983) 'Organizational culture and counterculture: an uneasy symbiosis', *Organizational Dynamics*, 13, 52-64.

Martinko, M.J. and Gardner, W.L. (1984) 'The observation of high-performing educational managers: methodological issues and managerial implications', in J.G. Hunt, D.-M. Hosking, C.A. Schriesheim and R. Stewart (eds), *Leaders and Managers: International Perspectives on Managerial Behaviour and Leadership*, New York: Pergamon.

Maslow, A.H. (1943) 'A theory of human motivation', *Psychological Review*, 50, 370-96.

Melcher, A.F. (1977) 'Leadership models and research approaches', in J.G. Hunt and L.L. Larson (eds), *Leadership: The Cutting Edge*, Carbondale, Illinois: Southern Illinois University Press.

Meyer, J.W. and Rowan, B. (1977) 'Institutionalised organisations: formal structure as myth and ceremony', *American Journal of Sociology*, 83, 340-63.

Meyer, J.W., Scott, W.R. and Deal, T.R. (1981) 'Institutional and technical sources of organisational structure', in H. Stein (ed.), *Organisation and the Human Services*, Philadelphia: Temple University Press.

Meyer, M.W. (1979) 'Organisational structure as signalling', *Pacific Sociological Review*, 22, 481-500.

Miles, R.E. (1965) 'Human relations or human resources', *Harvard Business Review*, 43, 148-55.

Miles, R.H. and Petty, M.M. (1977) 'Leader effectiveness in small bureaucracies', *Academy of Management Journal*, 20, 238-50.

Miller, D. and Friesen, P. (1984) *Organizations: A Quantum View*, Englewood Cliffs, N.J.: Prentice-Hall.

Miner, J.B. (1975) 'The uncertain future of the leadership concept: an overview', in J.G. Hunt and L.L. Larson (eds), *Leadership Frontiers*, Kent, Ohio: Kent State University Press.

Miner, J.B. (1978) 'Twenty years of research on role-motivation theory of managerial effectiveness', *Personnel Psychology*, 31, 739-60.

Miner, J.B. (1982) 'The uncertain future of the leadership concept: revisions and clarifications', *Journal of Applied Behavioural Science*, 18, 293-307.

Mintzberg, H. (1973) *The Nature of Managerial Work*, New York: Harper & Row.

Mintzberg, H. (1982) 'If you're not serving Bill and Barbara, then you're not serving leadership', in J.G. Hunt, U. Sekaran and C.A. Schriesheim (eds), *Leadership: Beyond Establishment Views*, Carbondale, Illinois: Southern Illinois University Press.

Mitchell, T.R. (1973) 'Motivation and participation: an integration', *Academy of Management Journal*, 16, 670-9.

Mitchell, T.R. (1979) 'Organizational behaviour', *Annual Review of Psychology*, 30, 243-81.

Mitchell, T.R., Green, S.G. and Wood, R.E. (1981) 'An attributional model of leadership and the poor performing subordinate: development and validation', in L.L. Cummings and B.M. Staw (eds), *Research in Organizational Behaviour, Volume 3*, Greenwich, Conn.: JAI Press.

Mitchell, T.R. and Kalb, L.S. (1981) 'Effects of outcome knowledge and outcome valence on supervisors' evaluations', *Journal of Applied Psychology*, 66, 604-12.

Mitchell, T.R., Larson, J.R. and Green, S.G. (1977) 'Leader behaviour, situational moderators, and group performance: an attributional analysis', *Organizational Behaviour and Human Performance*, 18, 254-68.

Mitchell, T.R. and Liden, R.C. (1982) 'The effects of the social context on performance evaluations', *Organizational Behaviour and Human Performance*, 29, 241-56.

Mitchell, T.R. and Wood, R.E. (1980) 'Supervisors' responses to subordinate poor performance: a test of an attributional model', *Organizational Behaviour and Human Performance*, 25, 123-38.

Moore, L.F. and Beck, B.E.F. (1984) 'Leadership among bank managers: a structural comparison of behavioural responses and metaphorical imagery', in J.G. Hunt, D.-M. Hosking, C.A. Schriesheim and R. Stewart (eds), *Leaders and Managers: International Perspectives on Managerial Behaviour and Leadership*, New York: Pergamon.

Morley, I.E. (1984) 'On imagery and the cycling of decision making', in J.G. Hunt, D.-M. Hosking, C.A. Schriesheim and R. Stewart (eds), *Leaders and Managers: International Perspectives on Managerial Behaviour and Leadership*, New York: Pergamon.

Morris, R.T. and Seeman, M. (1950) 'The problem of leadership: an interdisciplinary approach', *American Journal of Sociology*, 56, 149-55.

Morse, N.C. and Reimer, E. (1956) 'The experimental change of a major organizational variable', *Journal of Abnormal and Social Psychology*, 52, 120-9.

Mouzelis, N.P. (1967) *Organization and Bureaucracy*, London: Routledge & Kegan Paul.

Mowday, R.T. (1978) 'The exercise of upward influence in organizations', *Administrative Science Quarterly*, 23, 137-56.

Mulder, M. (1971) 'Power equalization through participation?', *Administrative Science Quarterly*, 16, 31-8.

Mulder, M. and Wilke, H. (1970) 'Participation and power equalization', *Organizational Behaviour and Human Performance*, 5, 430-48.

Nelson, P.D. (1964) 'Similarities and differences among leaders and followers', *Journal of Social Psychology*, 63, 161-7.

Nightingale, D.V. (1981) 'Participation in decision-making: an examination of style and structure and their effects on member outcomes', *Human Relations*, 34, 1119-33.

Nystrom, P.C. (1978) 'Managers and the hi-hi leader myth', *Academy of Management Journal*, 21, 325-31.

Oldham, G.R. (1976) 'The motivational strategies used by supervisors: relationships to effectiveness indicators', *Organizational Behaviour and Human Performance*, 15, 66-86.

Osborn, R.N. and Hunt, J.G. (1975) 'Relations between leadership, size, and subordinate satisfaction in a voluntary organization', *Journal of Applied Psychology*, 60, 730-5.

Ouchi, W.G. (1982) *Theory Z*, New York: Avon.

Page, C.H. (1946) 'Bureaucracy's other face', *Social Forces*, 25, 89-91.

Pelz, D.C. (1951) 'Leadership within a hierarchical organization', *Journal of Social Issues*, 7, 49-55.

Pennings, J. (1973) 'Measures of organization structure: a methodological note', *American Journal of Sociology*, 79, 686-704.

Peppenhorst, S. (1983) 'Make authoritative decisions with this situational model', *The Rainbow*, 2, 132-5.

Perrow, C. (1972) *Complex Organizations: A Critical Essay*, Glenview, Illinois: Scott Foresman.

Peters, T.J. and Waterman, R.H. (1982) *In Search of Excellence*, New York: Harper & Row.

Pettigrew, A.M. (1973) *The Politics of Organisational Decision-Making*, London: Tavistock.

Pfeffer, J. (1977) 'The ambiguity of leadership', *Academy of Management Review*, 2, 104-12.

Pfeffer, J. (1978) 'The micropolitics of organizations', in M.W. Meyer and Associates (eds), *Environments and Organizations*, San Francisco: Jossey-Bass.

Pfeffer, J. (1981a) *Power in Organisations*, Boston: Pitman.

Pfeffer, J. (1981b) 'Management as symbolic action: the creation and maintenance of organizational paradigms', in L.L. Cummings and B.M. Staw (eds), *Research in Organizational Behaviour, Volume 3*, Greenwich, Conn.: JAI Press.

Pfeffer J. and Salancik, G.R. (1975) 'Determinants of supervisory behaviour: a role set analysis', *Human Relations*, 28, 139-54.

Phillips, D.L. (1973) *Abandoning Method*, San Francisco: Jossey-Bass.

Phillips, J.S. (1984) 'The accuracy of leadership ratings: a cognitive categorization perspective', *Organizational Behaviour and Human Performance*, 33, 125-38.

Phillips, J.S. and Lord, R.G. (1981) 'Causal attributions and perceptions of leadership', *Organizational Behaviour and Human Performance*, 28, 143-63.

Phillips, J.S. and Lord, R.G. (1982) 'Schematic information processing and perceptions of leadership in problem-solving groups', *Journal of Applied Psychology*, 67, 486-92.

Podsakoff, P.M., Todor, W.D., Grover, R.A. and Huber, V.L. (1984) 'Situational moderators of leader reward and punishment behaviours: fact or fiction?', *Organizational Behaviour and Human Performance*, 34, 21-63.

Podsakoff, P.M., Todor, W.D. and Schuler, R.S. (1983) 'Leader expertise as a moderator of the effects of instrumental and supportive leader behaviours', *Journal of Management*, 9, 173-85.

Pondy, L.R. (1978) 'Leadership is a language game', in M.W. McCall and M.M. Lombardo (eds), *Leadership: Where Else Can We Go?*, Durham, NC: Duke University Press.

Powell, R. and Schlacter, J.L. (1971) 'Participative management: a panacea?', *Academy of Management Journal*, 14, 165-73.

Preston, L.E. and Post, J.E. (1974) 'The third managerial revolution', *Academy of Management Journal*, 17, 476-86.

Pugh, D.S., Hickson, D.J., Hinings, C.R. and Turner, C. (1969) 'The context of organization structures', *Administrative Science Quarterly*, 14, 91-114.

Ramsay, H. (1976) 'Participation: the shop floor view', *British Journal of Industrial Relations*, 14, 128-41.

Rauch, C.F. and Behling, O. (1984) 'Functionalism: basis for an alternate approach to the study of leadership', in J.G. Hunt, D.-M. Hosking, C.A. Schriesheim and R. Stewart (eds), *Leaders and Managers: International Perspectives on Managerial Behaviour and Leadership*, New York: Pergamon.

Rice, R.W. (1978a) 'Construct validity of the least preferred co-worker score', *Psychological Bulletin*, 85, 1199-237.

Rice, R.W. (1978b) 'Psychometric properties of the esteem for least preferred co-worker (LPC) scale', *Academy of Management Review*, 3, 106-18.

Rice, R.W. (1979) 'Reliability and validity of the LPC scale: a reply', *Academy of Management Review*, 4, 291-4.

Rice, R.W. and Chemers, M.M. (1975) 'Personality and situational determinants of leader behaviour', *Journal of Applied Psychology*, 60, 20-7.

Rotter, J.B. (1966) 'Generalized expectancies for internal versus external control of reinforcement', *Psychological Monographs*, 80, No. 609.

Ruble, T.L. (1976) 'Effect of one's locus of control and the opportunity to participate in planning', *Organizational Behaviour and Human Performance*, 16, 63-73.

Runyon, K.E. (1973) 'Some interactions between personality variables and management styles', *Journal of Applied Psychology*, 57, 288-94.

Rush, M.D., Thomas, J.C. and Lord, R.G. (1977) 'Implicit leadership theory: a potential threat to the internal validity of leader behaviour questionnaires', *Organizational Behaviour and Human Performance*, 20, 93-110.

Rychlak, J.F. (1963) 'Personality correlates of leadership among first level managers', *Psychological Reports*, 12, 43-52.

Sadler, P.J. (1970) 'Leadership style, confidence in management, and job satisfaction', *Journal of Applied Behavioural Science*, 6, 3-19.

Salancik, G.R. and Pfeffer, J. (1977) 'Constraints on administrator discretion: the limited influence of mayors on city budgets', *Urban Affairs Quarterly*, 12, 475-98.

Sashkin, M. (1976) 'Changing toward participative management approaches: a model and methods', *Academy of Management Review*, 1, 75-86.

Sashkin, M. (1984) 'Participative management is an ethical imperative', *Organizational Dynamics*, 14, 5-22.

Sashkin, M. and Garland, H. (1979) 'Laboratory and field research on leadership: integrating divergent streams', in J.G. Hunt and L.L. Larson (eds), *Crosscurrents in Leadership*, Carbondale, Illinois: Southern Illinois University Press.

Scandura, T.A. and Graen, G.B. (1984) 'Moderating effects of initial leader-member exchange status on the effects of a leadership intervention', *Journal of Applied Psychology*, 69, 428-36.

Schein, E.H. (1980) *Organizational Psychology*, Englewood Cliffs, N.J.: Prentice-Hall, 3rd edn.

Schneier, C.E. (1978) 'The Contingency Model of leadership: an extension to emergent leadership and leader's sex', *Organizational Behaviour and Human Performance*, 21, 220-39.

Schriesheim, C.A. (1979) 'The similarity of individual directed and group directed leader behaviour descriptions', *Academy of Management Journal*, 22, 345-55.

Schriesheim, C.A., Bannister, B.D. and Money, W.H. (1979) 'Psychometric properties of the LPC scale: an extension of Rice's view', *Academy of Management Review*, 4, 287-90.

Schriesheim, C.A. and De Nisi, A.S. (1981) 'Task dimensions of the effects of instrumental leadership: a two-sample replicated test of path-goal leadership theory', *Journal of Applied Psychology*, 66, 589-97.

Schriesheim, C.A., House, R.J. and Kerr, S. (1976) 'Leader initiating structure: a reconciliation of discrepant research results and some empirical tests', *Organizational Behaviour and Human Performance*, 15, 297-321.

Schriesheim, C.A., Hunt, J.G. and Sekaran, U. (1982) 'The leadership-management controversy revisited', in J.G. Hunt, U. Sekaran and C.A. Schriesheim (eds), *Leadership: Beyond Establishment Views*, Carbondale, Illinois: Southern Illinois University Press.

Schriesheim, C.A. and Kerr, S. (1977) 'Theories and measures of leadership', in J.G. Hunt and L.L. Larson (eds), *Leadership: The Cutting Edge*, Carbondale, Illinois: Southern Illinois University Press.

Schriesheim, C.A. and Murphy, C.J. (1976) 'Relationships between leader behaviour and subordinate satisfaction and performance: a test of some situational moderators', *Journal of Applied Psychology*, 61, 634-41.

Schriesheim, C.A. and von Glinow, M.A. (1977) 'Tests of the path-goal theory of leadership: a theoretical and empirical analysis', *Academy of Management Journal*, 20, 398-405.

Schriesheim, J.F. (1980) 'The social context of leader-subordinate relations: an investigation of the effects of group cohesiveness', *Journal of Applied Psychology*, 65, 183-94.

Schriesheim, J.F. and Schriesheim, C.A. (1980) 'A test of the path-goal theory of leadership and some suggested directions for future research', *Personnel Psychology*, 33, 349-70.

Schuler, R.S. (1976) 'Participation with supervisor and subordinate authoritarianism: a path-goal theory reconciliation', *Administrative Science Quarterly*, 21, 320-5.

Scott, W.R. (1981) *Organizations: Rational, Natural and Open Systems*, Englewood Cliffs, N.J.: Prentice-Hall.

Selznick, P. (1943) 'An approach to a theory of bureaucracy', *American Sociological Review*, 8, 47-54.

Selznick, P. (1957) *Leadership in Administration*, , New York: Harper & Row.

Sergiovanni, T.J. (1984) 'Cultural and competing perspectives in administrative theory and practice', in T.J. Sergiovanni and J.E. Corbally (eds), *Leadership and Organizational Culture*, Urbana: University of Illinois Press.

Shartle, C.L. (1957) 'Introduction', in R.M. Stogdill and A.E. Coons (eds), *Leader Behaviour: Its Description and Measurement*, Columbus, Ohio: Ohio State University, Bureau of Business Research.

Sheridan, J.E. and Vredenburgh, D.J. (1978) 'Predicting leadership behaviour in a hospital organization', *Academy of Management Journal*, 21, 679-89.

Shiflett, S.C. (1973) 'The contingency model of leadership effectiveness: some implications of its statistical and methodological properties', *Behavioural Science*, 18, 429-40.

Siehl, C. and Martin, J. (1984) 'The role of symbolic management: how can managers effectively transmit organizational culture?', in J.G. Hunt, D.-M. Hosking, C.A. Schriesheim and R. Stewart (eds), *Leaders and Managers: International Perspectives on Managerial Behaviour and Leadership*, New York: Pergamon.

Simon, H.A. (1957) *Administrative Behaviour*, New York: Macmillan (2nd edn).

Sims, H.P. (1977) 'The leader as a manager of reinforcement contingencies', in J.G. Hunt and L.L. Larson (eds), *Leadership: The Cutting Edge*, Carbondale, Illinois: Southern Illinois University Press.

Sims, H.P. and Manz, C.C. (1984) 'Observing leader behaviour: toward reciprocal determinism in leadership theory', *Journal of Applied Psychology*, 69, 222-32.

Sims, H.P. and Szilagyi, A.D. (1975) 'Leader reward behaviour and subordinate satisfaction and performance', *Organizational Behaviour and Human Performance*, 14, 426-38.

Sims, H.P. and Szilagyi, A.D. (1979) 'Time lags in leader reward research', *Journal of Applied Psychology*, 64, 66-71.

Singer, J.N. (1974) 'Participative decision-making about work: an overdue look at variables which mediate its effects', *Sociology of Work and Occupations*, 1, 347-69.

Singh, R. (1983) 'Leadership style and reward allocation: does LPC scale measure task and relational orientation?', *Organizational Behaviour and Human Performance*, 32, 178-97.

Smith, J.E., Carson, K.P. and Alexander, R.A. (1984) 'Leadership: it can make a difference', *Academy of Management Journal*, 27, 765-76.

Staw, B.M. and Ross, J. (1980) 'Commitment in an experimenting society: a study of the attribution process from administrative scenarios', *Journal of Applied Psychology*, 65, 249-60.

Stewart, R. (1967) *Managers and Their Jobs*, London: Macmillan.

Stewart, R. (1982) 'The relevance of some studies of managerial work and behaviour to leadership research', in J.G. Hunt, U. Sekaran and C.A. Schriesheim (eds), *Leadership: Beyond Establishment Views*, Carbondale, Illinois: Southern Illinois University Press.

Stewart, R. (1983) 'Managerial behaviour: how research has changed the traditional picture', in M.J. Earl (ed.), *Perspectives on Management*, Oxford: Oxford University Press.

Stinson, J.E. and Johnson, T.W. (1975) 'The path-goal theory of leadership: a partial test and suggested refinement', *Academy of Management Journal*, 18, 242-52.

Stinson, J.E. and Tracy, L. (1974) 'Some disturbing characteristics of the LPC score', *Personnel Psychology*, 27, 477-85.

Stogdill, R.M. (1948) 'Personal factors associated with leadership: a survey of the literature', *Journal of Psychology*, 25, 35-71.

Stogdill, R.M. (1950) 'Leadership, membership and organization', *Psychological Bulletin*, 47, 1-14.

Stogdill, R.M. (1963) *Manual for the Leader Behaviour Description Questionnaire - Form XII*, Columbus: Ohio State University, Bureau of Business Research.

Stogdill, R.M. (1974) *Handbook of Leadership: A Survey of Theory and Research*,

New York: Free Press.

Stogdill, R.M., Goode, O.S. and Day, D.R. (1962) 'New leader behaviour description subscales', *Journal of Psychology*, 54, 259-69.

Stogdill, R.M., Goode, O.S. and Day, D.R. (1963a) 'The leader behaviour of United States senators', *Journal of Psychology*, 56, 3-8.

Stogdill, R.M., Goode, O.S. and Day, D.R. (1963b) 'The leader behaviour of corporation presidents', *Personnel Psychology*, 16, 127-32.

Stogdill, R.M., Goode, O.S. and Day, D.R. (1964) 'The leader behaviour of presidents of labour unions', *Personnel Psychology*, 17, 49-57.

Stogdill, R.M. and Shartle, C.L. (1948) 'Methods for determining patterns of leadership behaviour in relation to organization structure and objectives', *Journal of Applied Psychology*, 32, 286-91.

Strauss, G. (1969) 'Human relations, 1968 style', *Industrial Relations*, 7, 262-76.

Szilagyi, A.D. (1980) 'Causal inferences between leader reward behaviour and subordinate goal attainment, absenteeism, and work satisfaction', *Journal of Occupational Psychology*, 53, 195-204.

Szilagyi, A.D. and Keller, R.T. (1976) 'A comparative investigation of the Supervisory Behaviour Description Questionnaire (SBDQ) and the Revised Leader Behaviour Description Questionnaire (LBDQ - Form XII)', *Academy of Management Journal*, 19, 642-9.

Szilagyi, A.D. and Sims, H.P. (1974) 'An exploration of the path-goal theory of leadership in a health care environment', *Academy of Management Journal*, 17, 622-23.

Tannenbaum, A.S. (1966) *The Social Psychology of the Work Organization*, London: Tavistock.

Tannenbaum, R. and Schmidt, W.H. (1958) 'How to choose a leadership pattern', *Harvard Business Review*, 36, 95-101.

Taylor, J.C. (1974) 'Technology and supervision in the post-industrial era', in J.G. Hunt and L.L. Larson (eds), *Contingency Approaches to Leadership*, Carbondale, Illinois: Southern Illinois University Press.

Taylor, J. and Bowers, D. (1972) *The Survey of Organizations: A Machine Scored Standardized Questionnaire Instrument*, Ann Arbor, Michigan: Institute for Social Research.

Taylor, P. (1983) 'Beliefs are imperatives', *Financial Times*, 31 December, 15.

Thompson, J.D. (1967) *Organizations in Action*, New York: McGraw-Hill.

Thornton, G.C. and Byham, W.C. (1982) *Assessment Centres and Management Performance*, New York: Academic Press.

Tinnin, D.B. (1982) 'The American at the wheel of Porsche', *Fortune*, 5 April, 78-87.

Tjosvold, D. (1984) 'Effects of leader warmth and directiveness on subordinate performance on a subsequent task', *Journal of Applied Psychology*, 69, 422-7.

Tolbert, P.S. and Zucker, L.G. (1983) 'Institutional sources of change in the formal structure of organizations: the diffusion of civil service reform, 1880-1935', *Administrative Science Quarterly*, 28, 22-39.

Tosi, H. (1970) 'A re-examination of personality as a determinant of the effects of participation', *Personnel Psychology*, 23, 91-9.

Tosi, H.L. and Slocum, J.W. (1984) 'Contingency theory: some suggested directions', *Journal of Management*, 10, 9-26.

Trice, H.M., Belasco, J. and Alutto, J. (1969) 'The role of ceremonials in organizational behaviour', *Industrial and Labour Relations Review*, 23, 40-51.

Trice, H.M. and Beyer, J.M. (1984) 'Studying organizational cultures through rites and ceremonies', *Academy of Management Review*, 9, 653-69.

Uttal, B. (1983) 'The corporate culture vultures', *Fortune*, 17 October, 66-72.

Vaill, P.B. (1984) 'The purposing of high-performing systems' in T.J. Sergiovanni and J.E. Corbally (eds), *Leadership and Organizational Culture*, Urbana: University of Illinois Press.

Vecchio, R.P. and Gobdel, B.C. (1984) 'The Vertical Dyad Linkage model of leadership: problems and prospects', *Organizational Behaviour and Human Performance*, 34, 5-20.

Vroom, V.H. (1959) 'Some personality determinants of the effects of participation', *Journal of Abnormal and Social Psychology*, 59, 322-7.

Vroom, V.H. (1976) 'Can leaders learn to lead?', *Organizational Dynamics*, 4, 17-28.

Vroom, V.H. (1984) 'Reflections on leadership and decision-making', *Journal of General Management*, 9, 18-36.

Vroom, V.H. and Jago, A.G. (1974) 'Decision making as a social process: normative and descriptive models of leader behaviour', *Decision Sciences*, 5, 743-69.

Vroom, V.H. and Jago, A.G. (1978) 'On the validity of the Vroom-Yetton model', *Journal of Applied Psychology*, 63, 151-62.

Vroom, V.H. and Yetton, P.W. (1973) *Leadership and Decision-Making*, Pittsburgh: University of Pittsburgh Press.

Wall, T.D. and Lischeron, J.A. (1977) *Worker Participation*, London: McGraw-Hill.

Weber, M. (1947) *The Theory of Social and Economic Organisation*, Chicago: Free Press.

Weber, M. (1948) 'Bureaucracy', in H.H. Gerth and C.W. Mills (eds), *From Max Weber: Essays in Sociology*, London: Routledge & Kegan Paul.

Weed, S.E., Mitchell, T.R. and Moffitt, W. (1976) 'Leadership style, subordinate personality, and task type as predictors of performance and satisfaction with supervision', *Journal of Applied Psychology*, 61, 58-66.

Weick, K.E. (1969) *The Social Psychology of Organizing*, Reading, Mass.: Addison-Wesley.

Weick, K.E. (1976) 'Educational organisations as loosely coupled systems', *Administrative Science Quarterly*, 21, 1-19.

Weiner, B. (1979) 'A theory of motivation for some classroom experiences', *Journal of Educational Psychology*, 71, 3-25.

Weiner, B., Frieze, I., Kukla, A., Reed, L., Rest, S. and Rosenbaum, R.M. (1972) 'Perceiving the causes of success and failure', in E. Jones, D. Kanouse, H.H. Kelley, R. Nisbett, S. Valins and B. Weiner (eds), *Attribution: Perceiving the Causes of Behaviour*, Morristown, N.J.: General Learning.

Weiner, N. and Mahoney, T.A. (1981) 'A model of corporate performance as a function of environmental, organizational, and leadership influences', *Academy of Management Journal*, 24, 453-70.

Weiss, H.M. (1977) 'Subordinate imitation of supervisor behaviour: the role of modeling in organizational socialization', *Organizational Behaviour and Human Performance*, 19, 89-105.

Weiss, H.M. and Adler, S. (1981) 'Cognitive complexity and the structure of implicit leadership theories', *Journal of Applied Psychology*, 66, 69-78.

Weissenberg, R.J. and Kavenagh, M.J. (1972) 'The interdependence of initiating structure and consideration: a review of the evidence', *Personnel Psychology*, 55, 119-30.

Wexley, K.N., Singh, J.P. and Yukl, G.A. (1973) 'Subordinate personality as a moderator of the effects of participation in three types of appraisal interviews',

Journal of Applied Psychology, 58, 54-9.

White, R. and Lippitt, R. (1960) 'Leader behaviour and member reaction in three "social climates"', in D. Cartwright and A. Zander (eds), *Group Dynamics: Research and Theory*, 2nd edn, London: Tavistock.

Whyte, W.F. (1943) *Street Corner Society*, Chicago: University of Chicago Press.

Wood, R.E. and Mitchell, T.R. (1981) 'Manager behaviour in a social context: the impact of impression management on attributions and disciplinary actions', *Organizational Behaviour and Human Performance*, 28, 356-78.

Woodward, J. (1965) *Industrial Organisation: Theory and Practice*, Oxford: Oxford University Press.

Woodward, J. (ed.) (1970) *Industrial Organization: Behaviour and Control*, London: Oxford University Press.

Yukl, G.A. (1971) 'Toward a behavioural theory of leadership', *Organizational Behaviour and Human Performance*, 6, 414-40.

Yukl, G.A. (1981) *Leadership in Organizations*, Englewood Cliffs: Prentice-Hall.

Yukl, G.A. and Nemeroff, W.F. (1979) 'Identification and measurement of specific categories of leadership behaviour', in J.G. Hunt and L.L. Larson (eds), *Crosscurrents in Leadership*, Carbondale, Illinois: Southern Illinois University Press.

Yukl, G.A. and van Fleet, D.D. (1982) 'Cross-situational, multimethod research on military leader effectiveness', *Organizational Behaviour and Human Performance*, 30, 87-108.

Yunker, G.W. and Hunt, J.G. (1976) 'An empirical comparison of the Michigan four-factor and Ohio State LBDQ leadership scales', *Organizational Behaviour and Human Performance*, 17, 45-65.

Zahn, G.L. and Wolf, G. (1981) 'Leadership and the art of cycle maintenance: a simulation model of superior-subordinate interaction', *Organizational Behaviour and Human Performance*, 28, 26-49.

Zaleznik, A. (1977) 'Managers and leaders: are they different?', *Harvard Business Review*, 67-78.

Zimmerman, D.K. (1978) 'Participative management: a reexamination of the classics', *Academy of Management Review*, 3, 896-901.

AUTHOR INDEX

Adair, J., 38, 39, 121, 123
Adler, S., 74, 202
Albanese, R., 80, 202
Aldrich, H.E., 175
Alexander, R.A., 196-7
Allen, M.P., 195
Alutto, J., 177
Andrews, I.R., 106
Anon, 186
Anthony, W.P., 88
Argyle, M., 96-7, 101, 104
As, D., 92
Ashour, A.S., 134-5, 137

Baetz, M.L., 27, 100, 101, 105, 147
Bales, R.F., 23, 84, 188, 202-3
Bannister, B.D., 134
Barnes, J.S., 76
Barrett, G.V., 33
Barrow, J.C., 24, 53, 54, 59, 75, 105, 118-19, 145
Bartlem, C.S., 203
Bass, B.M., 18, 19, 20, 21, 22, 24, 27, 33, 34, 59, 97, 100, 102, 105, 116, 118-19, 120, 161
Baumgartel, H., 95-6
Beck, B.E.F., 188
Beer, M., 77
Behling, O., 2
Belasco, J., 177
Bennis, W.G., 6, 16, 107, 185, 187, 188-9, 206
Beyer, J.M., 205
Bird, C., 18, 20, 25
Blake, R.R., 75-8, 85

Blanchard, K., 17, 77, 111-12, 147-50, 158
Blau, P.M., 3, 57, 59
Blout, H.D., 104
Blumberg, M., 14
Bolton, A.A., 38
Bowers, D.G., 62, 68-72, 73, 74, 81, 91, 92, 161, 176
Bragg, J., 106
Bray, D.W., 29-33
Brown, M.C., 195
Brownell, P., 98, 104-5, 123-4
Bruni, J.R., 73
Bryman, A., 7, 27, 88, 144, 171, 186, 187, 206,
Burger, P.C., 33
Burns, J.M., 194, 201
Burns, T., 135, 170
Burtt, H.E., 39, 44, 57-8, 176
Bussom, R.S., 61, 190-1
Butler, M.C., 73
Butterfield, D.A., 184
Byham, W.C., 32, 33

Cage, J.H., 156-7
Calder, B.J., 183, 185
Cammalleri, J.A., 104
Cammann, C., 98-9, 122
Campbell, D.T., 12, 13, 200
Campbell, J.P., 77
Campbell, R.J., 29-33
Carey, A., 38, 65
Carson, K.P., 196-7
Carter, L.F., 19
Cartwright, D., 68

227

SUBJECT INDEX

233